Knickerbocker Essays

Knickerbocker Essays

VOLUME I:
FOOD AND DRINK

VARIOUS AUTHORS

*Knickerbocker Essays, Volume 1:
Food and Drink (1833-1865).* —

"The Knickerbocker" Series

© 2022 Full Well Ventures

ISBN-13: 978-1-62834-028-0

Preface

THIS VOLUME features articles selected from "The Knickerbocker: or, a New-York Monthly Magazine," a literary magazine that was published in New York City from 1833 to 1865. Knickerbocker writers, who included such literary greats of mid-19th century America as Washington Irving and Lewis Gaylord-Clark, played a prominent role in the building of a young nation, the United States of America. Given the enduring legacy of "The Knickerbocker" for any student of mid-19th century America, it is believed that providing the materials in this Knickerbocker series, compiled and arranged according to a variety of themes, will allow readers to find a treasured place on the bookshelf for those beloved and time-tested passages that are found to be so useful and interesting for so many Americans and students of every age. Although this thematic collection features its many entertaining nonfiction essay, which encapsulate a flavor of the past, thus the choice of "Essays" in the Series title, with some poetry and fictional short stories included as well to give the reader a more thoroughly "Knickerbockeriana" experience. The words of these accomplished American writers and editors continue to may echo down through the centuries of American history. The Knickerbocker series begins with the theme of "Food and Drink," a vital preoccupation of American life in every age.

The Editor,
Volume I, June 2014

Table of Contents

PART ONE

PART TWO

Part One

I

Will You Dine With Me?

BEING THE LONGEST INVITATION UPON RECORD.

NOVEMBER 1860

THE SHORTEST being the 'Chops and Tomato Sauce' of the great Pickwick Oyer, and the finest the twentieth sonnet of Milton:

'Lawrence, of virtuous father virtuous sons,'

And proximate to that, the twenty-first:

'Cyriac, whose grandsire on the royal bench;'

and the most meritorious for precision a note, in 1756, from Warburton to Hurd, asking him to come to Bedford Row, 'where a college preparation shall be made for you; that is to say, a bed, a dish of tea, and a piece of mutton, while you stay with us.' Although there are others which are notable, like that which Ferdinand was accustomed to proffer to the Grand Admiral Henriquez: 'Stop and dine with us; we are to have a chicken for dinner today.' Not to forget Kit Marlow's 'Smooth Song':

'The silver dishes for thy meat,
As precious as the gods do eat,
Shall on an ivory table be
Prepared each day for thee and me;'

Or that roistering solicitation of the student in 'Faust': 'Come up to Burgdorf! — there you are sure to find good cheer: the handsomest girls, and the best of beer; and 'rows,' too, of the very first water.' Nor must we pass over, though it express not indeed

11

the preliminary summons, that excellent incitement in Heywod and Broome's 'Late Lancashire Witches':

> 'GENTLEMEN, welcome! 'tis a word I use;
> From me expect no further compliment,
> Nor shall you find,
> Being set at meat, that I'll excuse your fare,
> Or say, I am sorry it falls out so poor;
> And had I known your coming, we'd have had
> Such things and such; nor blame my cook to say
> This dish or that hath not been served with care,
> Words fitting best a common hostess' mouth
> When there's perhaps some just cause of dislike,
> But not the table of a gentleman.'

The quotation is a long one, but for my own part, I think it should be engraved upon all modern trenchers and tankards capable of receiving it without abridgment. There was a neat courtesy exhibited by Sir John Leach when he asked Lord Eldon to dine upon some grand occasion, and begged to be informed if there was any dish his lordship had a fancy for; when the Chancellor, like the son of a Newcastle collier, replied: 'Liver and bacon.' Somebody gives an account of a Sheik of the Lebanon, who placed before one of his European guests, for his sole consumption, a kid roasted whole, with the quiet remark, that 'having observed on a former occasion that GOD had blessed our hakim with a good appetite, this dish had been provided especially for him.' The Sheik was perfectly serious; and I confess that I have often thought of him with feelings of reverence when seated at the well-regulated board of my prudent friend, Mrs. McUdor. I have no doubt of the fact that strawberries, for instance, do not agree with the small McUdors; and that this interesting fact alone, and not the ruling price, occasioned their exclusion from the scene of festive enjoyment. Still, would it not have been well to have purchased a few for the adults, and thus to have given the minors a lesson of self-denial! I suspect that I should find this view of the case ably sustained in Miss Edgeworth's excellent Treatise on Practical Education, could I but summon courage to read that admirable work. I have no reason to deny that early diet may affect even the juvenile morality. All I have to say is, that George the Fourth was nurtured upon the royal turnips and mutton chops of Kew. But as I wish to create no doubts in the maternal bosom, I say no more.

I know that it is not well bred to leave the house of a friend, and afterward to speak ill of his larder, kitchen, or cellar. It is what no one should do and what everyone does. How can you refrain? If the dinner were finished when it were finished, then it were well, it were finished quickly. Unfortunately, it is not so. Are there not the mental agonies of disappointment? Are there not the physical pangs? Are you not bereaved of the raptures of reminiscence? Do not tell me that wise men never think of these things! I know better. Lord Eldon was esteemed a tolerably wise man in his day; and on the twenty-fourth of June, 1824, Lord Eldon dined with the Duke of Wellington, and dined badly. 'Did not get there,' says his Lordship, 'till past eight — all the turtle gone, alas! Ditto all the fish! Very splendid; not comfortable; open window on my left side — got a cold thereby.' How many poor creatures in Chancery, do you suppose, the cold dinner at the Duke's disappointed? Then notice, if you please in fine, sun-shiny contrast with the Chancellor's growl, the genial confession of Sidney Smith: 'I shall not easily forget a matelote at the Rocher de Concale, an almond tart at Montreuil, or a *poulet a la Tartare* at Grignon's. These are impressions not to be obliterated.' Then there is the criticism of a dinner, by Samuel Johnson, (who only a few years before, in writing to old Cave, had subscribed himself, 'Yours, *Impransus,*') who said, 'That was a good dinner enough, to be sure; but it was not a dinner to ask a man to;' in which remark I venture to say there is infinitely more philosophical acumen than in the Doctor's disquisitions upon Shakespeare. All diaries — the honestest species of writing — arc Diaries of Dinner. The three meals of the day are the events of the day from milky babyhood to the time when a man must cry with Barzillai: 'I am eighty years old. Can thy servant taste what I eat or what I drink?' I once thought to count the dinners in Tom Moore's Life and Correspondence, but my arithmetical powers are limited, and I gave over the task.

So it is with Political Economy. To be poor, means not to have enough to eat; to be rich, to have more than enough. PROVIDENCE smiles upon the crop, and my Lord Fitzfool stays in; a vile fly ravages the corn, and my Lord goes out. What is there for a poor man to do but to die? Malthus said it long ago. 'A man,' he declares, 'who is born into a world already possessed, if he cannot get subsistence from his parents, on whom he has a just demand, and if the society does not want his labor, has no claim of right to the smallest portion of food, and in fact, has no business to be where he is. At Nature's mighty feast there is no cover for him. She tells him to be gone, and will quickly execute her own orders, if he do not work upon the compassion of some of her guests.' When there is a bit of meat in every man's pot, and a loaf of bread in every man's oven, all goes well. But when Ceres is cruel, the happiest land is transmogrified, and in every smiling valley, and on every softly swelling hill, all is, as at the breaking up of Goldsmith's club, 'dam — blood—fire — whizz — blid — tit — rat — trip — riot — nonsense and rapid confusion.' 'I know why you come here,' said Jean Jacques Rousseau when someone visited his cottage; 'it is to see how little there is in the pot. Well, look in the pot.' And I suppose he took off the cover cynically. Alas! Had there been more and better in the pot, Blacksmith Louis might have made locks at Versailles to the last; fish-women might not have stuffed grass into the dead mouth of that poor Fermier-General; there might have been no Napoleon the First, and (oh! happy consequence!) no Napoleon the Third. Given Pat with potatoes; and how many English statesmen would have been saved from endless and empty management, from makeshift and mischievous meddlement, from an exhibition. Alas! too common in this world, weary of its own inanities — an exhibition of fatuity exalted and of selfishness in authority! Given Pat with potatoes, and what Vinegar Hill battles, contributions of rent, bad lyrics, worse speeches, and hopeless, pitiable, floundering failures, should we have escaped! Alas! no Act of Parliament ever did or can legislate potatoes into any human stomach, when in all the land no potatoes were, or are, either for love or lucre, to be had. 'A belly-full!' is the eternal shibboleth of all statesmanship. Down through vistas of history comes the resounding cry of 'Victual!' Over the clangor of hostile steel, and the reverberations of artillery and polyglot slogans of defiance, and the babblement of senates and synods; from the city and from the hamlet; from lands that the high sun wastes and from lands that a low sun leaves to stiffen in unchanging sterility; from the terribly refined to the terribly rude; from master and from bondman; from hideous masses of humanity writhing like vipers in a pot, and from dwellers in lone places and mountainous solitudes; from besieged cities full of wailing mothers, and from haunts of hunger where a sightless foe stretches the inexorable cordons of barrenness; from storm-stricken ships weltering at will; from prisons in which strong men waste day by day in the arms of starvation; in all these times, from all these scenes, from all these empty mouths, comes Nature's primal cry for food! Man is ever the same prodigal, ever wasting or wanting, be he dandy dawdling over his breakfast at the club, or sooty and smeared Esquimaux filling himself with blubber to distention.

Indeed, between this same polar gormandizer and a certain notable person called Louis the Fourteenth, I find a kind of essential resemblance and human link. Our Hyperborean friend cannot, as it appears, content himself, in plenteous seasons, with less than five pounds of blubber at a sitting, and must have ten pounds for his *per diem,* the magnitude of which fact will become more evident to the reader, if he will remember that Cornaro, the noble proto-Grahamite of Venice, allowed himself for many years only one pound of food daily. The Esquimaux, as I learn from Captain Parry, 'becomes distended, and suffers considerable pain.' We will leave him in disgust, and seek relief at Versailles.

Madame de Baviere affirms that she saw Louis the Fourteenth, at a sitting, 'eat four dishes of different soups, an entire pheasant,' a partridge, a great plateful of salad, mutton hashed in its own gravy with garlic, two good pieces of ham, a plate of pastry, with fruit and comfits.' This, I think, surpasses even the trencher triumphs of Clodius Allinus, who ate for his breakfast five hundred figs, one hundred peaches, ten melons, one hundred beccaficoes, and four hundred oysters. Poor Madame de Maintenon, who had the care of her royal husband's soul and stomach, mourns:

'Nothing but the extraordinary health and strength of the King could be a consolation for the manner in which he treats those he best loves. If he made me eat half as much as he eats himself, I should not be long alive.' Afterward, she writes, still in trouble: 'The King eats as much as ever, especially at night, which makes me tremble.' Our poor Esquimaux should have come to Paris and turned courtier.

From gilded galleries to Grub Street may be a violent transition, but the good nature of my reader, unless, indeed, he long ago, provoked by my lucubrations, threw down his KNICKERBOCKER and went off to dinner — must bridge the gap. Poets have jibed with sad hearts, I fear, in all times, at their own poverty. The world would never have known so much of it, if they had not most unfraternally betrayed each other's squalid secrets. With the quarrel — and when have not men of letters quarreled? — always came the cruel charge, from either side, of beggary. It would seem to be the most trenchant thing a poet can say of his enemy, that he does not have enough to eat. Thus Landor, in sheer scorn, offered 'a hot penny-roll and a pint of stout for breakfast to any critic who could write one of his imaginary conversations.' There is a touching passage in Goldsmith's Animated Nature, very suggestive of his goodness of heart and of his own bitter experience. 'Some men,' he says, 'who have long lived by chance, and whose every day may be considered a happy escape from famine, are known at last to die of a disorder caused by hunger, but which in common language is often called a broken heart. Some of these I have known myself, when very little able to relieve them.' Better days have come than those of 'witty want.' Poets who can passably sing, need not now want some

'AXYLUS, hospitable, kind and good,'

to entertain them for their strumming, 'some Holland House,' as Byron sings,

'WHERE Scotchmen feed and critics may carouse,'

reminding us, in a modern way, of that Phaeacian Feast of Homer, when Demodocus was placed by Pontonius 'on a seat with silver knobs, in the midst of the banqueters, with his back against the tall central pillar; and the herald hung from the peg the high-toned lyre above his head, and signified that he should take it in his hands; and he placed beside him a basket and fair table, and wine, beside the repast, to drink of whenever his spirit urged him.'

But before we conclude our dinner, good gentlemen, it is but fair, I think, that we remember the cooks. We have, indeed, reverend authority for so doing. The excellent Dr. Isaac Watts, who was the best of men, and led the most comfortable of lives, did not disdain, pausing from that sacred singing which generation has since caught from generation, and which will subside into silence only when our English language subsides into eternal silence; he did not disdain, I say, to celebrate a cook — she, probably, who cared for his wants and ministered to an appetite which was always delicate. Here is his little offering:

> 'The cook, who in her humble post,
>   Provides the family with food,
> Excels those empty dames that boast
>   Of charms and lovers, birth and blood.'

And it is true, every word of it, good Dr. Watts! 'We beg your pardon, O pious shade! But we are now about to mention Theresa, cook and mistress of one J.J. Rousseau, and perhaps you had better leave the room. 'Of Theresa,' says Lord Brougham, 'the Comte d'Eschery speaks with constant scorn and dislike, as of a most silly, vulgar, and mischievous person, having only the one accomplishment of being a very good cook. But Rousseau never suffered her to sit at table.' And the more shame to him, say I, the crazy, vain, selfish monster! To drive her from the meal she had prepared — she the concoctor of his savory messes and the mother of his children! He should have been compelled

> 'To eat the pudding that he made himself.'

Montaigne had an admirable cook, and an admirable description he has left of him. There are some verses by Shenstone, very coarse and different from his usual silken style, upon his cook, but we cannot quote them. Of a very old cook, or rather of his shade, the veracious Captain Lemuel Gulliver has given us an account in the voyage to Laputa. 'I prevailed,' he says, 'upon the Governor to call up Heliogabalus's cooks to dress us a dinner; but he could not show us much of his skill, for want of materials. A helot of Agesilaus made us a dish of Spartan broth, but I was not able to get down a second spoonful.' I think that Mary may now be dismissed.

But I fancy I hear some impatient person exclaiming in a pet: 'Pray, what would the man be at? He began by asking us to dinner; he has been talking as if it were on the table before us; and yet, with all our eyes and all our appetite, not a morsel can we discover.' Restrain yourself, my friend! Mortify your carnal man! Learn philosophy, and cultivate your intellect! I value little that man's friendship; I think I may say that my friend KNICKERBOCKER values even less than I do that man's friendship — you are to understand that we have now had, figuratively speaking, six bottles apiece or so — and I say, I value very little anybody's friendship, who cannot dine, and I will go farther and I will say breakfast, so to speak (cheers) upon what I may call, if my venerable friend KNICKERBOCKER (cheers) will permit — I see that my esteemed friend KNICKERBOCKER (cheers) permits—who cannot make three meals a day, or even four, or even two, or I will go farther, and say one on the most inferior article; if I may be allowed such a superlatively silly, and I may say, ridiculous expression, that ever appeared in the pages of THE KNICKERBOCKER MAGAZINE. (Immense and prolonged cheering.)

Hillo! Where are we?

Absolutely, my friend, I do not know. All I know is, that, as D'Alembert was wont to relate, Madame and Mon. Dacier once cooked a dish in concert by a receipt found in Apicius, and both sat down and ate of the same till both were very sick.

Really, they were a very pretty pair of Grecians, but I hope our ragout will not prove to be like theirs.

II

Ode to Java Coffee

By J. Clement

MAY 1847

Of all the isles that gem the Indian seas,
    Fair Java smiles the enviable queen;
There Flora's train, kissed by the tropic breeze,
    Give vernal life and beauty to the scene:
And one of modest mien, yet matchless grace,
    Madonna of the fragrance-breathing throng,
Whose virtues all of excellence embrace,
    May claim this humble mead, a tribute song.

Bards of the bloodshot eye and reeling brain
    May give libations rich of reeking verse;
To bloated Bacchus swell the foaming strain,
    And fancied merits of the vine rehearse;
To Java's peerless plant my lay I pour,
    Whose juice no gods defile with lecherous lip:
Give me my cup of Coffee, brimming o'er,
    And Jove unenvied may his nectar sip.

No headaches huddle there like lurking foes,
    No serpent-passions coil around the brim;
Beneath its power the stream of feeling flows,
    More soft and gentle than a Naiäd's hymn.
And manly Thought, in river's crystal-clear,
    Sparkles with truth and foams with eloquence,
And far from bluffs of Bombast, bleak and drear,
    Meanders through the verdant vales of Sense.

19

ODE TO JAVA COFFEE

Come, then, sweet Flora! At thy incense shrine
    Call forth thy blooming daughters, angel bright;
Bid them unveil their beauties, all divine,
    To fill the gazer's eye with new delight:
And while they bow in reverence round thy throne,
    And breathe from honeyed lips an odor-shower,
Bid them the worth supreme and beauty own
    Of Java's glorious and immortal flower.

J. Clement,
Buffalo

III

Tea and Coffee

DECEMBER 1859

SO UNIVERSAL has the use of infused beverages become that, in America at least, one cannot sit at table, public or private, without replying to the question: 'Tea, or coffee?' Not in the sense of' 'Do you wish tea or coffee,' but which do you prefer? At many private tables throughout the country, if one happens to be abstemious, or has conscientious scruples as to the moral effects of artificial drinks, or from any cause desires to quench his thirst with 'the nectar which Jupiter sips,' he must put the hostess to the inconvenience of sending for a pitcher of water; and then, ten to one, he must swallow a weak solution of carbonate of lime, with nothing to disguise its raw, earthy taste. Doubtless many timid reformers are deterred from teetotalism by its inconvenience, and by the extra trouble they must necessarily occasion others, in order to its practice.

A popularity so universal have the infused beverages attained, and so great an influence do they exert upon the human race, that the question of their use, abuse, or disuse, is worthy the consideration alike of philosopher and philanthropist. Their use can be superseded and their influence overcome neither by the enthusiasm of the radical reformer nor by statistical appeals to the economy of the race. The fact that the annual expenditure for tea and coffee in the United States alone, is upwards of twenty-five millions of dollars, does not prevent the poor widow from purchasing her ounce of tea, though she possesses but a handful of chips with which to steep it. It is useless to tell the *gourmand* that his luxuries cost more than his necessaries, for men ever have expended and ever will expend most for the gratification of their governing appetites. So long as human nature retains its humanity, nothing else can be expected. Habits and appetites inculcated during a lifetime, whose predisposing causes may well dispute priority with the cradle itself, are not so easily eradicated, even though conscience be pitted against them; and until the appetite for stimulants, which is nonetheless strong because it is abnormal, be overcome, reformers may have science, experience, and economy entirely in their favor, and yet labor in vain. The stimulant users of the present day were born, speaking in a general sense, and ninety-nine in a hundred of them will die with their present appetites and indulgences. The change — for undoubtedly, sooner or later, change will come — must be effected through the rising and future generations. In their behalf, and in behalf of those who have not yet wholly surrendered themselves at the shrine of habit, let us examine the question candidly and in the light of science and reason.

The infused beverages are divided into three classes: first, teas, or infusions of leaves; second, coffees, or infusions of seeds; and third, cocoas, which are thin soups or gruels rather than infusions.

A tradition respecting the origin of the tea-plant, handed down from the third century, runs thus: 'A pious hermit, who, in his watchings and prayers had often been overtaken by sleep, so that his eyelids closed, against his will, in holy wrath against the weakness of the flesh, he cut them off and threw them on the ground. Well pleased with this mark of his devotedness, a god caused a tea-shrub to spring out of them, the leaves of which exhibit the form of an eyelid bordered with lashes and possess the wonderful gift of hindering sleep.'

A similar tradition exists concerning the origin of the coffee-plant.

The Chinese claim for tea that, 'it is of a cooling nature, and if taken in excess, produces exhaustion and lassitude.' It increases the flow of animal spirits, and imparts a feeling of cheerfulness. Its three principal ingredients are theine, tannic acid, and a volatile oil. The first contributes its enlivening properties; the second, its astringency; and the third its narcotic principle, which last is very powerful in recently prepared tea. The Chinese never use that which is less than a year old, thus allowing the volatile oil partially to escape. This oil is not a natural constituent of the plant, but is generated during the roasting process. Tea lessens the loss of the system by perspiration, arrests the metamorphosic decomposition of the tissues, and thereby lessens the quantity of nutriment necessary to the repair of the body.

Coffee resembles tea in its chemical constituents, theine or caffeine, for the terms are synonymous, and a volatile, empyreumatic oil forming the prominent principles. As is the case with tea, the oil is produced during the roasting process. Chemists have assayed to determine to which of these substances the peculiar effects of the beverages are due; but, practically considered, such investigations are no better than scientific nonsense. When the devotee of the bowl raises the potion to his lips, he does not pause to ask what part of the chemical formula for alcohol ($C_4 H_6 O_2$) it is that burns his palate, nor does the hungry man care whether it be empyreumatic oil or oil of vitriol that satisfies his craving as he sips his cup of coffee. In the same manner as tea, coffee lessens the excretions and arrests metamorphosis.

The ingredients of cocoa are similar to those of tea and coffee, with the addition of cocoa butter and a greater proportion of starch and gluten. A volatile oil is produced by roasting, as with tea and coffee, and a peculiar principle, called theobromine, corresponds to theine. Cocoa has no qualities superior to those of the two beverages already mentioned, with the exception that it is more nutritious. On account of the large percentage of cocoa butter, it taxes the digestive organs more than either of the other beverages.

Everything in the great realm of nature has been created, and is sustained on the principle of growth and decay, of supply and waste. Reverse this law and the result is destruction and death; and just in proportion as this process is retarded does the organism suffer deterioration. In the vegetable kingdom the process is continually repeated. Without it neither man, nor beast, nor tree could exist for a single day. Without constant change, a process of inhalation and exhalation — to use a more classical term, a perpetual metamorphosis — the human body would soon become a loathsome mass of putrefaction. The old and worn-out particles must be thrown off to give place for new material, which, in turn, after performing its office in the vital laboratory, is displaced by a new supply. As soon as the supply is stopped, the vital domain suffers. Emaciation and dissolution result from its protracted refusal. It follows, that any substance which serves to arrest the constant waste and renewal of the tissues, while it actually diminishes the quantity of nutriment necessary to the support of the system, it vitiates the quality of the tissues by causing them to retain particles which are effete and should be excreted. The rule will hold good in every case, and with all substances: just in proportion as we decrease the *quantity* of material necessary to supply the waste of the system, do we depreciate the *quality* of the tissues. These beverages tax the organs of excretion by furnishing new substances, theine, tannic acid, etc., to be expelled; and these latter in their eliminatory passage serve to constringe and clog the excretory ducts, thus causing other extraneous matters to be retained. It may be laid down as an axiomatic aphorism in physiology that, whatever is gained in quantity is lost in quality, if the gain be through the agency of arresters of metamorphosis.

Again, we must beware of accepting the abnormal action of the system consequent upon the use of stimulants as the direct action of the stimulants themselves. Vital action and reaction must not be mistaken for specific action. Increase the ordinary load of your draught horse slightly, and he will step a little more firmly; double it, and he will put forth uncommon effort and move faster than with an ordinary load; apply the whip, and he will strain his muscles to their utmost, and probably break his harness; but it would be absurd to argue that the increased demand for exertion and the prompting of his driver produce a corresponding increase in the strength of the animal. The human organism acts upon the same principle. It performs its ordinary labor quietly. The vital machinery, if unimpeded, moves with very little friction from the dawn of life until stopped by the chill of death. When any substance, deleterious to its delicate tissues, is introduced into the system through the digestive organs, intelligence is at once telegraphed to the capital of the vital domain, and an extra force is dispatched to defend the structures and dislodge the intruder. The channel of ejection is determined by the nature and potency of the substance introduced. Sometimes the repulsion is attended with very little commotion: a slight perspiration, or slight increase through some other of the excretory channels, as in case of weak stimulants and 'tonic' preparations; sometimes with violent perturbations throughout the whole system, as in case of strong narcotics and small doses of poison; and sometimes the vital forces are entirely overthrown, as in case of fatal poisoning. In every case the action is forced and abnormal.

An old physician — and old physicians are too often deemed the best authority, simply on account of age — is said to have replied, when asked if tea really is a slow poison: 'Certainly, very slow indeed; I have been dying of it myself for the last seventy years.' He told the truth, though in a metaphorical way, for it matters very little with the result whether we vitiate or abbreviate life. To those having a high ideal of physical purity, there is no avoiding the inference; and the moral is more nearly allied to the physical than most men care to admit.

After all that can be said against the use of these beverages, the fact that nature will adapt herself to circumstances continually contravenes the philosophy of the radicals. Almost unlimited provision has been made for the exigencies and emergencies of this physical life. The human constitution is well nigh invincible. Abuse it as we may, still the machinery of life moves on, not generally without complaint, but always with fidelity. Adepts in the art of arsenic-eating perceive no inconvenience from doses which would prove fatal to an inexperienced taster; and thus, whatever habits we may indulge, or in whatever circumstances we may be placed, if the former are regular and systematic, and the latter are permanent or habitual, we shall find our natures gradually accommodating themselves to their condition, even though it be not strictly physiological.

IV

Tea: The Cup that Cheers but not Inebriates

BY SUSAN PINDAR

AUGUST 1847

'No riches I covet, no pleasures I want,
　　Ambition is nothing to me;
But one thing I beg of kind Fortune to grant,
　　For breakfast, a good cup of tea!'

IMPROVED READING.

Let others quaff their sparkling wine,
　　And praise its roseate hue,
Nor think, though mirth is in the cup,
　　There's madness in it too;
Be mine the humbler task to sing,
　　Neglected herb! Of thee,
Whose nectar-draughts no poison bring,
　　Invigorating Tea!

In vain some envious minds have sought
　　And idle tale to frame,
With base, malicious meaning fraught,
　　To sully thy fair fame;
They say, when maiden ladies meet
　　In groups of two or three,
They find a dish of scandal sweet,
　　Washed down with cups of Tea!

TEA

They tell not how the married man,
    When with a friend he sups,
Comes reeling home with noisy voice,
    Uproarious in *his* cups;
While quietly his lady wife
    Sits sipping her bohea,
Nor finds a cause for angry strife
    In twenty cups of Tea!

The social circle gathers round,
    While fiercely roars the storm;
Thy fragrant breath perfumes the air,
    The toast is buttered warm;
The board is spread, a goodly show
    Of tempting viands see,
And kindly hearts still kindlier grow
    Beneath the power of Tea!

Though many strive, with envious spite,
    To write thy virtues down,
So long as Woman owns a tongue,
    She'll trumpet thy renown;
Some gratitude we ought to show
    Those wonderful Chinese,
To whose unwearied skill we owe
    The luxury of Teas.

Susan Pindar.
June, 1847.

V

The Ladies' Dinner

WE WERE very aristocratic in Summerfield—oh! very. We were a New England society, with very many reminiscences of the 'Mayflower,' every house having some article from that heavily freighted craft. We almost all of us had an old brocade, that had belonged to some ancestress of wonderful beauty, and some of us had a picture of a gentleman in powdered wig, broad cuffs, and other insignia of respectability. We were not rich; but then we were high-born, and that was a great consolation to us, as we sat in our little back-parlors and turned our old dresses, and spoke of the magnificence that *had been.*

So we watched with jealous and suspicious eyes all newcomers into our village. We did not wish to see the old aristocracy broken up. So when handsome Mrs. Ames, the railroad contractor's wife, came to town, we pronounced her vulgar and lowborn, and would not call upon her. But her handsome face showed itself so frequently at the doors of the poor and the sick, that we began to suspect the existence of virtues even among the lower classes. Then she wore very pretty collars and dresses, the patterns of which we admired and wanted, but would have died rather than asked for. At last. Dr. Ingersoll, our rector, asked us to call upon her, saying she was very intelligent and agreeable.

We called an especial tea party to consider of the matter, and having all adopted our best sponged and turned black silks, reported ourselves at Mrs. Pendleton's, who was the *siné qua non* of Summerfield aristocracy.

Mrs. Pendleton was a stern, uncompromising old aristocrat, poorer and prouder than any of us. She had waged a fierce war with Summerfield society when she entered it herself, having been suspected of having sewed for lucre at one period of her youth. But this may have been a slander. At any rate, once in, she defended the barriers of the order with spirit and acrimony worthy of Oliver Cromwell himself. She had ruled us all with a rod of iron for many years. Church and State alike bowed before her mighty nod. The Church suffered particularly, for woe be unto the new rector if his wife did not become Mrs. Pendleton's slave; his pillow was one of thorns, carefully picked and stuffed for him by Mrs. P. State fared better, for the men could vote and legislate somewhat as they pleased; but even here her power was felt, and Mr. Peirson always attributed the loss of his election to her, because she had a son-in-law who wanted his place, and got it.

This formidable female convened, therefore, a tea party, to take into consideration Mrs. Ames's case.

Mrs. Hanson came early. She was our wit and woman of letters. We always regretted that she could not in some way reach the throne; for virtuous as we were, we felt that she would have been a Pompadour, had she had the chance. The evil whispered that Mrs. Hanson liked a flirtation, and there had been a chronic one in progress for many years. Still Mrs. Pendleton affected Mrs. Hanson, so we bore with it in silence, and really admired her wit and talent very much.

Then came Mrs. Stearns, who was somewhat richer than the rest of us, and therefore (such is the weakness of even the most exalted characters!) quite deferred to by the younger and least aristocratic of the villagers, (Summerfieldians, forgive me! I should have said, *community*.) It required (as Sydney Smith said) a surgical operation to get a joke into Mrs. Stearns's understanding, and I think that had any such operation been undertaken, even with the influence of chloroform, it would have been fatal, as almost any sizable idea would have distended her mind entirely beyond the natural dimensions. Her literal interpretation of any remark made it sometimes awkward to talk with her on general topics, but she was aristocratic to a great degree, and her ancestors, in some remote age, came from Boston.

Then came Mrs. Wentworth, whom we thorough aristocrats looked upon with suspicion. She was one of us by birth and position, but she was always breaking out and doing improper things, like calling on new people, and we felt that if such people as Mrs. Wentworth were encouraged, anarchy and confusion would come next. Some of us had said as much, and had remonstrated with her; but she said, 'Humbug!' and went on her way, with her bright blue eyes full of mischief and determination.

She was the only woman in the village who did not dread Mrs. Pendleton, and the occasional rebuffs which that monarch met with from Mrs. Wentworth were, perhaps, the only instances of downright rebellion she had ever had to contend against.

We had tremendous talk at the tea party. After exhausting the interesting events of village news, and after listening to two or three well-told anecdotes from Mrs. Hanson, Mrs. Pendleton majestically commenced making tea, and giving out the law at the same moment.

'Ladies, I presume you have all heard of the advent in our village of a Mr. and Mrs. Ames, and I am not ignorant that our worthy rector, or rather I should say, our late rector, Dr. Ingersoll, has requested all the ladies to call and see her. I have inquired about the woman, and have seen her, and I unhesitatingly pronounce her vulgar and low-bred, and I need not say that I presume none of you will call upon her.'

Mrs. Pendleton paused and looked around on her quaking subjects until her eye reached Mrs. Wentworth, who was trotting her cup up and down and looking from the window and smiling.

Now Mrs. Wentworth was very tall and handsome, and could by no means do any thing that was not noticed. So Mrs. Pendleton's attention was arrested immediately, and a look of alarm ran round the room, for we knew 'the hour of battle was near, and the trumpets sounded even to the combat.'

'May we inquire what amuses Mrs. Wentworth?' said Mrs. Pendleton, with knitted brows.

'I was bowing to poor Mrs. Ames,' said that undaunted individual.

'May I inquire how you happen to know Mrs. Ames?' said the autocrat, paling with wrath.

'I called yesterday, and found her a charming person, and I intend to know her better, and I trust all of you ladies will hasten to cultivate her, and give yourselves the great pleasure of knowing her,' said Mrs. Wentworth, still smiling, and looking about with her bright courageous eyes.

Mrs. Pendleton was a skillful general; she knew that a dignified silence was more impressive than a vigorous denunciation, so after a pause, she asked Mrs. Wentworth to take another cup of tea.

Although it seemed almost impossible to touch pitch and not be defiled, yet we all wanted to hear about Mrs. Ames, and Mrs. Hanson, presuming on the protection of Mrs. Pendleton, asked a few questions.

'She has an English way of speaking,' began Mrs. Wentworth; 'she is very well educated, and I particularly noticed the beauty of her hands. She asked me if there were any young ladies who wished to take lessons on the piano; she says she should like a few scholars; she was trying to mend an old coat when I went in —'

'Whose coat was it?' asked literal Mrs. Stearns.

'Her husband's, I suppose. She laughed very prettily, and asked me to show her how it was done, saying she didn't know very well how to mend old clothes.'

'Very creditable to a poor man's wife,' growled Mrs. Pendleton.

'I wonder if she ever heard of Burns' mother, who made 'auld claithes look 'maist as gude as new,' sighed Mrs. Hanson.

'Do you know,' burst out impetuous Mrs. Wentworth, 'she looks to me as if she had a history!'

'What history?' interrupted Mrs. Stearns. 'I have Robertson's and Gibbon's.'

'No, a story, a romantic story. I think she has seen better days. I wonder if anybody knows anything about her.'

'Dr. Ingersoll,' suggested a modest voice in the corner.

Now Dr. Ingersoll was a character. He was a man of great talents, but had not applied them much. He had been educated abroad, and perhaps that unfitted him for the duties of his New-England parish. Certainly, though for many years our rector, he had not corrected some very important faults in our community, but was whimsically fond of bringing them to light; he was a man of great humor, learning, and eccentricity, and having enough to live on, he had retired from the ministry, being a little lazy withal, and had been succeeded in turn by several young men, to torment whom was the honey of Mrs. Pendleton's existence.

Just at the moment of this last question, Dr. Ingersoll was announced. He was evidently much amused internally, and had dropped in to hear the result of the ladies' congress.

Mrs. Pendleton had retired from the Ames conversation, and was talking with Mrs. Hanson with dignified contempt, every now and then catching a remark of ours, but appearing stone deaf to the whole thing. She did not dislike Dr. Ingersoll; he was an ancient institution, an aristocrat, and treated her with profound respect. She had an innate suspicion that he laughed at her, but as she frequently said, 'Dr. Ingersoll had a vein of levity in his composition which prevented his becoming a distinguished man,' she probably comforted herself in that way.

At length Mrs. Wentworth found an opportunity to ask the Doctor about Mrs. Ames. He pleaded profound ignorance, except that he believed she was of English birth. 'But I have some startling news for you, ladies,' said the Doctor, taking his spectacles from his pocket; 'we are to have another neighbor.'

To quiet the storm of 'When?' 'Who?' 'How?' that followed, the Doctor read us a letter, dated May first, Granton Ticarage, D—shire, England:

'DEAR SIR: I want to ask your kind services and attention for my friend and parishioner, Miss Lydia Hedd, who has taken the eccentric determination to go to your country to reside, owing, perhaps, to the sad associations which surround her home, lately a very happy one, but now desolated by the death of her father, and the ill-conduct of a relative. I have advised her to try your village at first, as I entertain agreeable remembrance of it, and I know you will receive her with a welcome. She is elderly, quite rich, and connected with some of the best families in the county. What she is mentally and morally you will soon discover — one of the wittiest and wisest of women, and when not too much prejudiced, one of the best. She wishes me to add, that if it is not too great an effort, she wishes you would take a house for her for one year, as she always travels with a retinue.

'How is my friend Rose? Blossomed yet? Not plucked from the parent stem, I trust, though my ungallant memory informs me that she approaches the sere and yellow leaf of sixteen. Ah! Old friend, when you and I measured wits at Edinboro' we did not feel as stiff as we do now; but one of us, at least, has kept the stiffness from the vital organs, and still is yours, as of yore,

GEORGE SINCLAIR.'

We immediately began to run over in our minds the houses in the village which would suit a lady 'connected with the best families in the county.' There were but two empty ones. One was the Crampton House, a large red brick house, with stiff rooms on either side the hall, a stiff yard, and fence in front. It had belonged to a gentleman lately deceased, and was waiting for a purchaser. Another was the little rambling cottage at the end of the street, with rooms in all sorts of out-of-the-way places, built by some low-bred man who delighted in prospects; we immediately concluded that the high-born lady would prefer the Crampton House, as that was much nearer a ducal residence in our minds than any other attainable.

Dr. Ingersoll, with his usual obstinacy and eccentricity, decided upon the cottage.

By the first of July we had all called upon and seen Miss Lydia

Hedd. She was forty or more, tall, thin, and not handsome. We thought we saw traces of noble blood in her sallow countenance, but we felt a little offended at her *freedom of speech*. For instance, when we suggested that we thought the Crampton House would have been a more fitting residence for a lady of her importance, she called it a miserable-looking, stiff nonsensical house, with no views from it except the opposite stable; while she spoke of her cottage as an ugly, ill-contrived little *bungalow*, but with pretty views, and quiet, and away from the village.

'Bungalow' puzzled us for some time, but at length we discovered that it meant something East Indian, but why it should be applied to a Christian cottage, in the highly-intelligent town of Summerfield, we could not imagine, or at least Mrs. Stearns could not.

Still we liked her very much. She was witty, well informed, and hospitable. She instituted a very agreeable custom of giving a dinner once a week to seven ladies, herself being the eighth. No gentleman was allowed to show his head at these entertainments, though Dr. Ingersoll was permitted to come in the evening, for we staid to supper. Sometimes one or two gentlemen were permitted to follow the Doctor, but Lydia preferred to have the gentlemen save themselves for her whist-parties, which were semi-weekly.

These dinners were great events in Summerfield. The dishes were very new and very delicious, but we ate them with commendable self-respect, and pretended to have eaten them all before.

Lydia enjoyed Dr. Ingersoll very much, and Rose, his only daughter, was her especial favorite. She took much notice of her; drove her frequently in her little carriage; read with her, and did much to add to the very good education the Doctor 'had given his darling: and one of our most delightful dinners was given by Lydia, on the occasion of the recovery of Rose from a fit of illness, during which, Lydia had nursed her with the greatest affection.

Perhaps we should state that Miss Hedd had requested many of us to call her by her Christian name, before she had been long with us. Among the privileged persons were Dr. Ingersoll and Rose, and, from hearing them so call her, we all followed, when speaking *of* her.

Lydia received us — the fortunate seven — in a pretty little room looking out on the garden. She had now been with us nearly a year. The lilacs were in full bloom about the cottage, and Rose Ingersoll sat on the sofa, in her sweet white dress, looking beautifully delicate and convalescent. Mrs. Wentworth had arrived. Mrs. Hanson came, in great outward adornment and much manner, with juvenile vivacity and kittenish buoyancy, which hardly fitted her five-and-forty years. She rushed at poor Rose, embraced her violently, called her her dear lily of the valley, her white Rose, and other endearing terms.

'You must *excuse me*, dear Miss Hedd, I am so enthusiastic, I never could contain myself.'

'Heaven forbid that you should, Madam,' said Lydia, in her rough way. 'I always think if people feel so, it is best to let it out.'

The party being complete we went to dinner. We had to descend two steps to the dining room.

'Here we go, *Hedd* foremost,' said our hostess, who loved a pun.

'Why, no one has fallen!' said Mrs. Stearns, with a frightened air.

We forbear to mention the delicacies which tempted us on that occasion. Women are supposed not to eat; and for fear some budding Byron may read these pages, and find his theory disturbed, we will not refute that belief.

But no one ever believed that women remained silent, so we may narrate the conversation.

'Rose, try these sweetbreads,' said Lydia.

'Ah! That reminds me of poor Mrs. Ames,' said Rose. 'Lydia, you must let Williams carry one of those to poor Mrs. Ames.'

'Yes, Rose, but you must explain it; for you know I have never seen her yet, and I fear it might seem officious.'

Poor Mrs. Ames, indeed. Early in the winter a little Ames had made his appearance in this cold and wicked world, and the young mother had passed a weary winter of illness and trial.

Kind Mrs. Wentworth, with her great heart, had been all that she could to the poor stranger, and many other ladies had forgotten aristocracy and Mrs. Pendleton, and watched by her sick bed. But owing to these causes, Miss Hedd had never seen our bone of contention. Rose, too, had been a prisoner nearly all winter, so that Mrs. Ames had one comforter the less.

Mrs. Hanson told us a very romantic but rather improbable story about Mrs. Ames's husband, whom we rarely saw, as he rose early and drove to the railroad which was being constructed near Summerfield. She said he was throwing a stone one day out on his works, when a ring came off his finger, and was lost. He showed a great deal of anxiety, and said he would have rather lost five pounds than that ring, and immediately hired an Irishman to look for it.

'Now that shows me that he is English,' said Mrs. Hanson. 'Yankees don't talk about five pounds.'

Mrs. Wentworth said, 'Why shouldn't he be English?' She had never asked Mrs. Ames about herself, for there was a sort of reserve about her that forbade it, but she had no sort of doubt that Mr. and Mrs. Ames were English people, and she almost thought they had run away and been married clandestinely, for she was sure Mr. Ames did not look at all like a working man, or seem to know much about common life.

'Williams, pour me a glass of wine,' said Miss Hedd, looking distressed.

We all remembered that Dr. Ingersoll's letter had spoken of the ill conduct of some of Miss Hedd's relatives, and we concluded this remark had caused unpleasant recollections.

She shook them off, as one of the ladies began rallying Rose Ingersoll on the subject of the young rector, who was rather inclined to admire her.

'What a charming tableau you made the other morning, Rose, with Mr. Thurston sitting at the head of your sofa, and your papa looking benignly on,' said Mrs. Wentworth, laughing.

Lydia did not like Mr. Thurston.

'What! Rose Ingersoll! Did you allow that Mr. Thurston to sit and talk to you?'

'Yes, Lydia; dear, sentimental Mr. Thurston!' said Rose, for she liked a joke. 'The window was open, and the lilacs peeped in and filled the parlor with fragrance. I reclined on a sofa, looking delicate and interesting. The hummingbirds flew about, the very bees sang and buzzed in a loving manner: why should not Mr. Thurston and I join the voices of the season, and sing and buzz of love!'

'Nonsense, Rose. I see you don't care for that silly fellow; but if I ever hear of your talking under any description of lilac bush, and encouraging stupid young clergymen, I will write to Lord John directly and tell him not to come.

'Did Rose ever tell you of Lord John?' addressing us all.

'Never,' burst from twelve anxious lips.

'Well, Lord John C— is my near relative, and the finest young man in England. He is not only handsome and accomplished, but he is good and great. He entertains the belief that some peerless woman is growing up for him somewhere, and so do I. He is in this country now, and is coming here to see me. If Rose behaves herself, I intend to marry him to her, and raise her to the peerage — but no more flirtations with young clergymen. Rose! I will not stand it!'

Now Lydia had no more idea of marrying Rose to Lord John, than she had idea of marrying him herself She knew very well that my Lord John's papa would not relish the idea of an unentitled daughter-in-law, and in many a conversation with Rose had she talked of the feeling which existed in England against *mésalliances*. With her it was merely a joke, and she perhaps had a whimsical idea that when she brought these young people together, they might inconveniently fall in love, and all this joking of hers would prove Rose's effectual safeguard in case they did.

Fate had provided a more certain heart-armor for Miss Rose than even Miss Lydia had been able to construct, and that was an undefined sentiment of regard which that young lady felt for one Mr. Gordon Lee, a dark-eyed young gentleman, who had passed one of his vacations in Summerfield, and made some use of it, in cultivating the acquaintance of Rose.

They were both extremely young, but that has not always prevented people from being extremely fond of one another; and although no one knew, of course, 'how far' matters had gone, we all married Rose to Gordon Lee, in our imaginations.

Fate, however, interfered once more in Miss Lydia's plans, and sent Dr. Ingersoll and Rose to the sea-side, for the better building-up of the health of the latter. And the first day at dinner, Rose's neighbor pointed out to her Lord John C—, who had come down with a party of young men to the hotel where they were staying.

Dr. Ingersoll immediately made his acquaintance, on the strength of mutual regard for Miss Lydia. Lord John desired an introduction to his lovely daughter; and very many walks, sails, and talks, was the natural result.

Alas! There was no Lydia, no Gordon Lee present. 'Both were young, and one was beautiful.' Rose was a very attractive girl; she had an American face, with an English figure. It was a combination Lord John had not met with; her grace, her tact, the almost inseparable accompaniments of the independent, self-reliant education she had had, charmed and surprised the young Englishman. He, too, was very agreeable; he was not as handsome as Gordon Lee, so Rose observed to herself, as they returned from a boating party, as the young Lord's healthy English face glowed with the exercise and enjoyment; nor was he quite as intellectual: but how manly he was! How athletic, how strong!

One day he brought down his book of drawings to show her. She was astonished to find how accomplished he was; he, so modest, so silent on all that related to himself She turned over the leaves, one by one, and came to some female heads.

'Why, certainly, this is a picture of someone I have seen! Why, this is Mrs. Ames! No, it cannot be; but how like!'

Lord John turned pale. 'I did not know that was in existence; but whom did you say it resembled?'

'Mrs. Ames; the dearest, sweetest woman; she has lived in Summerfield a year or so, and has been very ill. No one knows her or her husband; that is, no one did. But papa and I, and a Mrs. Wentworth, have been to see her; and her husband came to see papa when they first came to our village; I don't know why, perhaps because he is a clergyman; and I believe he told papa about himself, but papa never would tell.'

'Resemblances are curious sometimes: these were mostly sketches made in Spain;' and Lord John took his portfolio and left the room.

Before the young people parted at the seashore, one soft summer twilight, Lord John took his ring from his finger, and showed the design carved on it. It was an arrow transfixing the stem of a rose, and apparently flying through the air with its fragrant prize.

'This is my crest, dear lady; my brave ancestors had to win their roses with more deadly weapons than we are called to use; but I trust we are to be no degenerate ancestors, and that we may win our roses with devotion and love, instead of arrows!'

Rose did not reply; she certainly liked Lord John very much, but did she love him? Did not a pair of dark eyes sometimes come in and destroy the pleasant picture of sailing off to England, and living in a turreted castle, like those she had seen in landscapes?

He took her hand, and gently slipped the ring on it. 'Wear it, at least, dear lady, till we meet again: 1 shall see you before many weeks. You do not make any promise by consenting to wear it; you will but remember the owner, and this evening, when you see it.'

That evening. Lord John had a long interview with Dr. Ingersoll; but there was not one word spoken about Rose.

The first person Rose saw when she reached home was Gordon Lee, the second was Lydia, the third was Mrs. Ames.

Lydia was overwhelmed with confusion, delight, and wonder, at the account of Lord John. Rose was a woman, and therefore quite capable of throwing dust in her (Lydia's) eyes, on the subject of Lord John's admiration; beside, a walk with Gordon Lee had quite convinced her that Lord John's ring must be returned.

Sweet Mrs. Ames was very happy to see her friend, and listened to the account of her visit with pleasure. She had her little son in her arms, and was walking up and down the room with him, while Rose described. Lord John, and the remarkable resemblance which that picture of his bore to Mrs. Ames.

'It was fuller than you, Mrs. Ames, and more smiling, and was dressed in a riding habit; but so like you!'

Mrs. Ames hid her face on the baby's little white shoulder, and walked up and down silently. Rose talked on, admired the baby, and got up to go home. As she shook hands at parting, Mrs. Ames screamed with delight, as she saw Lord John's ring.

'My husband's ring! Where was it found, dear Rose? The very one I gave him before we were married! Poor George! How he sorrowed when he lost it; almost the last relic of happier days! Did that Irishman bring it to you?'

Rose was very much confused. A whole history came out with these words, and she had not time to connect the links, nor did she want to tell the romantic story of the ring. Mrs. Ames looked anxiously at her, never doubting that the ring was the one lost by her husband, and wondering at her confusion.

Rose at length found voice and courage to say: 'Mrs. Ames, this is not yours; it is one that Lord John C— put on my finger.'

It was now Mrs. Ames's turn to be confused. What had she done? What a dreadful disclosure she had made!

'Rose, dear, you have unfortunately become possessor of a secret: may I depend upon you? Will you keep it secret? You shall know more soon; but, dear Rose, what have I to hear — can it be possible? What strange links bind us all together!'

Rose walked home, bewildered and almost stunned. She was not particularly imaginative, and her mind was very much disturbed with her own affairs. The Ames mystery perplexed her greatly. She walked up to her own little room, and tried to unravel the complicated affair.

The next day, on returning from a walk with Gordon Lee, she ran in to see Lydia, who was sitting in her little parlor, crying.

'O Lydia!' said Rose, 'don't do that, I beg of you! Everybody is in trouble; everybody is saying and doing strange things, and I came in to see you, hoping that you at least were all right! Papa is walking up and down in great perturbation; I am walking up and down in great distress; you are crying, and Mrs. Ames—!'

She had nearly forgotten her promise!

'Go home, dear child, go home! I can't tell you anything, but your papa will!'

Rose walked home; went to her papa's study. There stood Lord John, with his arms around Mrs. Ames!

The Doctor was 'walking up and down,' as Rose had described him, wiping his eyes and working off an immense deal of feeling.

'Come in, Rose,' said Mrs. Ames; 'come in! The days of mysteries are over!'

Lord John disengaged himself, and came forward to receive the lady of his heart.

'Mrs. Ames is my sister, dear Miss Ingersoll; and one day she chose to run away with a certain Captain A—, whom her papa and brother did not approve of. I came to America, partly to learn her fate and to take care of her, if she needed it; but I did not mean to see her. Your few words, when you saw her picture in my portfolio, the compassion which your face expressed, awoke the brother in me so keenly, that I have altered my intention, as you perceive.'

'And you, papa, have known this lady's history from the first?'

'Yes, my dear, and a dreadful time I have had of it; but then it was great comfort to hear the ladies determine not to call on her, on account of her *low birth!*'

'And Lydia?'

'Is Mrs. Ames's aunt; and when she was sent here by that curious fatality which always brings people together who wish to stay apart, I had to tell her that her runaway niece, whose conduct was the reason of her leaving England, was here, in fear some sudden interview might take place and kill them both on the spot!'

'And has Lydia not forgiven her?'

'Hardly. It was a great blow, for I was almost a daughter to her,' said poor, weeping Mrs. Ames.

'Here she comes, up the street!' said the fidgety Doctor, looking from the window.

The kindly Ingersolls left them together, the offended and the offending. Peace was the result. Mrs. Ames had 'given the world for love, and considered it well lost.' Nothing remained for them but to forgive. There was an implacable father still left to appease, but Lord John would be a good mediator; and better than all to the poor wife, they, at her solicitations, forgave her husband.

And how did it fare with Lord John, the good, the generous, the unselfish? As it fares but too often with the good, Lord John was the only one who went away with a heavy heart.

'And how is that happy ring, dear Miss Rose, which I see still on the finger where I placed it?' said Lord John, when evening found them alone together.

Poor Rose had never refused anybody; she did not know *how* in the least. She felt as if she were going to faint; but she was a brave, good girl, and seeing now plainly her own heart, and which way it leaned, she only sought to save her kind and noble admirer all the pain she could.

She took the ring off and handed it back to its owner.

'I cannot keep it, Lord John, and I trust I shall not seem coquettish to you. You were the first cultivated man, the first traveled, accomplished man of the world I had ever seen. I was fascinated by that nameless something which the world gives, and which we rustics have not; and your kindness, your preference for me added a new charm to our intercourse. I should have known from the first, too, how far we are apart, how unfitted I am for the exalted station which you occupy. Your father, he must not be called on to sorrow over unequal marriage!'

Lord John was not at all disconcerted by all this; on the contrary, he was looking very much pleased; and poor Rose found she had not discarded him at all.

'My dear Rose — permit me to use the word — I know all about these matters better than you. You are no *bad match* (to use your own suggestion) for anybody. Oh! If anything about me has touched your heart, if you love me in the least, trust the rest to me! Believe me, I can make it plain and right, and happy for you. I have a conviction so deeply seated that I can make *you* happy, that

I beg of you to say that one little word that can make *me* happy.'

Must she then put the truth into *words*, that delicate, unspoken truth which she hardly acknowledged to herself? How could she frame it in *words?* — But she must.

'Dear Lord John, much as I like you, greatly as I admire you, I am afraid I *love* another.'

Lord John did not attempt to refute this argument. It was a great blow to him; for her confusion, her self-depreciation had won him very much, and given him every encouragement. She could not have done it worse; but fortunately he was as straightforward and as generous as she was, and liked her all the better for it *the next day.*

'So Mrs. Ames is the Lady Geraldine C—, whose elopement we all read about two years ago! Ah! Truth is stranger than fiction, and the human heart a mysterious thing,' sighed Mrs. Hanson, at the next tea party.

'I wonder if her brother left her any money?' said Mrs. Stearns.

'He offered himself to Rose Ingersoll,' said Mrs. Wentworth.

'What is title, and wealth, where the heart is unmoved?' put in Mrs. Hanson.

'I think it a good deal,' said Patty Patterson; 'and I suspect the poor little fool will find it out, before Gordon Lee gets ready to marry her.'

Patty was a little older and less handsome than Rose.

'Mrs. Ames looks ten years younger,' said Mrs. Pendleton. 'I went round to advise her about the baby, yesterday.'

'Have *you* been to see her?' said Mrs. Wentworth, laughing.

'Certainly, several times,' said the autocrat, who never made any acknowledgment of defeat, but ignored everything she did not wish to remember.

Lydia gave a 'ladies' dinner,' shortly after these tremendous events. Mrs. Ames, forgiven and beloved, sat at her right hand; Rose at her left. She liked Rose all the better for having refused Lord John. Rose and Lydia smiled at the deference and admiration with which even the oldest aristocrat regarded Mrs. Ames.

Dr. Ingersoll arrived to supper. Lydia offered him oysters. 'No,' said he,

> 'Save me from all *eating* cares,
> Wrap me in soft *Lydian* airs.'

'O Doctor! You know you want some supper. I am too old to be taken in by your poetry.'

So the Doctor ate his oysters, and looked about with twinkling eyes, as he saw Mrs. Pendleton herself helping Mrs. Ames to some delicacy.

Mr. and Mrs. Ames, or rather Captain A— and his wife, left Summerfield very soon. Lord John had found something for Captain A— to do more fitted to his education than building railroads. We never saw them again; for the unforgiving father, having been called away to account for his own deeds, they went home to England, where they remained.

Lydia went with them, to the lifelong regret of Summerfield. She kept up a vigorous correspondence with Rose, who waited patiently for her Gordon, and at length married him, when his profession was promising, and his political prospects (then the great hope and interest of all young Americans of talent) were high. He got to be this and that in the state, all of which pleased Rose much better than if she had married a man of rank, and been borne down

> 'With the burden of an honor,
> Unto which she was not born.'

At last came a letter from Lydia, telling Rose of the marriage of Lord John (now Lord C—) to a lady of rank and fortune. Lydia said she was all they could wish, and her dear nephew was very happy.

'Now, dear Rose,' she wrote, 'I am getting old, and I want to see you before I die. Your old friend. Lord C—, and Lady C— both wish me to ask you and your husband to spend the summer in England, at his house, where I, a shadow, flit about at twilight, but keep out of the sunlight, as all ghosts do. Come, dear Rose, and gladden your old friend's heart. Geraldine, too, is within a morning's drive, and longs to see you.'

Mr. and Mrs. Lee found it agreeable to themselves to accept this invitation; and Rose, who had lost her dear old father, thought with tearful eyes of Lydia, who had been, next to him, the best friend of her youth.

"When Lord John gave Rose his arm, at the entrance of his stately house, he looked with surprise at her now perfected beauty.

'I think I shall not be ashamed to present my transatlantic friend to Lady C—!' he whispered to Rose.

They found Lady C— handsome and charming. Secure in her lofty lineage and position, and in her own natural gifts, she felt no annoyance at her husband's admiration for the beautiful American; but cordially assisted him to amuse his guests.

They drove over the beautiful country. They looked at ruins hallowed by story. They breathed the healthful air. They enjoyed that perfection of liberty, of hospitality — an English country house. They saw a delightful party of people gathered together in Lord C—'s house, walking, driving, talking, when they pleased; and acknowledged that social life in England was far more perfect than social life in America. But a strong spirit animated them both — to return and do what they could to improve their own dear land.

How proud and gratified was Rose, when she heard Gordon talking very well at dinner, in presence, too, of some of the best men of England. He was giving a rapid but graphic picture of the immense possibilities of America. He painted in few but glowing words her silver network of rivers, joining her scattered fragments in imperishable union. The wealth, which poured like Dane's shower into the hands of her hard-working people—the splendid pedestal which Industry and Energy were building, on which would some day rest the proud achievements of immortal Art.

Rose stole a furtive glance at Lord C—. He was looking at her with a world of meaning in his eyes. He smiled slightly, and gave her a little nod.

SUMMERFIELD has connections now with the nobility. We speak often of our titled friends. Lydia is always mentioned as 'the Honorable Miss Hedd;' and we respect Rose very much more, that she might have been 'My Lady.' Occasionally, some lady, more intrepid than the rest, gets up several side dishes, with infinite labor and pains, and we have a 'ladies' dinner.'

VI

The Proposal

BY FRANCIS COPCUTT

FEBRUARY 1852

You're late: the soup's gone!
    Dear Ellen! —Miss Leeds—
I—I—think that trout's spoiled—the cook's careless deeds.
I've something to say—Charles! The salt!—quite unusual,
And I hope—Superb sauce!—I shall have no refusal.
I'm relieved by that blush—This tomato's all seeds—
No, thank you; not yet, Charles: *first*, wait on Miss Leeds.
Would it not be as well—Will you have some baked beans?—
To avoid farther blushing? They'll notice these *scenes*.
Charles! That partridge! Some breast? This is very good
dressing—
I may say, since the day that I first had the blessing
Of seeing—Some pepper?—your face, that the passion
(Which e'er since the creation's been so much in fashion)
I feel, I felt then: and I hope you return it.
Well—thank you for that; for I feared you might spurn it.
By the way, I might say—Yes, I've done: take the plate—
As your *mother's* will only hangs *now* o'er our fate,
That I'm not *very* rich, and my income's not great,
But plenty to keep up respectable state:—
Charles! I've no spoon! —and as I hate fashion,
And observe that in that way you've almost no passion,
We'll have more than enough; you'll have no cause to sigh

49

THE PROPOSAL

For—Rice pudding? Or do you prefer pumpkin pie?—
Aught that you wish, 'twill be yours.—Which of these?
Nuts? 'Tis well, they are bad—these raisins, or cheese?—
I am just thirty-eight: I am frank, and—You've dined!—
In the morning I'll ask what's you're dear mother's mind;
And from doubt of the future no trouble I'll borrow—
No! No coffee—Good-bye until dinner tomorrow.

VII

Table Aesthetics

BY CARL BENSON

APRIL 1848

I AM GOING to write on a most important subject, one which concerns all classes and conditions of men every day of their lives, and has a direct influence on very weighty public and private affairs; which is intimately associated with ideas of joy and comfort and strength; three most pleasant things. It is the art, science and mystery of those acts which the Transcendentalists call 'appropriating to one's self a portion of the outer world;' in plain English, breakfasting and dining with their incidents and accessories; what for want of a better term, I call *table aesthetics.*

Now I am well aware at the outset, that many very worthy persons, either from defective education and want of opportunity to know better, or from inconsiderate conformity with those about them, (a common American fault,) or from want of accurate discrimination, confounding things which have some resemblance (another very common fault of our beloved countrymen) will consider my purpose in this essay frivolous at best, if not absolutely mischievous. So, as it is always well to clear the ground for a fair start, our preliminary step will be to hear what they have to say, and then endeavor to enlighten them a little.

'The art of eating and drinking!' cries one. 'Animal propensities! Sensual! Making a beast of one's self! Digging his grave with his teeth!' and much more in the same strain.

Hold hard, my friend, and don't talk rubbish. Do you mean to insinuate that table-asstheticism and gluttony are convertible terms? If so, you might just as well say that every man who goes to see the *Venus de Medicis* is a profligate. The very reverse is true in most cases. It is notorious that the most barbarous nations, those among whom table aesthetics, as well as all other arts, have made the least progress, are the most voracious feeders. The man who eats knowingly, generally eats at least one-fourth less than the average of those who eat at random. He seldom exceeds two meals a day and one of those not a hearty one. For my own part I would wager that if the readers who are tempted to turn up a frugal and virtuous nose at the title of this paper were put upon my daily diet by way of regimen, the majority would cry out for a change, and confess themselves half-starved in less than a fortnight. And on the score of health, worthy Cato, let me tell you that you are sadly mistaken. It is not the man who, after the toil and bustle of the day are over, leisurely refreshes himself with a dainty and judicious repast, irrigated with a moderate supply of the generous *latex Lyoeus,* and then reposes over his book or in pleasant conversation to digest it; it is not he who is bilious and dyspeptic. No, it is the man who at the unnatural and barbarous hour of one P.M., pitches into himself a variety of miscellaneous provender indiscriminately for fifteen minutes, and in fifteen more is at his business again. As to the intellectual side of the question, there are doubtless extraordinary occasions when a man has to get through a certain amount of head-work in a limited time, and is obliged to live like a hermit in order to keep his brain clear. Most persons have had some such experiences. I remember a period of three weeks during which I would willingly have dispensed with eating altogether, and did only take just enough to support the system. But this corresponds to the training of the pedestrian or the jockey, by which he is enabled to undergo a preternatural amount of bodily exertion; and the one is no more the normal state and habitual system of diet, than the other is of exercise. All the genial and natural products of a man's intellect, the happiest spontaneous effusions of his fancy and imagination, proceed from a well-nourished frame. *Satur est quum dieit Horatius, Evoe!*

As to the expense too, the argument in many cases makes all the other way. Economy, not a niggardly parsimony, but a sensible and prudent economy, enters into the calculations of the aesthetic. Good taste abhors excessive profusion, and good edibles are naturally less prone to be wasted than bad ones.[1] A clever French cook will make up nearly the difference in his wages by saving the fuel which would have been unprofitably expended by an Irish ignoramus, or *ignorama,* as I once heard a learned Boston lady call it. It is well known by those versed in military affairs, that a French regiment will subsist comfortably on rations which would drive an English regiment to mutiny, not because the French do not require as much nourishment as the English, whatever their novelists and dramatists may represent to the contrary, but because their superior skill in cookery enables them to make a given amount of animal matter go further. Let it be allowed, however, that aesthetic habitudes do involve more outlay of capital than a rude and haphazard way of supporting nature. It remains to be asked whether the advantages procured by them do not justify the additional expense. And this will be better considered in connection with the third objection which may be supposed, viz., that the pursuit is a frivolous one and not worthy the time and trouble which it requires.

Now if man be a social animal (as we have the highest authority for asserting that he is) and if table-aestheticism promotes sociability, then in truth is it no unimportant matter. A good dinner is the parent of good feeling, peace with one's self and with the world, benevolence and liberality. Wherefore the charitable societies of England do wisely give dinners, knowing that the purse is more open after a sumptuous banquet. On the other hand, what mortification, discomfort and misanthropy result from a bad dinner! What an awful infliction it is to be asked to partake in suffering one! And to say that any man with

---

1   In the hall of a New England college where I pretended to eat some twelve years ago, the expense of what was wasted would have kept a decent table. The students used to squander their supplies in very spite, they were so bad.

the requisite means can provide the needful by merely giving orders to his cook, confectioner and wine merchant, is absurd; for in the first place, it requires aesthetic discernment to choose *the* cook, *the* confectioner and *the* wine merchant. Moreover, we have observed that one part of the science is to manage your means and make the most of your resources, so that one instructed can give an agreeable banquet at the expense which would procure but a sorry set-out in the hands of the uninitiated. The truth is that table-aestheticism is a branch of the fine arts, a subordinate one indeed, but occupying its distinct and appropriate place; and you will generally find that the man who has a good taste in poetry, painting and music, will also have a good taste in all things pertaining to the management of the table. There are some people who think all the fine arts wicked, and incentives to bad passions; and others who, having no perception of the beautiful, think them expensive follies, and take credit to themselves for their insensibility, like Mr. Chief Engineer Jervis, who makes a merit of defacing and disfiguring the most beautiful river in the world. And there are men whose palates are naturally blunt, and to whom it makes not the slightest difference what they taste or imbibe, just as there are others again who would as lief talk to an ugly woman as to a handsome one; but you, reader mine, are not of that sort, I trust, nor happily are the majority of mankind, even in this utilitarian age. Still even these people may be led to see the excellency of table-aestheticism, if they will look at the power it confers on a master of it in society. What gives a man *prestige* and personal popularity, what softens criticism and wins partisans like being an irreproachable Amphitryon? No observant man can doubt that the Boston literati owe a great part of their reputation and influence to the fact of their understanding table aesthetics and habitually giving correct little banquets to each other and to casual visitors. I don't think anyone who ever dined with Shortbody could set himself down seriously to inquire whether the metaphors in Diaboline will hold water, and whether Trochaic Tetrameter Acatalectic is a natural and suitable metre in English or not. What weapon so powerful in the hands of a diplomatist as a *comme-il-faut* entertainment? Hence the Russians, whose diplomatic superiority is well known, give their ministers unlimited supplies that they may 'hang out' (pardon the vulgarity of the expression, as Jeames says) without limit. What keeps a political association together like good eating and drinking? There was a striking instance of this some years ago in the English parliament, where thirty radical members voted together in a body so long as two of their number (Molesworth and Leader) supplied the bond of union in the shape of dinners. When the dinners stopped the unanimity stopped also. Were I ever to become a politician I should, as the very first step import a first-rate *artiste* from Paris. A friend who, like Ulysses, had seen the cities and ascertained the dispositions of many men, made a remark the other day in connection with this point, which struck me as proceeding from a philosophic mind. 'Why,' said he, 'do the good people of Boston fret about the way things go on in Washington, and complain of the national politics? What's the use of slanging the President and passing resolutions? There is a far more natural and efficacious remedy open to them. Let them send down to the capital (by subscription or otherwise) one of their most aesthetic men; let him build an elegant house, give elegant parties, and induct the western and southwestern members into the refinements of civilization and especially of cookery. My life for it, they would do more in that way than by all the speeches that ever were made in Faneuil Hall, even though the god-like Daniel were one of the speakers. And the god-like would say so himself, for he understands the value of table-aesthetics.'

Such was the substance of my friend's remarks, and I commend them to the attention of those whom they most concern, as well worthy to be pondered upon.

There are some things connected with table matters, such as carving,[2] making salad, telling good wine from bad, without the

---

2   I mention carving particularly, being every day painfully reminded of the defects of my early education in this point. It is a natural consequence of the system practiced at most of our colleges of cramming the students

knowledge of which a gentleman's education cannot be said to be complete, and the subject generally I consider an essential part of education; very much more so than dancing, which some people consider the *sine qua non*, for everyone does not dance, and it is possible to live very happily without dancing, whereas everyone eats and drinks, and few people can live well without eating well; infinitely more so than that stump oratory, the acquisition of which seems to be the great object of half our young men, and which only renders them nuisances in conversation, and makes true oratory at a discount from the number of parodies upon it.

The above reflections, and many more of a like sort, were recently suggested to me with peculiar force by the perusal of a table classic, BRILLAT-SAVARIN's *Physiologie de Gout*. Although in the twenty-odd years which have elapsed since its publication many improvements have been made in the art of which it treats, it has still a right to be considered one of the standard works on table aesthetics. Whether it has ever been translated into English or not I will not undertake to say; but if there is a translation in our vernacular, I have never met with it; and at any rate, the book is not very well known among Anglo-Saxons. BRILLAT-SAVARIN was an advocate, and afterward a judge of the *Cour de Cassation*. Proscribed in the Revolution, he took refuge first in Switzerland and then in America. In our good city of Gotham he passed two years, supporting himself as a musician and a teacher, and gaining popularity, as he says himself, by taking care not to appear cleverer *(n'avoir plus d'esprit,)* than the Americans. Condescending Gaul! It is gratifying to find that such self-sacrificing modesty met with its reward. Better days dawned at home; he was restored to his old post of judge, and for the last twenty-five years of his life lived on the fat of the land. His great work, 'The Physiology of Taste, or Transcendental Gastronomy,' of which I shall try to give

---

into an uncomfortable hall, and feeding them on the coarsest fare, that they should contract a pernicious and not easily eradicated habit of scarifying and mangling dishes without care or decency. On this theme alone a treatise might be written, Bad fare naturally and inevitably induces a disrespect for the table and a neglect of its proprieties.

the benevolent reader some general idea, was first published in 1825, just before his decease. By way of prolegomena to the book we have twenty *fundamental axioms,* some of the most important of which I proceed to transcribe, with such comments as naturally present themselves.

'2. Animals *feed,* man *eats;* it takes a clever man to know how to eat.'

Accordingly, we hear the most unaesthetic and unrefined persons calling their dinners, etc., *food.* The word is awfully prevalent in Connecticut. The tutors at Yale used to talk about *food* till they made me sick. And that nuisance of modern English society, the 'fast man,' who is always very much of a Goth in his eating as well as his dress, never says that he is going to a dinner or a supper at so-and-so's, but to a 'feed' at so-and-so's; and certainly the expression is appropriate enough for such donkeys.

'3. The destiny of nations depends on the manner in which they are nourished.'

This is illustrated in the body of the work itself, where the author says: 'In the state of society at which we have now arrived it is difficult to imagine a people living exclusively on bread and vegetables. Such a nation, did it exist, would infallibly be subjugated by carnivorous invaders, as the Hindoos have been successively the prey of whoever has chosen to attack them.' The inferiority in warlike prowess of the abstemious Spaniards and Italians to the more substantially nourished French, Germans and English, is notorious. And the Mexicans — poor mortals! — who live on *frijoles* and *tortillas,* are ridden over roughshod by our beef and venison-fed soldiery. Apart from mere physical capacity, we can trace many of the mental characteristics of different nations to their different meats, beverages and condiments. The influence of beer and tobacco on the German mind — the stolid acquiescence in the present and dogged conservatism induced by the former, the mistiness of speculation fostered by the latter, are self-evident. The national light wines and indispensable coffee point to several elements of the French character; and it has often seemed to me that the windy loquacity and speech-making propensities of a certain class of our countrymen are distinctly referable to their large consumption of cold water.

'4. Tell me what you eat, and I will tell you who you are.'

In compliance with and as a test of this philosophic dictum, I offer the following problem: Given, a gentleman whose favorite viands are 'Anguilles a la Tartare,' 'Dindon déssosé' and 'Beignets de Pommes,' (which being interpreted, are fried eels with mustard sauce, boned turkey and apple fritters,) and whose pet 'vanity' in the way of drink is, in winter, Mazanilla sherry, and in summer dry champagne half and half with iced water: required, the character of the individual.

'10. Those who get indigestions [why could we not say, *who indigest themselves? —* a felicitous expression, that *s'indigèrent,*] or get drunk, do not know how to eat or drink.'

Cf. sis, (as the classical editors say,) our remarks *ante* on the error of confounding table-aestheticism with gluttony.

'14. A dessert without cheese is like a belle who has lost an eye.'

Various nations employ cheese in very various ways, The Italian takes it in soup, and with the national *minestra* of macaroni or vermicelli it is a great improvement; but with any other kind of soup, detestable. The Frenchman serves it at the other end of his dinner, among the fruit and the bon-bons. The Englishman eats it — often accompanied by salad — between the meats and the pastry; arid with a very large number of Englishmen it supplies the place of pastry or dessert altogether; cheese being to John Bull what pie is to Brother Jonathan. With us 'crackers and cheese' are the ordinary tavern and steamboat lunch, and you may also see the traveling public devouring much cheese at *tea,* along with smoked beef, cake and preserves — awful catachresis of eatables! I saw with my own eyes a man do this who was then in the legislature, and has since gone abroad on a diplomatic mission. I hope he will learn better in Europe. On our dinner tables cheese is seldom seen, the national taste being decidedly in favor of closing with a variety of sweets; and as a general rule, our custom seems preferable; yet there are some occasions when cheese makes the most appropriate termination; for instance, when you drink hock. I said, *when;* for on more accounts than one, hock is not to be drunk every day. At such a time you cannot do better than follow the example of my venerated aesthetic friend 'JOHN WATERS,' and let your *roti* be succeeded by nothing but some delicate Neufchatel with exquisite little dry biscuits and the finest butter; for sweets destroy German wine, and any sweets except fresh fruit and those indispensable sponge biscuits familiarly denominated finger-cakes, are detrimental to your perception of Bordeaux and Burgundy.

'16. THE INDISPENSABLE QUALITY OF THE COOK IS PUNCTUALITY: IT SHOULD ALSO BE THAT OF THE GUEST.'

I have written this in small capitals. Every guest and every host should have it by heart. Of the two a deviation from punctuality is worse on the host's part, as being less remediable. If a man doesn't come at the time appointed, you have always the resource of sitting down without him; but what escape is there for the unfortunates who are kept three-quarters of an hour in the drawing room hungry and listless, making painful endeavors to amuse each other, and looking anxiously round every time the door is opened to see if dinner is announced? The English used to have an absurd custom of understanding the time of dinner as two hours later than that named in the invitation; *e. g.,* if you were asked at six, the company assembled at half-past seven and sat down at eight. They are now wiser, and rarely wait more than fifteen minutes beyond the specified time,[3] which indeed is a very liberal allowance; five for difference of watches, five for accidents, such as detention in the road, etc., and five out of pure grace. The Parisians are generally punctual to the minute. With us there is no fixed rule; some hosts are punctual, and some not. The consequence is extreme confusion, for a corresponding uncertainty is produced on the part of the guests; and the results are frequently very awkward. For instance, an invited one assists

---

3   Of course there are some exceptions to this rule, as there are to most rules. Thus, if a commoner expected a peer to dine with him, honest John's inherent flunkeyism would probably make him wait considerably beyond the fifteen minutes.

with extreme punctuality at two or three entertainments in the beginning of a season, and has to wait three-quarters of an hour at each. He becomes tired of the fun, and on the next invitation, should he have any business on hand, says to himself: 'There's no use of hurrying,' and accordingly arrives perhaps half an hour after the period specified; but this time he has to do with a punctual host, and finds to his confusion that the soup and fish are already despatched, or what is worse, that the dinner is waiting *for him*, and the guests staring at him, as at a guilty creature, when he enters. At Washington the old English unpunctuality is the rule; at least it was a very few years ago. You were asked to breakfast at ten, and on arriving found no one up to receive you. It once befell me to be invited to dinner at the 'White House.' The card of invitation named an early hour — half-past five, I think. For forty minutes I enjoyed an uninterrupted opportunity of examining the furniture and calculating whether the appropriations made for it were extravagant or not. At ten minutes after six a member of the President's family made his appearance; in half an hour more the company began to assemble, and at a quarter past seven we sat down to table. Now this was of no consequence in the case of a nobody like myself, but the very same might have happened, and I have no doubt has happened more than once, to some foreigner of distinction. All delays on either side are bad. Waiting for a guest spoils the dinner; waiting for a dinner may half-starve the guests. It makes an important difference in a man's morning arrangements whether he is to dine at five or at seven, as in the latter case some slight mid-day refreshment is necessary. Note also the next axiom.

'17. *To wait too long for a late guest is a want of respect for those who are present.*'

The lion of the party has a sort of prescriptive right to be waited for, *but it is very bad manners in him to avail himself of the privilege.* Whenever the [Olympian gods/fate] shall place me in a dinner-giving position, I don't intend to wait for anyone, lion or not.

'18. He who receives his friends without giving any personal attention to the repast which is prepared for them, does not deserve to have friends.'

'19. The mistress of the house should always make sure that the coffee is perfect; and the master, that the liqueurs are of the best quality.'

Alas! With us it would often puzzle master and mistress both to make sure of the coffee. It is astonishing that out of so many civilized countries all consuming the beverage to a greater or less extent, there are only two in which you ordinarily and habitually get good coffee; France, to wit, and Belgium. The French seem to have a peculiar genius for the preparation of this article. Our author's receipt is: 'Pour boiling water upon coffee placed in a silver or china vase perforated with very small holes. Take this first decoction, warm it up to the boiling point, strain it again, and you have as clear and good coffee as can be made.' I used to dispense with the perforated vessel, and consequently with the first straining; instead of which 1 followed the ordinary plan of mixing an egg with the ground coffee. My instructors in the art were an Englishman and an American, who in this way made as good coffee as I ever drank in Paris; but I never could come up to their mark, except on a few lucky days, though I made coffee for myself nearly a year; which confirms me in the belief that the art is born with one. But while thus frankly owning my deficiencies, I believe myself capable of giving some not altogether useless hints on the subject. The *first* great and general fault in English and American coffee making is, *not putting in enough coffee*. At hotels universally, and at private houses generally, there is one-half or two-thirds too much water. The next great and common error is *over-roasting the berry,* which imparts a bitter and nauseous flavor. By carefully avoiding these dangers, you may make very palatable coffee without its being quite clear, though of course complete claridity is essential to its perfection. The coffee should be *roasted and ground just before it is used*. This is one great secret of the superiority of the Parisian article. If it be too much trouble to prepare the coffee every day, the best way of keeping it is *after it is made*. You may bottle up enough for a week, (taking care to cork it tight,) and warm it over as you want it. This sounds strange, but I have tried the experiment with entire success.

The remark upon liqueurs is worthy of attention. Not long ago I was at a dinner where the host had imprudently left the care of this matter to the butler; and the consequence was, that instead of Maraschino and Curaçoa, we were presented with—anisette and cherry-bounce! Not that cherry-bounce is by any means a despicable variety, under certain circumstances, but it is not *exactly* what you would select for a *chasse-café*.

The English are very ignorant of the use and theory of coffee and liqueurs. You will see an Englishman take two large cups of coffee, flooded with milk, and should a *chasse* be introduced — which is not generally the case — he will make no scruple of tossing off two or even three glasses. Just before leaving the fast-anchored isle, I concentrated my aesthetic resources into three dinners: conceive my dismay, when after the second I perceived one of the guests — a young Eton-bred Cantab, but quite old enough to have known better — seizing my last bottle of Maraschino and drinking it as if it were table claret! Fortunately I had presence of mind enough to divert his attention by throwing some champagne in his way. And Lady Blessington, who must have seen good society in her time, talks in one of her novels of a nobleman tossing off two bumpers of Curaçoa.

The earlier part of M. Brillat-Savarin's first volume treats chiefly of matters physiological and anatomical, which in a treatise not professedly scientific may as well be passed over. The third of his chapters, or 'meditations,' as he calls them, comes directly to *gastronomy*, which is defined as 'the scientific knowledge of all that relates to man in the matter of nourishment: its subject matter is all that can be eaten: its end the preservation of the species by the best possible sustenance.' He then shows the connection of gastronomy with other sciences, natural history, physics, chemistry, political economy, etc., and particularly its influence in promoting the intercourse of different nations. A feast knowingly set out is like an epitome of the world, where each quarter has its representatives. Gastronomic knowledge is of great utility to all classes, but especially to those in easy circumstances, and who are forced by their position to give frequent entertainments. To take the lowest view of the case, it saves them from being pilfered at will by their dependants. In illustration of this he introduces, as his way is, an appropriate anecdote.

'The Prince de Soubise meant to give a fête one day. It was to close with a supper, the bill-of-fare of which he demanded to see. The maitre-d'hôtel appeared at his bedside with a beautiful bill, headed by a vignette, and the first article which the prince cast eyes on was '*Fifty hams.*' 'Eh? What, Bertrand!' he exclaimed, 'are you mad? Or do you mean to treat my whole regiment? 'No, my lord; there will only appear one on the table, but the remainder is no less necessary, for my *espagnole,* my *blonds,* my *garnitures,* my —' 'Bertrand, you are cheating me, and this item shall not be allowed!' 'Ah! My lord!' said the *artiste,* keeping his temper with difficulty, 'you don't know our resources! Only say the word, and these fifty hams, which trouble you so, shall all go into a glass vial no larger than my thumb.' What answer could be made to so positive an assertion? The Prince smiled and submitted; the item was allowed.'

Next come some remarks on the appetite, and the danger of disobeying its calls. To illustrate this, there is a most awful story, which I cannot detail in cold blood. That any man, however high a public functionary he might be, should leave his company *four hours and a half* in the agonies of hunger and expectation while he was at a cabinet council, seems a pitch of depravity incredible even in a Frenchman; and that the company should have waited out the infliction without pillaging his house, or setting fire to it, or even adopting the extremely lenient course of walking off and dining elsewhere, seems an equally praeter-Gallic observance of those *convenances* which form the French moral code. Afterward we have some anecdotes of great appetites, derived from the author's personal observation; among others one of a cure, who used to consume in his midday meal a capon and a leg of mutton, not to mention the trifling accessories of soup, salad and cheese. It must be remembered, however, that the French *gigots* are decidedly diminutive, and not to be named in comparison with the legs which English clowns eat for wagers.

The next 'meditation' is on the respective nourishment and other different effects of different kinds of aliment. One remark is curious. That an icthyophagous [fish-eating] population is blessed with abundance of infants is generally known; but it is not so generally known that the female infants preponderate in the proportion of nearly ten to one. Savarin's inference is that a fish diet is debilitating. That it produces leanness there is little doubt. 'Jockeys, in *wasting,* are never allowed pudding when fish is to be had,' says an English authority; a Quarterly Reviewer, if I am not mistaken.

We have now arrived at particular dishes; first, of course, soup, about which we have somewhat to say by-and-by. Then the *bouilli,* that ghost of meat, which French economy has made a national dish. Our author sees that it is a great mistake, and observes with pleasure that it has been banished from the best-conducted tables, and replaced by fish. This was in 1825. At present there is little danger of encountering *bouilli* at a Parisian dinner. The national introduction of fish being *just before the roast* instead of just after the soup, a complete French dinner now involves *two* courses of fish at these two different periods. To us Anglo-Saxons, fish after soup seems a natural sequence; but it is difficult to give any *a priori* reason for it, and it may be only the force of habit. On another point we have less hesitation in condemning the French: their acceptance of cold fish; which in any shape is an abomination.[4] Indeed, considering the French gastronomic skill, it is singular that they admit into their catalogue of edibles three of the most insipid viands: *bouilli,* cold fish, and veal. The last may be tolerated on account of the badness of their beef. Good beef is only to be obtained in the very first cafés of Paris. Even at private houses in the metropolis it is generally detestably tough. As to their mutton, it is worse than ours; which is saying a great deal. Indeed, the sheep is only to be found in its perfection in the British isles; while,

---

4   Of course there is no reference here to anchovy in Mayonnaise, which is a condiment not a basis.

in spite of all that is said about 'the roast-beef of Old England,' you will get *on an average* of hotels and private houses, better beef in our Middle States than in Queen Victoria's dominions. But I am running miles ahead of my subject.

The observations on game I do not intend to remark upon or quote from, being fully persuaded that we are the only people in the world who know how to cook game. The English keep it too long and the French do it too much; added to which, the French game is not so good as ours, to begin with. Our blacks especially have a natural talent for the preparation of this delicious nutriment. And being deeply sensible of our many aesthetical deficiencies, I take an honest pride in being able to insist on this superiority, which I have too often seen, heard and tasted the verification of, to be in any doubt about it. Never did I meet foreigner so prejudiced as to resist the argument of a canvass-back.

Our author alludes to the practice of beginning a dinner with oysters as an ancient custom, which had become disused in his time. It has since been revived, and deserves all encouragement, as the very best way of preparing for your repast, however delicate a soup you may have in prospect; *only don't eat two dozen,* or even one dozen. Three oysters of the size we have them, or six like the European ones, give the proper whet. To this rule of course there are individual exceptions. One of BRILLAT-SAVARIN'S friends used to eat *thirty-two dozen,* ('say three hundred and eighty four,') and then was just ready for dinner.

The speculations on the truffle are amusing. Savarin suspects that the reputation of this famous edible is owing partly to its rarity and partly to what he learnedly denominates its *genesiac* powers. But give whatever weight you may to the fact of its being an exotic and an erotic, it must be confessed to impart an exquisite flavor to those dishes into the composition of which it enters, though nothing very wonderful in itself. With all due deference to the great authorities, and the general opinion the other way, I do *not* think that the dried and bottled truffles are *very* inferior to those freshly dug. I have eaten the latter at Rome, where they are as common as potatoes, and could not detect any great difference. Talking of truffles reminds one of mushrooms, which are to us almost as great a rarity as truffles. Herein we are much to blame for not properly cultivating our national resources. A very short residence in England or France will convince anyone of the importance of this fungus in cookery, and — it may be unfashionable, reader, but I never attempt to disguise my opinions — the cook who has plenty of good mushrooms at command need not, *me judice,* much regret the absence of truffles.

Of coffee I have discoursed already. Chocolate finds great favor with our author, who perhaps, amid his well-merited eulogiums, slurs over rather too much the fact that with some people it promotes biliousness. The Spanish preventive against this is to follow the chocolate with a glass of water. On this account the beverage is not so well adapted to our summers; but in winter there is no better breakfast than a copious cup of chocolate with a roll or some dry toast. It is very nourishing, and very light at the same time. Whether a man is going to exercise his head or his legs, whether he means to read, write or walk, or particularly if he is going to travel, there is nothing like the chocolate.

Passing over some more 'meditations' upon 'sugar,' 'the theory of frying' and other matters, (for one is obliged to omit something,) we come to the important subject of *thirst,* which naturally leads to the means of appeasing it. Now, having said some things already which may appear rather impudent, I am going to say one which certainly will appear so. I believe M. Brillat-Savarin to have been rather a take-in in the matter of drinks. I do this, not because he holds forth on the virtues of *eau sucrée,* as a beverage 'refreshing, wholesome, agreeable, and sometimes salutary as a remedy;' for the French passion for that most insipid of beverages which turns the stomach of an Anglo-Saxon, is an inexplicable idiosyncrasy, which must be put into the same category with their delight in veal. No, my reasons are first that he says comparatively little on the whole subject; and second, that he promulgates this as one of his fundamental axioms.

'It is a heresy to pretend that one must not change wines: the tongue becomes saturated, and after the third glass the best wine excites only an obtuse sensation.'

As if one could not drink four consecutive glasses of Latour without wanting to cross it with some other wine! The very reverse of BRILLAT-SAVARIN'S assertion holds good. It is the mixing of liquors, and crossing them back and forward, that satiates and confuses the palate, and *moreover it is the surest and quickest way of getting drunk;* an important consideration. Stick to one wine during each course. The only *wine of intervals,* if I may be allowed the expression, is champagne.

The most sagacious remarks I ever met with in the use of champagne are to be found in Walker's Original. Walker was an eccentric character, but he had some very correct ideas on the subject of dinner-givings. By the way, did you ever know a Walker who was not an original in some way or other? I never did. The eccentricities of the celebrated HOOKHAM, (familiarly called HOOKY, and related to the distinguished Chinese philosopher HOW QUA,) are too well known to need more than an allusion. And this reminds me of a story (I don't know where I shall get to with all these digressions) relative to the said HOOKHAM WALKER. It was once my good fortune to dine with six jolly Englishmen, among whom was Romano.[5] Over the mahogany, an exciting discussion came off between the Rum'un and another of the company suspected of being a mason. The conversation became animated, and at last my friend was tempted to terminate a period by the emphatic and sweeping assertion that 'Masonry was all Walker!'

Now our eighth man was a quiet middle-aged parson, not altogether at home in his position, for the rest of us thought and talked rather too fast (in the natural as well as the slang sense of the term) for him, and he did not always perfectly understand the subject on the *tapis.* Just after Romano had uttered his oracular condemnation, there was a momentary pause, when our clerical

---

5   For a full account of this gentleman, see the *American Review,* vol. v., p. 631.

friend, bending forward, observed in a slightly hesitating tone, 'I understand you then to say that this author, WALKER, whom you quote, considers Masonry to be a delusion?'

'Just so,' responded the Rum'un, sustaining his gravity by a mighty effort, while the remainder of us stuffed our napkins into our respective mouths in very imperfectly suppressed laughter.

Well, Walker says of champagne, that to go round with it only once or twice (as is often the case in English and French dinners and sometimes even in American dinners,) is tantalizing and mere aggravation. It should go round once during each course, that is to say, three, four, or five times according to the length of the dinner, *making its appearance with the fish,* and not (a very common fault) in the middle of the dinner.[6] And thus judiciously employed, it has a marvelous effect in enlivening and spiriting up a party. With us generally the fault is the other way, and our Amphitryons 'lay on' the beverage too freely, which is also, though not equally, a mistake, for the best champagne when drunk pure, cloys upon the palate sooner than any other wine. Dry is less cloying than sweet, and accordingly all *savans* prefer it. With champagne diluted with iced water in the proportion of one-half or two-thirds as a summer beverage, the case is different. It is the most cooling and refreshing of drinks, and there is no satiety or headache in an ocean of it. Therefore, reader mine, when you give a dinner in hot weather put a bottle of champagne (or at least a pint bottle) and a saucer of ice by every gentleman.[7] Never mind the looks: it removes all fear of deficient supply, and saves John and Thomas a vast deal of trouble in running round with the wine.

On the intellectual effect of champagne drunk continuously, BRILLAT-SAVARIN remarks, that 'this wine which is exciting in its first

---

6　　We suppose that the goblets are of a proper capacity. Some of the old-fashioned tapering glasses scarcely hold a thimble full.

7　　It is taken for granted that every man has his carafe of water. How ridiculous that at large dinners bread and water, the two first necessaries of life, should often be the hardest things to get! Your servants should be instructed to put two pieces of bread into each napkin, and carafes of water to each guest are indispensable to a well-regulated dinner of any size.

results (*ab initio*) is stupefying in its after results (*in recessu.*) This conclusion he founds partly on theory, arguing from the presence of carbonic acid gas, and partly on his observation of particular cases. For which reason as well as for that above mentioned, it should never be continued into the desert.

In the preparation of cold drinks we Americans excel. I had the honor of first introducing sherry cobbler, if not into England, at least to 'Young England' in the universities, and the beverage created a perfect *furore*. In hot compounds, the English have the advantage of us. Egg-sherry is better than eggnog, and bishop and cardinal (*alias* mulled port and mulled claret) are perfect in their way. The French have adopted punch with great zest. Our author speaks of it in the highest terms, always with the accompaniment of — what do you think? — *toast*, literally *buttered toast*, another English importation which the Parisians were then beginning to relish. Talking of punch, let me give you a hint; the best cold punch is *kirsch* — no liquor but kirsch. You can get it to perfection at Delmonico's. *In that punch there is no tomorrow;* a most important consideration.

If John Waters sees this he will never forgive me for insinuating that there is any punch in the world but his; but the truth must be told at all risks, in a matter of such importance.

Under the head of *gastronomic tests,* some bills of fare are presented to us which will not be without interest to the aesthetic reader. Here they are:

'I. *Moderate, circumstances; say, five thousand francs income:*

'1. A fillet of veal *piquée* and cooked in its own gravy.

'2. A turkey stuffed with chestnuts.

'3. Fat pigeons properly larded.

'4. A dish of sour-crout and sausages. [?]

'5. *Œufs à la neige.*

'II. *Easy circumstances; say fifteen thousand francs income:*

'1. A fillet of beef piqué, and cooked in its own gravy.

'2. A forequarter of roebuck with cucumber sauce.

'3. A leg of mutton à la provencale.[8]

---

8   Of this dish I confess my entire ignorance.

'4. A truffled turkey.

'5. New peas.

'III. *Wealth; say thirty thousand francs income or more:*

'1. A dish of poultry, seven pounds weight, stuffed with perigord truffles till it becomes a globe.

'2 An enormous *paté de foie gras.*

'3. A great carp à la chambord.

'4. Quails truffled and basted with marrow, upon toast with basil.

'5. A pike *piqué,* and *farci,* with cray-fish sauce.

'6. A pheasant, kept just long enough, piqué on toast.

'7. A hundred sticks of the largest asparagus with gravy sauce.

'8. Two dozens ortolans *à la provençale.*

'9. A pyramid of meringues *à la vanille* and *à la rose.*'

These bills of fare suggest at once several reflections. The first which naturally presents itself to the financial mind of an American is the difference between Gallic and Anglo-Saxon ideas of wealth. Would any man in England or America, with six thousand dollars or twelve hundred pounds a year, think of giving such dinners as that last? I shouldn't like to try it, even as a bachelor. The next is the absence of all mention of soup. Can it be possible that all the delightful varieties of this article have been invented within twenty-two years? It must be so, for it would be absurd to suppose that if they had existed, a professor of the art like M. BRILLAT-SAVARIN, would have said nothing about them. The *bisque d'ecrivisse,* for instance, which makes the taster of it for the first time experience a new and unimagined sensation, is one of the last things that an aesthetic writer would pass over. But the matter is put beyond doubt by a preceding chapter, wherein he speaks of *potage* as a single and simple article, and no more thinks of dividing and classifying *potages,* than one would now of discoursing on different kinds of bread; though even on that subject a not uninstructive chapter might be written, without going into as much detail as Athenaeus has done.[9]

---

9   Since the above was written, I have ascertained on more minute inquiry that the Trios Frères Provencaux, then boasted twelve varieties

The English are not *au fait* at the theory of soup. Not but that some of their soups, such as hare and turtle, are very delicious; but they are soups to make a dinner off, not to begin a dinner with. After consuming a copious plateful of either, you should not attempt to partake of anything except a little game. To be sure the English don't follow the rule, but after *two* supplies of rich and satisfying turtle, will go on through three or four courses; but the English are certainly gross diners. Bearing in mind this peculiarity of their *potages*, it is often a good plan when among them to eschew soup entirely; for it is possible to make a very good dinner without soup, (though I have a friend who when he reads this won't believe it.) Such a one is even now present to my imagination. I enjoyed it with a comrade at Windsor, just three years ago. It consisted of only three dishes, mutton cutlets with tomato sauce, chicken curry and apple fritters. The cutlets came up on plate, piping hot, the fritters ditto, the curry was dexterously prepared, the ale (so grateful after curry) of the best: to make our banquet perfect we only wanted good wine, but that is not to be had at an English hotel 'for love nor money.'

It is astonishing how badly off the English are for wine, considering the great quantity they drink and the high price they pay for it. They literally do not know what Madeira is. I lived among them six years, and in that time knew one corporation and two individuals who had the article as it should be. They boast of their sherry; but how often does an American find what he would call a good glass of sherry in England? Observe, I am not speaking of hotels merely, but of private families. They principally pride themselves upon their port, which is really no wine at all, but an artificial preparation, which ought only to be used in mixtures, such as bishop and negus, and then with discretion. But it is time to go back to our author and his *cartes*.[10]

of soup. It has now—how many? Probably seventy at least. Such is the progress of science.

10   He does not speak of them as bills of fare, but as series of gastronomic tests; so that we must suppose them to include only the striking and principal dishes; which will account for the omission of entrées, dessert, etc.

It will also be observed that in the third bill the epithets prefixed to the dishes signify a *profusion* of good cheer. Indeed, that there shall be no mistake on the subject, he subjoins an observation:

'For a gastronomic test to produce its effect with certainty, it must be comparatively in large quantity. Experience, founded on knowledge of the human heart, teaches us that the most delicate rarity loses its influence when not in exuberant proportion; for the first impression which it makes upon the guests is naturally checked by the fear that they may be shabbily helped, or in certain cases be obliged to refuse out of politeness.'

Now it seems to me that in this, as well as in everything, there is a limit. Profusion will no doubt often produce a startling effect, but it is generally at the expense of good taste. I for one do not like to be set down with seven more to a dinner for twenty. Moreover, small dishes, except at a *very* large party, (which is always a mistake,) look more aesthetic and manageable than large ones. It is very easy for any man with ordinary judgment to hit the proper medium; (of course we are speaking of dinners and regular meals; at stand-up collations, ball-suppers, and the like, there must be a great deal of waste, and a great allowance for waste;) but the fault is on the right side, and one may be well forgiven for running into it who has witnessed the meanness with which game is often distributed at very pretentious dinners. Titmarsh's sketch of three people, with one quail among them, is hardly a caricature of what often occurs. Speaking of game, Walker has a truly original idea about its introduction. He says, that by being brought on late in the dinner after the guests' appetites are nearly sated, it loses its rank as a delicacy and becomes only equal to an ordinary dish in the beginning of the dinner; therefore he advises that the game should make its appearance *first*; and if there is not game enough for an entire dinner[11], joints afterward. The suggestion is a bold

---

11   Walker was evidently from his writings a moderate and judicious eater. Thus he speaks of having dined one Christmas on a woodcock and a slice of plum pudding; a menu which almost frightened the *Quarterly Review* into fits.

one. Meat after game would strike most people as startling; and beside, as it is not right to be *too* hungry when attacking a dainty, it appears more reasonable to stay the first edge of appetite on something more substantial; that is, supposing the diner to be sharp-set at the beginning, which he ought to be. The best plan is now and then to give a *game-dinner exclusively,* introducing your venison (how seldom, alas! can one obtain good venison in New York!) immediately after the soup, then your small birds of various species, and a great display of ducks to conclude. Dinners of this kind, all in one vein, are very effectual for a change. The fish dinners of Greenwich and Blackwall have a great reputation; very unduly, in my opinion. Water-zouchy is most unsatisfactory stuff; you don't know whether it is fish or soup, hot or cold; whether you are to eat it with a spoon or a fork. Of eels they understand so little as actually to serve them plain fried, without any kind of sauce; and the much vaunted white-bait is not superior to, indeed hardly equal to smelt. Of the eight or ten dishes usually comprised in the first courre, the only one worth remembering is the salmon cutlets, which are really excellent; and the best part of the whole affair is the cooling and agreeable 'cup,' composed, I conjecture, chiefly of sherry and cider, pleasantly flavored with various herbs, and iced to the point. By way of contrast to a comparison with our French *ménus,* let us look at one of Walker's for a bachelor party of eight:

'1. Turtle-soup and punch.

'2. White-bait, brown-bread and butter, and champagne.

'3. Grouse and claret.

'4. Apple fritters and jelly; claret continued.

'5. Ices and fruit; claret continued indefinitely.'

The 'Quarterly Review' objected to the turtle, not without reason. The sweet punch which the English always drink, with turtle soup is terribly out of place; and so is, between you and me, reader, the Roman punch introduced at our dinners before the game; at least if you intend to eat any game after it. It may do for the women, who are not always able to appreciate venison and canvass-backs.

To come back to Brillat-Savarin's observation, which has set us wandering so far. The last clause of it brings to mind a very correct hint, which the considerate reader will not despise because it is quoted (from memory) out of a book of etiquette; for however snobbish it may be generally to refer to such manuals, it does occasionally happen that they are written by gentlemen, and you may sometimes find in them judicious and appropriate observations.

'There is no error more common among half-bred people than that of refusing to take the last piece upon a dish, 'out of manners,' as it is called. This is a direct insult to your host, as it insinuates that he is not able to furnish a fresh supply when the first is exhausted. It is better even to go out of the way for the sake of taking the last piece.'

To which it may be added, that if the host is such a curmudgeon as not to have made sufficient provision, his meanness ought to be exposed in the most unmistakable way. *Item,* if a very small pie or pudding, or any dish which is expected to 'go all round,' be put before you to help, don't worry yourself with trying how many infinitesimal divisions you can make of it, but distribute it in reasonable portions so long as it will hold out, and let the rest go without. It is the host's fault, not yours. I once saw this experiment tried with complete success. Half the guests were pieless that day, but the master of the house always took care in future to have his tarts of a proper size.

Some men, according to our author, are gourmands by nature, others by position. Of the latter in France he enumerates four classes: financiers, doctors, literary men, and *dévots,* or what we should call 'Professors of Religion.' Such a catalogue would hardly answer for our meridian, or even just across the channel. It appears that the different orders of French nuns are distinguished for different kinds of confectionary. English parsons are not altogether without the reputation of understanding the things which pertain to good eating and drinking. The Fellows of Cambridge are right hearty livers, clever in the dishes they have, and most liberal and Catholic in their acceptance of new ones. I

74

well remember how, after the fatigues of one examination, worn out and half delirious, (not having slept and scarcely having eaten for five days and nights,) I went to the rooms of a fellow classic to take a quiet cup of tea and read poetry to him. This double process had pretty well soothed me down, and I was on the point of departing at nine P.M., or thereabout, when Horace called me back.

'Won't you stay and read some more Tennyson, Benson, and have something to drink? I have some capital cognac that was sent me *by an old parson in the country.*'

At these last words I reseated myself in well-founded confidence. Better cognac never came out of France. The morning was considerably advanced when I fell asleep in his armchair, gloriously oblivious of my recent annoyances.

We have already adverted to the influence of gastronomy and table aesthetics upon the destiny of nations. M. Brillat-Savarin returns to this head, and illustrates it by a striking example from the history of his own country.

After 1815, the conquered and humbled French were obliged to pay more than *fifteen hundred millions of francs* in three years. Men naturally feared that this enormous drain on the finances would ruin the country; but the very reverse proved true. During those three years, *more money came into France than went out of it.* The secret of this lay in the excellence of the Parisian cookery, which attracted thousands of strangers and kept them there. One individual instance of temporary loss and ultimate profit is positively gigantic. When the invading army passed through Champagne, they helped themselves to *six hundred thousand* bottles of M. Möet's wine. In the ten years succeeding, the additional orders which he received from the north of Europe more than repaid him for this enormous pillage.

We now come to a most important topic; not that M. Savarin's remarks upon it are very copious or striking, for he was writing for a people who had some knowledge and consideration in the matter; but an infinitely important topic for us Americans, who in relation to it show more 'crass' ignorance, as Lord Brougham calls it, or willful and sinful carelessness, than any people professing to be civilized. An American seems to think he is losing time by taking his dinner at a decent pace and preserving a decent composure and tranquility after it. Accordingly, one man rushes to his country house before the last morsel is fairly down; another chooses that time of day of all others to take a walk — such a walk, too! — as if his dinner was before instead of in him, and he were walking for it; a third chooses the half-hour preceding his departure on a journey for the important meal, and after shoveling in his last piece of pie, runs off to catch the boat; a fourth jumps into a skeleton buggy and tears over the Third Avenue, his fast-trotter pulling his arms half off. If you are asked to make up a riding party, ten to one the time specified is, 'after dinner.' Suppose you are in the country, at a friend's house. How many of my readers can realize the truth of a picture like this? You sit down to table at the early hour of three; not too early, however, for you have risen with whatever American bird corresponds to the skylark, and breakfasted with the chickens. Well, at four, instead of enjoying a leisurely cup of coffee and a cigar — if so inclined — on the piazza, and admiring the scenery in luxurious and dreamy repose, some fidgety character proposes to 'see the grounds,' and forthwith you are dragged off two or three miles, up hill and down, part of the way under a broiling sun, and by way of finish, are put into a very imperfectly cleaned and still more imperfectly bailed boat, and set to work at rowing of all exercises the most laborious to a man not perfectly accustomed to it—for an hour or more; or, as I said before, you are called on to mount and ride. (N.B. — A ride does *not* mean a drive, which latter diversion, if you have a Christian horse, and not one trained on 'b'hoy' principles, is a very legitimate and wholesome occupation after dinner in warm weather.) Now until our countrymen and countrywomen reform these things; until the great truth can be inculcated upon them that *after a copious meal, abstinence from anything approaching to severe bodily or mental exercise is indispensable for at least one hour;* until then, I say, all the teetotalers and Grahamites that ever prated will not save them from bile and dyspepsia. Not but that bad liquor, pickles, hot buttered cakes, salt meats, and other things either atrocious in themselves or mischievous in their excess, do undoubtedly cause a great deal of harm; but the prime evil of all is, that whatever they eat they do not take time to digest it.

The English are as gross and nearly as undiscriminating feeders as we; but they understand perfectly this matter of digestion. The hardest reading student at the university, the most plodding barrister at the inns of court, the shrewdest and most diligent merchant, all eschew on principle hard work of any sort for the hour or two succeeding their prandiation; and this praiseworthy custom may divide with their regular and systematic exercise the merit of that magnificent health and strength which characterize all the upper and middle classes of England.

These remarks upon the post-prandial period naturally bring up another great question, to which, reader mine, I do entreat your attention. We used to practice the good old English custom of 'seeing mahogany;' that is, in twenty minutes or half an hour after dessert is placed on the table, the ladies retire and the gentlemen remain at table for about an hour longer. But it is with sincere grief and mortification that I am compelled to observe and confess that within a few years this ancient usage has been invaded and nearly displaced by the continental custom, according to which both ladies and gentlemen rise very soon after the dessert has appeared; before in fact the more deliberate part of the guests have done justice to it or begin to appreciate the Bordeaux. Now I maintain that for the real purpose and object of a dinner party — which is not to make a great display of plate and china, and bully your guests under the pretence of hospitality, nor to 'kill off' people who have invited you before, in conformity with the usages of a heartless and hollow etiquette, but *to bring people together that they may enjoy themselves;* and accordingly BRILLAT-SAVARIN nobly and philosophically declares, that 'to invite anyone to dinner is to take charge of his happiness for the time that he remains under your roof' — for the real purpose and object of a dinner party, I say, the English is *on all accounts* preferable. It is not always possible nor desirable that all your guests should be intimate associates to begin with; one great use of a dinner is to make pleasant and clever people acquainted with each other, and give them the opportunity of becoming friends if they mutually suit. Now this opportunity is much better promoted by the English plan, because, FIRST, there are certain subjects on which gentlemen are most disposed to talk out, and draw one another out, and converse easily and naturally, which are mere bores to the ladies. Such are, first, politics; secondly, some particular branches of science and literature which are *generally* out of a lady's line; third, different kinds of business and commercial affairs. In like manner, the women have their peculiar topics; for instance, nice points of dress and millinery, about which few gentlemen take much interest or have much knowledge. So that nothing throws your company together and makes them talk out and lets them within each other, so to speak, like separating the sexes for a time and letting each converse on its own topics.

SECONDLY. A man is naturally inclined immediately after dining to some little *abandon* of attitude and manner. He likes to lean back in his chair or to turn it half round to his neighbor's, or perhaps, if he has well dined, to let out a button or two of his waistcoat. Nor do I believe that some corresponding latitude is altogether unpleasing to the fair sex, and that they object to reclining in their *fauteuils* for a while and gossiping at leisure among themselves without the trouble of having to try to look interested at fine gentlemen speeches. Then there are men who like to smoke after dinner; and though not an habitual smoker myself, I know enough of the effects of the cigar to sympathize with those who find it an exceeding comfort about that time. There are some also who like their half-bottle of Bordeaux after dinner, and others (like myself) who like to sip their glass or two very leisurely. Now by letting a man do these things (which he can do only when the English plan is adopted) you make him feel at home at once: he grows genial and natural, and disposed to talk other things beside mere drawing room commonplace, and lets you see something of what manner of man he is. Thus you may find out more about a person, his *specialités,* strong and weak points, good qualities, hobbies, etc., by dining once with him, English fashion, than fifty times French fashion, in which latter case, indeed, unless you sit near him you may never come to know him at all.

Nevertheless, in spite of these potent and unanswerable reasons to the contrary, the non-mahogany system is fast gaining ground among us, being urged and supported by two classes, the Gallomanic fashionables who *will* follow the French blindly in everything (though even the French are not so abrupt as their imitators here, and do not rush away from the table in ten minutes after the fruit and ices are put on) and the stingy fine people who are shy of their wine. I dined once with a character of the latter sort, and it was amusing (or rather it would have been to any but a sufferer) to watch how carefully he abstained from taking any notice of the decanters before him (of course through mere absence) and how spirited his conversation became with those immediately on each side of him. Having a presentiment that there was but a quarter of an hour before us, I vainly strove to catch his eye with looks that almost magnetized the decanters themselves and brought them down of their own accord. It was only throwing away so much ocular indignation and entreaty. At length when he had nicely calculated his time, he started the wine with a great flourish and it had just gone once round when *Mesdames* rose, the host started with his lady, and we as in duty bound did the same. Now if a man only drinks one glass of wine at his dessert he likes not to have to do it in a hurry. But the truth is that most diners-out like more, if they will act in truth, and not play hypocrites to themselves and one another. And without any fear of falling into the former English habits of vinous excess (which honest John has now happily amended) a guest may well and comfortably, during the hour of social relaxation, when the chairs of the well-dined banqueters are drawn close together, imbibe his half-bottle of red wine, preceded and followed by a glass of Madeira or Sherry. (This is a very good rule, a glass of white wine as a foundation for the claret, and another as a preparation for the coffee: it was one of BRUMMELL'S.) There is surely nothing indelicate, or ungallant or discourteous in a man's drinking more than a woman, any more than there is in his eating more, which everyone takes as a matter of course. Indeed the latter fact necessarily leads to the former.

And now, should the reader be afflicted with the too prevalent epidemic of Anglophobia, he may begin to chafe, so it will to appease him with some of our Frenchman's maxims for a dinner, which however I shall take the liberty of accompanying, as in a former instance, with such commentaries as they suggest. BRILLAT-SAVARIN introduces them with the appropriate observation that 'however delicate the meats, and however sumptuous the accessories, there is no enjoyment at table, should the wine be bad, the guests collected indiscriminately, and the meal consumed with precipitation.'

'The number of guests should not exceed twelve, so that the conversation may be general.'

Connu et agrée. I will not positively affirm that it is *impossible* to conduct a large dinner on aesthetic principles, as I have never dined with very great people, and am not prepared to say what the union of colossal fortune and highly cultivated taste may not accomplish; but I am sure it must be very difficult. One reason immediately suggests itself. At a very large table there must be a considerable interval between each course, and supposing that the guests are so felicitously grouped as to be able to amuse themselves during these intervals, with or without the assistance of music, (and this is not probable where the guests are numerous,) the whole period of the dinner must ultimately be protracted to a tedious length. For a bachelor dinner, eight is an excellent number. By the way, when the head of a family gives a bachelor party, he should either pitch his tent at a restaurateur's for the occasion, or contrive that *Madame* shall dine with her relations. One woman among seven men is awfully out of place, and sure to be bored herself without adding anything to their pleasure.

'The guests should be so selected that their pursuits shall be various, while their tastes are analogous, and with such points of contact that you will not be obliged to have recourse to the odious formality of introductions.'

A magnificent expression of profound wisdom: 'The guests should be so selected that their pursuits shall be various while their tastes are analogous;' that is to say, they must be gentlemen and liberally educated men in the highest sense of those terms; and then, however diverging their lines of business or pleasure, they will be sure to find points of contact. 'The odious formality of introductions' is a strong phrase, but not too strong for the occasion. *We* have carried this absurdity to its height. I don't know whether the elaborate presentation and solemn hand shaking that one has to undergo everywhere is more annoying or ridiculous. How much better they manage these things in England! There you meet a stranger at dinner; over the wine you hear him talk and perhaps talk to him; you learn his name indirectly and he yours; you take a survey of the man, physically, intellectually, and socially; and afterward it is at your option to know him or not when you next meet. Whichever you do he has no right to be offended.

'The dining room should be brilliantly lighted, the table furniture of remarkable propriety, and the temperature between sixty and seventy degrees.'

The first hint needs no comment. The second may for a moment 'give us pause.' There are many things connected with the equipment of the table, involving more or less expense. It is not everyone who is the fortunate possessor of costly plate and sumptuous china. The most accessible luxury, and that which gives most pleasure in proportion, is elegant cut glass. The delicate form of a decanter and still more of a glass, adds a new zest to the generous liquor contained in it, and makes the aesthetic drinker linger goblet in hand. But the plate and china are very glorious things for those that have them. Only it is a fatal mistake (happily more common in Europe than here) to suppose that any display of these can atone for any deficiency in that which is upon them. On the contrary, the more exquisite your china and plate the more necessity that your cook should be irreproachable. Anything bad, or shabby, or scanty in the dinner, is only aggravated by the gorgeousness of the service, which is then felt to be but a bitter mockery. The temperature of the room will depend not merely on the quantity of fuel employed, but also on the number of guests in proportion to its size. I mention this apparently self-evident fact, because many people who give dinners do most certainly lose sight of it. Not unconnected with this is another fault which deserves the most serious animadversion; that of putting more people at a table than providence and the cabinet-maker intended should sit at it.[12] Doctor Whewell, the master of Trinity College, Cambridge, was a sad sinner in this respect. I used to think that his parties were given on the principle of solving some problem in physics like this: *Given a table of a certain size; required the number of individuals that can be brought around it in a sedentary posture.* It was once my felicity to give him a gentle hint. Being in the position of a trussed goose at his board, in some crippled movement, I contrived to knock over a tumbler. Whereupon he looked thunder-cloudish, and the uncivilized Cantabs there assembled began to laugh by way of restoring the stranger (it was the third month of my residence in England) to his ease. With a composed countenance I turned to the great W—, and assured him that 'accidents would happen in the best regulated families,' a pregnant proverb involving the inference that *à fortiori* were they likely to happen when people were packed together in that fashion.

'The men should be intellectual without pretension, and the women amiable without coquetry.'

Methinks I hear the reader say, 'It is very easy to give such rules as these, but to be able to comply with them is another thing.'

Perfectly right: it *is* difficult to follow this direction, and I am glad you appreciate the difficulty. Half the battle is to select your company. It is a work of thought for a bachelor party: when you ask couples the task becomes one of great nicety, and when you mean to invite the men and women separately, all your cleverness and all *Madame's* will be brought into play. To combine a party of young ladies and unmarried gentlemen, and make the dinner go

---

12   'Whereas armchairs are very pleasant on other accounts, they are particularly useful on this, that they prevent the possibility of over-crowding your table.'

off well, is the highest triumph of social genius.

On this most important subject a few suggestions may not be altogether out of place.

1. James Smith's rule for a literary bachelor party is, eight guests: six talkers; two listeners.

Scholium. The most valuable guest is he who can be a talker or a listener, according to the company he is in. This requires a man to be brilliant, sensible and modest, a rare and happy union of qualities.

2. Beware of bringing too many lions together: they are not apt to roar in perfect concert. This is a very natural error when you are feasting a stranger or foreigner. Anxious to show off to him the celebrities of your place and your acquaintance with them, you are tempted to ask all the men of note your room and table will hold, forgetting the first rule, that to give talkers their fair chance, there must be listeners.

3. Avoid all *bas bleus.*

4. Avoid all men who, as was said of Coleridge, 'have a talent for monologue.' Anyone who will monopolize the conversation, however great his talents and acquirements may be, is oppressive at a dinner. The places for such people are *soirées* and *conversaziones,* where they can lecture to circles of admirers.

5. One *fool positive,* that is to say an individual who persists in making stupid remarks, whether talked to or not, is enough to spoil a whole party.

6. Some of the very pleasantest parties are those made up of persons who have at some period of their lives been intimate; but who, by their daily pursuits or other circumstances are prevented from meeting very often. This is the remark of a shrewd English friend: it has a relation with BRILLAT-SAVARIN's precept, that the pursuits of the guests should be various and their tastes analogous.'

'The dishes should be most carefully selected and not too numerous, and the wines the very best, each of his kind.'

The other precepts I omit, because some of them, such as those relative to the coffee and the liqueurs, have been already anticipated, and others relative to temporary fashions, such as tea, toast and punch, which were then (in 1825) recently introduced English novelties. But the last one deserves attention.

'No one should go before eleven, but everyone should be in bed by twelve.'

This corresponds to the Englishman's rule who hung over the chimney-piece of his dining room: '*Come at seven, go at eleven.*'

But one day an erratic friend, who wished to prolong the festivities, inserted a monosyllable which materially changed the nature of the precept, for it then read: '*Come at seven, go* IT *at eleven.*' And they did 'go it' accordingly.

This closing precept takes it for granted that the guests have no other engagement that night. But from a dinner to an evening party or ball is a natural and customary progress, and therefore the natural arrangement seems to be that your carriage should come to take you *from* one just in time to take you *to* the other. And this reminds of another argument in favor of the English habit of remaining at table. It occupies an hour or two agreeably, which by the pseudo-Gallic innovation is utterly thrown away. What earthly use is there in breaking up your dinner party at eight or half-past eight when no one goes to a ball before ten? Or if there is no ball to go to, it is even worse. You reach home before nine: it is too early to go to bed, and your evening is just broken up. If I had quoted all SAVARIN's maxims, you would have seen that his post-prandial arrangements are not so directly antagonistic to those of the English. The *sederunt* is transferred from the dining room to the drawing room; there is whist for the gentlemen instead of politics, and punch instead of claret; but one of the great ends, repose and ease in the house where you have just dined, is attained by analogous, though different means.

Our next halting in the physiology shall be the meditations on corpulence. The reader must not be too startled at hearing that one cause of obesity is — eating and drinking too much. The quality of the aliment however, has as much to do with the matter as the quantity. *Bread is exceedingly fattening;* those therefore who are inclined to be corpulent should eat but little, and that little of *rye*. They should also avoid eggs, potatoes, rice, pastry and other farinaceous substances. (I am afraid this last sentence reads somewhat like the grocer's sign, — *Soap, candles, blacking and other vegetables for sale here.* Don't put down the confusion to BRILLAT-SAVARIN's discredit; it is all my fault. I am trying to condense the substance of his remarks as much as possible, for this grave treatise which set out to be eight pages, has run on to a length that frightens me; and hence you see *dum brevis esse laboro,* etc.) They must also have a horror of beer. So much for negatives; for positive remedies, they must eat radishes and celery and drink seltzer water and light French wines. The next precept seems somewhat inconsistent with this, for they are commanded to eschew vinegar, and the command is enforced by a touching history of a beautiful girl, who by drinking a glass of vinegar every morning in the foolish hope of thereby reducing her figure, brought herself to a premature grave at the age of eighteen. Finally, it will be well if they can rise early and take much exercise on foot and on horseback, but these recommendations, the author adds, are difficult to follow, and he therefore does not depend much upon them. The chapter in which he enlarges on the 'difficulties' of carrying out these most simple prescriptions are amusingly and at the same time painfully indicative of the Celtic character as contrasted with the Anglo-Saxon. What to an Englishman or Englishwoman is second, nay, *first* nature, is an out of the way and impracticable remedy to a French ditto.

Those unfortunates who suffer from the opposite defect, will of course adopt a contrary regimen, take eggs at breakfast, rice, potatoes and pastry at dinner, and plenty of bread at all times. They will drink beer, (which it is not considered vulgar to do in London and Paris, and which it is supremely absurd to consider unlady-like here, although there *are* dummies among us who if told that a young lady 'drank beer' would look at her as a sort of Lola Montez,) and pay proper attention to sponge-biscuits, macaroons and similar varieties of confectionary. The author expatiates with much feeling on the *régime incrassant,* commencing thus:

'Every lean woman wishes to grow plumper; we have noted the desire in a thousand instances; it is then to render a final homage to the all-powerful sex, that we shall endeavor to replace by real forms those fictitious charms of silk and cotton which one sees so profusely exposed in the shops, to the great scandal of all rigid moralists who pass by in a tremor and turn away their faces from these chimeras as sedulously as, nay, more so than if the reality were before them.'

Elsewhere in more homely and practical language he says, that 'it is as easy to fatten a woman as a chicken.'

Here is a delicious bit of aesthetic enthusiasm: 'Shun all acids, except salad *which rejoices the heart.*'

Salad as a great many Americans and almost all Englishmen make it, does anything but rejoice the heart. Will it be believed that in a cookery book published in this city and sold by several of the principal booksellers, there occurs a *receipt* for dressing salad which leads off thus: 'Take three spoonfuls of oil and *as many of vinegar.*' A mingled feeling of indignation and pity stops my pen. Whoever wrote down that receipt in cold blood ought to be sent forever to where we are about to accompany M. Brillat-Savarin.

Namely, *Lent.*

Not however with the intention of fasting; the more so as our author expressly condemns fasting as a very bad practice, wherein I take it for granted that my readers are good Protestants enough to agree with him. No, we will only touch on this meditation because it gives a sketch of the manner in which the Parisians at the middle of last century arranged their meals when they were *not* in Lent.

'We used to breakfast before nine on bread and cheese, fruits and sometimes cold meat. [Not in the order in which they are here enumerated it is to be hoped.]

Between twelve and one we dined on the habitual soup and soup-beef, with better or worse accompaniments as our means and other circumstances allowed.

At four there was a lunch, a light meal for the particular benefit of children and of those who piqued themselves on following the usages of antiquity.

But there were *supperish* lunches which began at five and lasted indefinitely.

'About eight came the supper; roast, side dishes, sweets, salad and dessert.'

That is what we should call a late dinner *minus* the soup and fish. Nature seems to dictate that the principal meal should be taken when the fatigue of the day is over; whether it be called *dinner* or *supper* is a mere fashion of the times.

From speculating on the usages of different ages, the transition is easy to a history of the art. Our author says a great deal about the cookery of the Greeks and Romans, and it would be easy for me to say as much more, and overwhelm you with an ocean of erudition, gossip and jokes, more or less bad, out of that inexhaustible Athenaeus. But nothing is farther from my intention, because, in the first place, our knowledge of the classical *cuisine* is very imperfect when *we come to details,* and secondly, what we do know in a general way does not impress one very favorably. With the deepest veneration for the poetry of the ancients, I have a very moderate opinion of their table aesthetics. The thick inspissated wines, the clumsy fashion of lying down at meals, which no modern but Fanny Kemble has ever been able to practice, the Romans' preference for pork — the Athenians were more aesthetic, and founded their suppers on fish and game — all these and various other peculiarities of theirs, are to us incomprehensible, if not barbarous. One or two things I will just allude to, as they show amusing resemblances in ancient and modern matters. The Greeks had regular bills of fare; so the prince of gossips tells us in his second book. 'When the host had reclined,' he says, 'there was presented a little writing, containing a sketch of the preparations, so that he might know what delicacies the cook was going to serve.'[13] And in one of the later books of this indefatigable gourmand there is a list of receipts for making cake, several of which on examination I have

---

13   DEIPNOSOPHISTAE II.

found to be, with the substitution of sugar for honey, very good receipts for those good old KNICKERBOCKER preparations, *krullers*, *doughnuts* and *oely-koeks*. Happening once to mention this to a Cantab friend, he remarked that one of the London University professors (let us say 'George Long;' for a story is only half a story unless there are some names in it;) had tried to put into practice these very receipts, and made an awful mess of them. Somewhat taken aback by this, I at length bethought me of inquiring whether Long had ever in his life before made cakes of any kind. To which the response being in the negative, 'Ah!' quoth we, 'that accounts for the milk in the cocoa-nut.'

There is one most luxurious practice of the ancients worthy of all imitation: that of delighting their guests, after the repast was over, with a display of the first professional talent. I commend this to the attention of the next millionaire in Gotham who is going to open a magnificent house in a magnificent manner, and to do the magnifico generally. Let him engage Truffi, Rossi and Benedetti, and entertain his company after dinner to the second act of Lucrezia Borgia.

Thirty-eight pages of manuscript, and we are only just at the beginning of the second part of the Physiology! What a pity we cannot linger on that second part! It would have been a rich treat, for here the author drops precept and argument entirely, and indulges himself in illustration and anecdote. I should have liked above all things to relate to you his preservation of a huge turbot's 'entirety' after it had puzzled the *bon vivants* of Villecrène as much as one of its species did Domitian's senate of old; and his Day with the Bernardines, which reminds us of the song about

    — 'The monks of old,
  What jolly good souls they were!'

and shows that some of the brotherhood at least have not deteriorated in this respect; and the consternation of the innkeeper when required to lodge and entertain a large arrival of English, 'for not more than six francs;' and a dozen other good stories; but it could hardly be done short of this whole number of the KNICKERBOCKER. Let me just give you one anecdote; not because it is by any means the best, but because it is the shortest. The author having been slightly 'done' by an apothecary is on the point of calling the worthy dispenser of drugs to account, when he is suddenly deterred by remembering the bad success of his friend General Bouvier in an encounter with one of the fraternity. This general sent for M. Brillat-Savarin to sustain him in the interview with his apothecary, who had overcharged him; and to the further intimidation of this redoubtable personage he had arrayed himself in full uniform, orders and all. He was just explaining this to our author, 'When even as he spoke the door opened, and we beheld a man of about fifty-five years enter, carefully dressed. He was of lofty stature and sedate step. His whole appearance would have presented a uniform aspect of severity, had not his eyes and mouth together betokened something sardonic in their connection.'

[What a novel Savarin might have written if he had tried! Did you ever see a character better introduced? It is a perfect opening of a mysterious chapter.]

'He approached the fireplace, refusing to take a seat, and the following dialogue ensued, which I have faithfully retained in my memory:

'THE GENERAL.

'Sir, this is a regular apothecary's bill that you have sent me, and—

'THE MAN IN BLACK.

'Sir, I am not an apothecary.

'THE GENERAL.

'And what *are* you then, Sir?

'THE MAN IN BLACK.

'Sir, I practice pharmacy.

'THE GENERAL.

'Very well, Mr. Practicer of Pharmacy, your boy ought to have told you—

'THE MAN IN BLACK.

'Sir, I have no boy.

'THE GENERAL.

'Who was that young man then?

'THE MAN IN BLACK.

'Sir, he is a pupil.

'THE GENERAL.

'Well, Sir, I wished to tell you that your drugs—

'THE MAN IN BLACK.

'Sir, I do not sell drugs.

'THE GENERAL.

'And what do you sell then, Sir?

'THE MAN IN BLACK.

'Sir, I sell medicines.'

'There the discussion finished. The general, ashamed of having committed so many solecisms and of being so little advanced in the knowledge of the pharmaceutic tongue, was thrown into confusion, forgot what he had to say, and paid all that was demanded.'

And now, reader, a word in your ear before we part. Do you prefer that Celtic or Anglo-Saxon principles to prevail in the world? If you have any tendency to the Puritan faith, if you undertake to be a strict moralist and a religious man, you can hardly help desiring that the latter should triumph. Very well; if you give up the science of table aesthetics, which has so important an influence on mankind, to the Celts, you leave in their hands a tremendous weapon and means of obtaining power. Ask a Frenchman the reason of his country's ascendency; and if a conceited man like Michelet, he will tell you that it is because France has lavished more blood and treasure and labor in the cause of humanity than all the other nations in the world together, which is very much after the manner of Michelet; or if you ask a more modest man, like our physiologist, he will say that it is because the French are so obliging in their intercourse with strangers as always to let themselves down to the level of their capacity; of the truth of which those who have traveled abroad can judge for themselves. But the true secret is, depend upon it, the progress which the French have made in the arts of dress and cookery, wherein, notwithstanding occasional absurdities, they on the whole very much surpass the rest of the world. By the former they gain the women; by the latter, both sexes. Will you yield them without an effort the whole of this advantage, or try to put yourself as nearly on an equal footing as you can? 'What's the reason the devil should have all the good tunes?' said some great divine; Calvin, was it, or Wesley? 'What's the reason the French should have all the good dinners?' says CARL BENSON.

VIII

Do Not Strain Your Punch

BY JOHN WATERS

MARCH 1850

ONE OF my friends, whom I am proud to consider such; a Gentleman, blest with all the appliances of Fortune, and the heart to dispense and to enjoy them; of sound discretion coupled with an enlightened generosity; of decided taste and nice discernment in all other respects than the one to which I shall presently advert; successful beyond hope in his cellar; almost beyond example rich in his wine chamber; and last, not least, felicitous to say no more in his closet of RUMS — this Gentleman, thus endowed, thus favored, thus distinguished, has fallen, can I write it? into the habit of — straining his PUNCH!

When I speak of RUMS my masters, I desire it to be distinctly understood that I make not the remotest allusion to that unhappy distillation from molasses which alone is manufactured at the present day throughout the West Indies since the emancipation of the Blacks; who desire nothing but to drink, as they brutally express it, 'to make drunk come' but to that ethereal extract of the sugar cane, that Ariel of liquors, that astral spirit of the nerves, which, in the days when planters were born Gentlemen, received every year some share of their attention, every year some precious accession, and formed by degrees those stocks of RUM, the last reliques of which are now fast disappearing from the face of Earth.

And when I discourse on PUNCH, I would fain do so with

becoming veneration both for the concoction itself, and, more especially, for the memory of the profound and original, but alas! *unknown* inventive Genius by whom this sublime compound was first imagined, and brewed — by whose Promethean talent and touch and Shakespearean inspiration, the discordant elements of Water, Fire, Acidity, and Sweetness, were first combined and harmonized into a beverage of satisfying blessedness, or of overwhelming Joy!

My friend then — to revert to him — after having brewed his Punch according to the most approved method, passes the fragrant compound through a linen-cambric sieve, and it appears upon his hospitable board in a refined and clarified state, beautiful to the eye perhaps, but deprived and dispossessed by this process of those few lobes and cellular integuments, those little gushes of unexpected piquancy, furnished by the bosom of the lemon; and that, when pressed upon the palate and immediately dulcified by the other ingredients, so wonderfully heighten the zest, and go so far to give the nameless entertainment and exhilaration, the unimaginable pleasure, that belong to Punch!

Punch! — I cannot articulate the emphatic word without remarking, that it is a liquor that a man might 'moralize into a thousand similes!' It is an epitome of human life! Water representing the physical existence and basis of the mixture: Sugar its sweetness: Acidity its animating trials: and Rum, the aspiring hope, the vaulting ambition, the gay and the beautiful of Spiritual Force!

Examine these ingredients separately. What is Water by itself in the way of Joy, except for bathing purposes? or Sugar, what is it, but to infants, when alone? or Lemon-juice, that, unless diluted, makes the very nerves revolt and shrink into themselves? or Rum, that in its abstract and proper state can hardly be received and entertained upon the palate of a Gentleman? And yet combine them all, and you have the full harmony, the heroism of existence, the diapason of human life!

Let us not then abridge our Water lest we diminish our animal being. Nor change the quantum of our Rum, lest wit and animation cease from among us. Nor our Sugar, lest we find by sad experience that 'it is not good for man to live alone.' And, when they occur, let us take those minor acids in the natural cells in which the Lemon nourished them for our use, and as they may have chanced to fall into the pitcher of our destiny. In short let us not refine too much. My dear Sirs, let us not strain our Punch!

When I look around me on the fashionable world, in which I occasionally mingle, with the experience and observation of an old man, it strikes me to be the prevailing characteristic of the age that people have departed from the simpler and I think the healthier pleasures of their Fathers. Parties, balls, soirees, dinners, morning calls, and recreations of all sorts are, by a forced and unnatural attempt at over-refinement, deprived of much of their enjoyment. Young men and maidens, old men and Widows, either give up their Pitchers in despair, or, venturing upon the compound strain their Punch.

Suppose yourself for the moment transported into a Ballroom in a blaze of light, enlivened by the most animating music, and with not one square foot of space that is not occupied by the beauty and fashion of the day. The only individuals that have the power, except by the slowest imaginable sidelong movement, of penetrating this tide of enchantment, are the Redowa-Waltzers; before whom every person recedes for a few inches at each moment, then to resume his stand as wave after wave goes by.

You can catch only the half-length portraits of the dancers; but these are quite near enough to enable you to gain by glimpses their full characteristic developments of countenance. Read them; for every conventional arrangement of the features has been jostled out of place by the inspiriting bob-a-bob movement of the dance.

Look before you — a woman's hand, exquisitely formed, exquisitely gloved in white and braceleted, with a wrist 'round as the circle of Giotto,' rests upon the black-cloth dress of her partner's shoulder; as light, as airy, and as pure, as a waif of driven snow upon a cleft of mountain rock, borne thither in some relenting lull or wandering of the tempest; and beautiful! Too beautiful it seems for any lower region of the Earth.

She turns toward you in the revolving movement, and you behold a face that a celestial inhabitant of some superior star might descend to us to love and hope to be forgiven! Now listen, for this is the expression of that face:

'Upon my word this partner of mine is really a nice person! How charmingly exact his time is! What a sustaining arm he has, and how admirably, by his good management, he has protected my beautiful little feet against all the maladroit waltzers of the set! I have not had a single bruise notwithstanding the dense crowd; and my feet will slide out of bed tomorrow morning as white and spotless as the bleached and balmy linen between which I shall repose. Ah! If he could only steer us both through life as safely and as well! But poor fellow! It would never do. They say he has no fortune, and for my part all that I could possibly expect from papa would be to furnish the house. How then should we be ever able to — strain our PUNCH!'

And he — the partner in this Waltz—instead of growing buoyant and elastic, at the thoughts that belong to his condition of youth and glowing health; — at the recollection of the ground over which he moves; — of the Government of his own choice, the noblest because the freest in the world, that rules it; — of the fourteen hundred millions of unoccupied acres of fertile soil, wooing him to make his choice of climate, that belong to it; — of the deep blue sky of Joy and health that hangs above it; — of the GOD that watches over and protects us all; — and, lastly, of this precious being as the Wife that might make any destiny one of happiness by sharing it what are the ideas that occupy *his* soul?

He muses over the approaching hour of supper, speculates upon his probable share of Steinberger Cabinet Wein, and doubts whether the Restaurateur who provides may or may not have had consideration enough to — strain the PUNCH.

Bear with me once more, gentle Reader, while I recite the title of this Essay: 'Do not strain your PUNCH."

JOHN WATERS.

IX

The Antique Goblet

BY CURTIS GUILD

OCTOBER 1850

I.

Hail! Massy old relic of years that have flown,
Of those merry old days that forever have gone,
When the bright gleaming bubbles that merrily swim
Have circled within thee and foamed at thy brim:
How oft in those old feudal times, at the board
Where sparkling in light the red liquor was poured,
And the armor and banners all hung on the wall,
In the flash of the torches that lighted the hall.

II.

The knights and retainers were gathered around,
And loud doth the peal of their revelry sound;
While the stout feudal baron, the chief of the band,
Hath raised thee, old goblet! On high in his hand:
The feast and the revel, the shout and the laugh,
The pledge of the gallants o'er wine that they quaff,
The clink of the goblets together that shine,
As the knights raise their cups with 'Success to the vine!'

III.

Then high at the head of the table doth stand,
With a smile on his lip and the cup in his hand,
The baron — the brave feudal baron of old,
Who drinks with his knights and retainers so bold:

But hark! the wild sound of the revel has ceased,
And hushed for a while is the din of the feast:
'Tis the voice of the minstrel whose melody rings,
'Tis his magical touch that sweeps over the strings.

IV.

Now sweetly he chants the soft music of love,
And the strains die away in the rafters above;
Then changing the measure, of battle he sings,
Till the hall with the shout of the battlefield rings;
Or when in sad numbers the sound of the dirge
Peals in deep solemn tone, like the moan of the surge,
Till waked from its sadness, the livelier strain
Flows on in glad measure of music again.

V.

How oft at such revels, odd cup! Hast thou been?
O, wouldst thou could tell of the sights thou hast seen!
Of the dark-bearded mouths that have pressed at thy rim,
Or the red lip of beauty that breathed at its brim:
Perchance thou hast held the dark poisonous draught
Which the victim of tyrants or treachery quaffed,
And e'en while a moment upheld in his grasp
The cold hand of death has unloosened his clasp.

VI.

Or perchance, by the sick, all pallid with pain,
Thou hast held the pure nectar that cheered them again;
In the hand of the maiden, the grasp of the knight,
And glowing with deep rosy wine in the light:
All, all hast thou seen, as ages have flown
And left thee, old goblet! Still gleaming alone;
And those that have drained thee, the young and the brave,
Have passed and have vanished; gone down to the grave!

VII.

And the deeds of the brave feudal barons of yore,
They glimmer but faintly in history's lore;
Their battles, their feasts, their retainers so true,
Have faded away from our memories, too:
But I'll think, as I gaze on this massy old cup,
Of those merry old days when the knights took it up,
And from it a bumper I'll drain with a cheer
To the knights of old times and their memories dear!

Boston, August 21, 1850.

X

Adulterations of Food: Bread

MAY 1859

WHAT SHALL we eat? What shall we drink? And wherewithal shall we be clothed? Continue to be considerations that exercise the carnal and worldly, notwithstanding the Divine injunction to the contrary.

In its persistency in the effort to secure a wardrobe, the wicked world has succeeded in a manner quite satisfactory. Doeskin and calico have accomplished the result. If, however, there be a great lack of the conscientious fiber in the French cloths manufactured in the Bay State, and Valenciennes and Brussels have not experienced the purifying properties of the sea air, the delusion is perfectly harmless. The pocket, it is true, may be depleted without adequate consideration; and self-love may wince under the conviction of a simulated and tawdry apparel, but in this there is nothing alarmingly fatal. The innocent possessors of sensibilities so delicate will survive the shock of the exposure. But *eating* and *drinking* require serious consideration. *What* it is that people eat and drink they scarcely know. There is a nomenclature, it is true, belonging to this great science of regaling the physical man; but with reference to their original application and use, the terms now employed are certainly misnomers. We speak more particularly of articles of food which undergo a process of preparation, and are somewhat removed from a condition of nature.

We find bread, for instance, compounded of potatoes, alum, beans, chalk, carbonate of magnesia, silica, pipe clay, bone-dust, plaster of Paris, sulphate of copper, etc.

Coffee is adulterated with chicory, roasted wheat, and beans, mangel-wurzel, acorns, etc. Tea is mixed with leaves of the beech, elm, willow, poplar, sand, starch, etc., and the dangerous auxiliaries, Venetian red, chrome yellow, carbonate and arsenite of copper, chromate and bichromate of potash, etc., are subsidized to give the counterfeit the requisite color.

That which is sold for sugar, contains sand and plaster of Paris. And the cerulean fluid yclept milk, if it be not elaborated in the diseased organisms of briefly caudated animals, is at least diluted with water and thickened with chalk, and in some instances with sheep's brains!

It may be interesting to the extractors of tobacco juice to know that while they are complacently enjoying an imaginary cud of placid contentment, they are in fact chewing a quid of

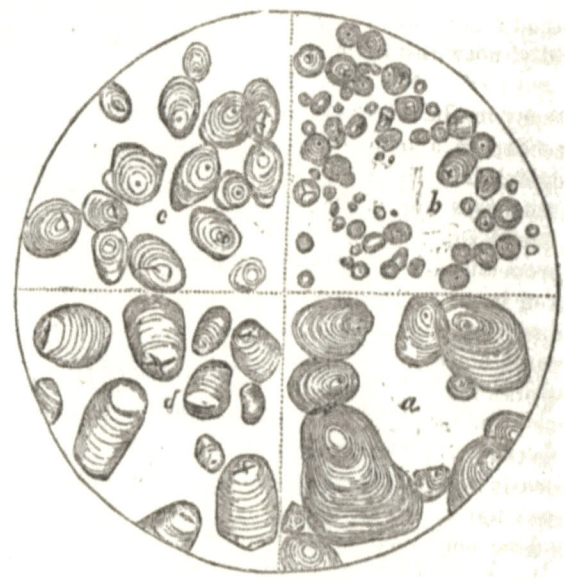

FIG. 1.

a, Granules of Potato-starch; b, of Tapioca-starch; c, West-India Arrow-root; d, Sago-starch.

bitter disappointment; and to those who resort to combustion of the delightful narcotic for visions of happiness in the upper regions of the blest, to learn that they are regaling themselves with the fumes of most unsentimental and uninspiring materials. Tobacco contains the following refreshing ingredients: bran, oakum, cabbage leaves, seaweed, roasted chicory root, beet root dregs, fuller's earth, sal-ammoniac, carbonate of ammonia, salt, potash, opium, etc. It was not long ago, that an importer in this city refused to pay the legal duties on a package of cigars at the Custom House, on the ground that *there was not a particle of tobacco in them!*

This system of adulteration, when extended to the depreciation of what supports life, or, worse, when it furtively intermixes a health and even life-destroying agent, should be exposed, in order that it may receive from the public the condemnation it merits; and legislation ought to be enlisted in the suppression and punishment of the baneful fraud. In this country as well as in Europe, the practice of adulteration extends to almost every article of food. Not only do luxuries possess the deleterious ingredients, but the commonest necessaries of life are contaminated; so that all ages, classes, and conditions are exposed to the noxious effects of this shameless outrage, the extent of which seems to be limited only — if at all — by the impossibility of finding materials valueless enough to be profitably used.

Scarcely anything that we eat or drink is free from falsification of some kind; either by mixture of a cheaper article of the same general alimentary character, in which case We only pay an exorbitant price for a given amount of really nutritious food, and are only cheated out of our money; by the substitution of harmless yet inferior and not equally palatable substances, in which case we are defrauded not only of our money, but of the proper amount of food, and the enjoyment of it; or, finally, which is far worse, by the addition of injurious, and often highly poisonous substances, for the purpose of giving a satisfactory color, improving the appearance, or of disguising certain products of decomposition in a damaged article. In this last case, we are swindled every way — in our pockets, our palates, and in our pancreatic functions.

The detection and exposure of a large class of these adulterations is within the province of chemical science, and the analyst can with the most unerring precision detect the existence of any of that class of substances called *inorganic*, and determine the quantity to the minutest fraction of a grain.

But in the determination of many *organic* substances, it becomes necessary to call in the aid of the microscope. Before this instrument was brought to the aid of chemistry, many adulterations of food of a most pernicious character were quite beyond the reach of exposure. Chemical reagents revealed very little respecting the use of organic matter in adulterations. The chemist was utterly powerless to distinguish the leaf of the veritable T. Bohea of celestial growth, from that of the willow or the hawthorn. He could not distinguish between pure ground coffee, and the semblance of it containing a large proportion of chicory. But the microscope, with its auxiliary use of polarized light, and the various superior appliances with which modern art has supplied it, has left no problem unsolved in this direction. It unravels the most delicate vegetable tissues, and by the peculiarities of their structure, designates the true and the false with unfailing certainty. All vegetable forms have definite organisms, these organisms varying in different parts of the same plant. The root, stem, leaf, and fruit, all exhibit a marked difference in their organic structure — a structure detectable in the minutest particle, even when it has been ground to impalpable powder, and terrified by excessive heat; so that, for instance, it would be impossible to adulterate the ground coffee-berry with other parts of the coffee-plant without detection. Even when there is a close resemblance in the organisms to be singled out from each other, there still exist slight shades of difference that enable the microscopist to decide with certainty between the real and the counterfeit. And so vigorously does this instrument, in the hands of a master, define the form, measure the size, and analyze the structure of the most delicate animal or vegetable organisms,

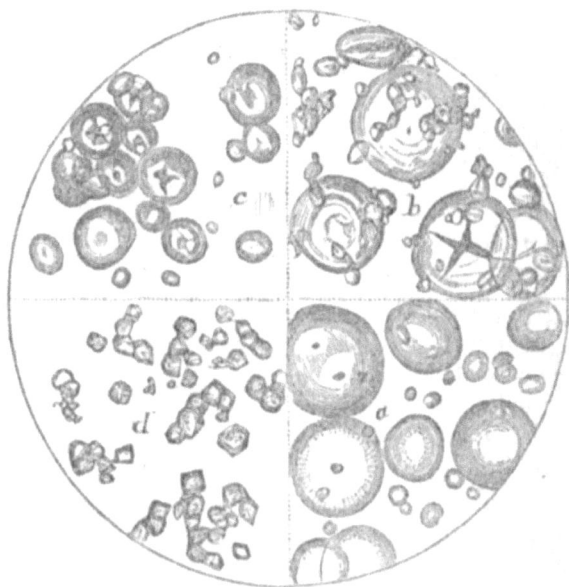

Fig. 2.

a, Starch granules of Wheat-flour; *b,* of Rye-flour; *c,* of Indian-corn; *d,* of Rice-flour.

that the most cunning adulterations are brought to light, leaving no escape for those who, in supplying our alimentary wants, are guilty of these criminal falsifications.

It then remains for the people at large to rebuke the fraud, to redress the high-handed wrong, and to punish, through the competent authorities, those who thus recklessly trifle with the public health. If by the publication of an extended series of chemical analyses of food, accompanied by the most searching microscopic examinations, we can expose 'the tricks of the trade,' and awaken in our own citizens a determination to live longer and better on pure food, the effort shall not be wanting; and the names of manufacturers and dealers who (so far as our investigations extend) are guilty of these adulterations, will be published. All that we desire is, the cooperation of honest manufacturers and dealers, and the sympathy of the suffering public.

The following list, taken from the results of the labors of

Hassall, Marcet, Mitchell, and others, of England, and corroborated by examinations in our own country, will give a condensed history, past and present, of the adulterations of the more common articles of food. Many of the substances used are not only harmless, but even nutritious, but their presence too often involves the addition of still other and more objectionable constituents, for the sake of preserving color, and improving the general appearance of the articles.

FLOUR: Rice, beans; rye, corn, and potato flour; alum, bone-dust, powdered flints, plaster of Paris.

BREAD: Mashed potatoes; rice, bean, rye, and corn flour; chalk, plaster of Paris, pipe clay, alum, carbonate of ammonia, sulphate of copper, sulphate of zinc.

SUGAR: Wheat and potato-flours, tapioca, starch, water, lead, iron, sand, chalk, pipe clay, plaster of Paris.

COFFEE: Chicory, roasted wheat, rye, and potato-flour, roasted beans, mangel-wurzel, acorns, burnt sugar.

COCOA AND CHOCOLATE: Maranta, East-India, and Tahiti arrowroots. Tous les Mois; the flour of wheat, corn, sago, potato, and tapioca; sugar, chicory, cocoa husks, Venetian red, red ochre, lard, tallow, mutton-suet.

TEA: Exhausted tea leaves, leaves of the horse-chestnut, sycamore, plum, beech, plane, elm, poplar, willow, etc.; lie-tea, sand, starch, black-lead, gum, indigo, Prussian blue, turmeric, Chinese yellow, China clay, soap-stone, rose pink, Dutch pink, chrome yellow, Venetian red, carbonate and arsenite of copper, chromate and bi-chromate of potash, carbonates of lime and magnesia.

TOBACCO: Water, sugar, molasses, salts, oil, rhubarb, potato, coltsfoot, dock, and other leaves, sawdust, earthy matter, sand, nitrate of soda, etc., etc.

VINEGAR: Water, burnt sugar, sulphuric acid.

PORTER AND ALE: Water, sugar, molasses, salt, Coculus Indicus, grains of paradise, capsicum, ginger, quassia, wormwood, calamus root, caraway and coriander seeds, orange powder, liquorice, honey, sulphate of iron, sulphuric acid, cream of tartar, alum, carbonate of potash, oyster shells, hartshorn shavings, nux vomica, beans.

GIN: Water, sugar, cayenne, cassia, grains of paradise, sulphuric acid, coriander seeds, angelica root, oil of almonds, calamus root, almond cake, orris root, cardamom seeds, orange peel.

COLORED CONFECTIONERY: East India arrowroot, wheat and potato flour, hydrated sulphate of lime, cochineal, lake, indigo, Prussian blue, Antwerp blue, artificial ultramarine, carbonate of copper, white and red lead, vermillion, chromate of lead of different shades, gamboge, sap green, Brunswick green, arsenite of copper, Indian red, brown ferruginous earths, etc.

PICKLES: Salts of copper.

PEPPER: Wheat and pea flour, ground rice and mustard seeds, linseed meal, pepper dust.

SNUFF: Chromate of potash and lead, ferruginous earths, red and white lead, carbonate of ammonia, lime, powdered glass, powdered orris root.

CAYENNE PEPPER: Ground rice, mustard-husk, salt, red lead, bisulphuret of mercury, Venetian red, turmeric, brick-dust.

GINGER: Wheat, sago, and potato flour, ground rice, mustard husks, turmeric powder.

HONEY: Flour, cane sugar, chalk, pipe clay.

LARD: Potato-flour, water, mutton-suet, salt, carbonate of soda, caustic lime alum potash.

MUSTARD: Wheat flour, turmeric, yellow ochre, chromate of lead.

Such are the results of the investigations to which we have referred. In view of the diversity of the constituents, which is shown by the above list to enter into our daily food, the naturalist might classify man as an omnivorous animal, in the broadest sense. Judging us by the amount of ferruginous earths, chalk, pipe clay, plaster of Paris, etc. that we are obliged to swallow in our daily bread, we might also appropriately be ranked with the clay-eaters of Siam or Kamtschatka. Fortunate indeed if we are not pinched with colic, prostrated with paralysis, and irrecoverably poisoned through the insidious effect of the most destructive metallic salts and oxides with which our food is seasoned.

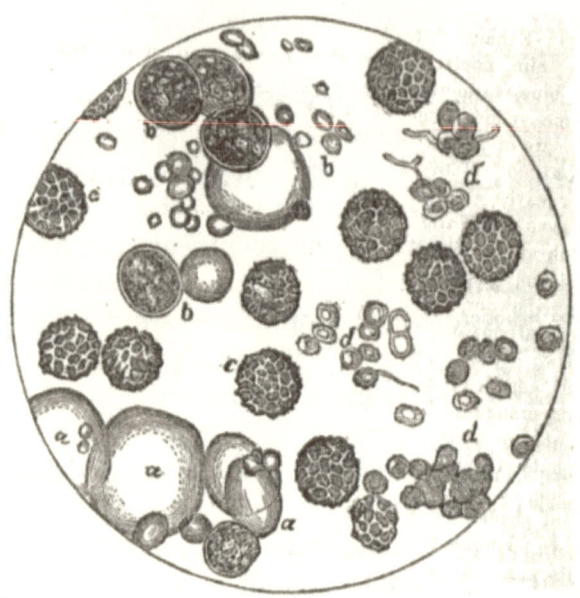

Fig. 8.

a, Starch granules of Wheat-flour; *b*, Puccinia Graminis (Sporules of;) *c*, Sporules of Uredo Caries; *d*, Sporules of Uredo Segetum.

Many foreign articles come to our markets surcharged with villainous compounds; while the modes of adulteration, in this country differ but little from those employed in England, except in cases where the required material is cheaper or less available.

The four varieties of starch represented in Fig. 1, as seen in the field of the microscope, will illustrate, though imperfectly, the discriminating power of that instrument: we say imperfectly, for it is impossible to represent in an engraving of this kind the more delicate shades of difference that characterize them in the eye of the observer. The difference in size, however, of these and other varieties of starch granules, is generally sufficient to distinguish them from each other, varying, as they do, from the one hundred and eightieth part of an inch — the size of potato-starch — to the twelve hundredth part of an inch, about the average diameter of the granules of buckwheat-starch.

The characteristic shapes exhibited by the granules of the

potato, sago, and tapioca starches, and West-India arrowroot, under the microscope, are sufficient, independently of their relative sizes, to distinguish them. The oyster-shape, and the distinctness of the concentric rings having their common focus, if we may so call it, at one end, mark the potato starch; the oblong form, truncated at one end, that of sago; the irregularity of form, sometimes even becoming triangular, that of maranta, or West India arrow-root; the more nearly circular form, and the tendency to compound granules, consisting of two, three, or even four united, that of tapioca. Thus by the microscope, and by that alone, we detect the adulteration of sago with potato flour; tapioca with potato-flour and sago-meal; and West-India arrowroot with all three.

Bread in itself contains nearly all the elements, and in almost the requisite proportions, indispensable to the sustenance of man: nerve and sinew, bone and adipose tissue, alike gather strength and fullness from its substance. It is, more than anything else, the universal pabulum of civilized man. Not inappropriately, then, has the word 'bread' become the synonym of food. Such is the universal necessity, such the unceasing demand for, and enormous consumption of, bread, that the adulteration, even to a moderate degree and with the least hurtful materials, becomes a great wrong to the public: but the revelations of the microscope and the test-tube show that the avarice of the dealer has not spared even the 'staff of life.'

Figure 2 represents the starch granules of different varieties of the f flour, as seen by the microscope, and illustrates the ease with which the more innocent modes of adulteration — the mixture of inferior with the more valuable farinas — are detected. The starch is readily separated from the gluten, by making a thick paste of the flour, wrapping it in a piece of cotton cloth, and kneading it with the fingers while a very small stream of water is running over it. The starch washes through the cloth, and will subside readily in the water, and may be easily transferred to the microscope. If it should be a sample of damaged flour, you may find scattered here and there in the field of the instrument, the

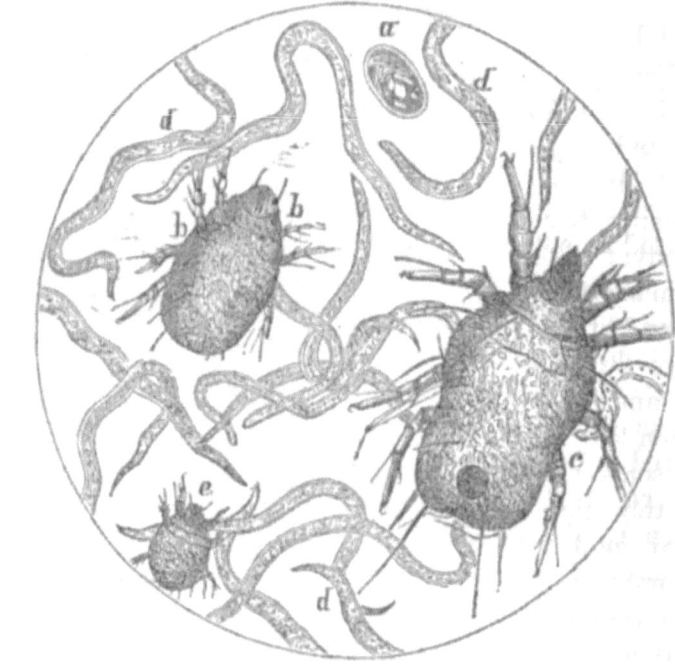

FIG. 4.

a, Ovum of Acarus Farinæ; *b, c, e,* Acarus Farinæ; *d, d,* Vibriones Tritici.

different varieties of fungus growths depicted in Figure 3, *b, c, d,* of which *b,* (Puccinia Graminis,) is commonly known as rust, *c,* (Uredo Caries,) as *pepper-brand,* and d, (Uredo Segetum,) as *smut.*

These fungi we have often detected in an examination of samples of inferior brands of flour in this city. They will seldom be found associated together in the same sample.

A still more uninviting picture is sometimes exhibited by the microscope, and one that is calculated to suspend the gnawing of hunger in a sensitive stomach. (See Fig. 4.)

The Vibriones Tritici exist usually in the blighted grains of wheat, as a cottony substance, exhibiting great activity except when perfectly dry. From this latter condition, however lifeless they appear, and though they crumble at the touch, they can be restored to a lively existence by simple moistening. It has been supposed that these animalcules do not find their way into flour through the meshes of the miller's bolting-cloths, but they certainly exist in the damaged article.

The Acarus Farina is another accompaniment of damaged flour; *a, e, b, c,* represent this mite in its different stages of development, from the ovum to the full-grown animal.

To the adulterations of flour and bread with the inferior farina, there is another class of substances superadded that can be detected only by the aid of chemical reagents. We refer to the extensive use of alum, sulphate and carbonate of lime, and more rarely perhaps, carbonate of magnesia. The use of alum serves a variety of purposes: First, it enables the baker to use a larger proportion of inferior flour without essentially affecting the appearance of his bread. Secondly, he can use with impunity damaged flour. Thirdly, it gives to bread, made even from the best flour, a whiter appearance. Carbonates of lime and magnesia are also used for the purpose of improving the appearance of bread and disguising an inferior quality of flour.

The effect upon health of the daily use of these substances, with some of which baker's bread is almost universally contaminated, is most pernicious. The continual use of food containing carbonate of magnesia is likely to result in the formation of the most painful calculi. We ask for bread, and they give us a stone.

The astringent effect of alum as a medicine should satisfy us of its evil effects as a constituent of food. The natural result from its continual use is acidity of the stomach, costiveness, dyspepsia. We may here state that, with scarcely an exception, alum is to a fearful degree a constituent of baker's bread in New-York City; and in many instances, lime and other deleterious substances are associated therewith.

The June number of the KNICKERBOCKER will contain carefully prepared analyses of twenty-five different varieties of baker's bread in New York, and the names of the bakers. [Editors's Note: This list not found.]

XI

An Essay
On Buckwheat Cakes

BY YADESSAC

OCTOBER 1851

'THERE IS nothing so closely interwoven in its consequences with the everyday existence of man as that unchangeable law. Change.' So spoke that distinguished moralist Keying Fum, admiringly styled in the chronicle, the 'Pride of Pe Kin, and the inexpressible delight of the Central Flowery Kingdom,' eight thousand years ago. Keying, by-the-bye, set up for a kind of celestial Fourierite, and being accused forthwith of heresy, was deprived by a peculiar process of both his eyes, (gouging did not originate in Arkansas, as the ignorant suppose; it is clearly of Chinese invention,) and at the same time of the whole of his estate, which, being neither bank stock nor state bonds, proved quite a godsend to the public treasury. It is also remarked by the historian, that immediately the vigilance of government was fearfully increased, and a great many prosperous gentlemen in the vicinity accused of the heretical taint and promptly deprived of their visuals, pigtails, and possessions. 'But in no single instance,' adds Hoang Tschu, the recorder, sneeringly, in a spirit of inexcusable malignity, 'was a poor man known to suffer.' The saying (as is always the case with the ancients; who dare contradict them?) is the very marrow of truthfulness, the purest distillation of wisdom, a quintessential drop of attar. Change is alike a concomitant to all our griefs and all our enjoyments. It sparkles the bosom of the exultant juvenile with visions of jacket and trousers obtrusive of long rows of

113

buttons gaily gilt. And then the quarter in the pocket: how he fumbles that pocket, how that coin expands to 'wealth beyond the dreams of avarice!' There's *change* for you. At the nuptial festival the one engrossing care, it filleth with reluctance the heart of age feebly pulsating toward its long rest. The wedding ring and trestle are alike its symbols.

But of all changes there is one, not the least afflictive, which, except at clinics and in treatises on indigestion, has not, we opine, been duly considered — change of diet.

Could we fathom the intimate relationship of mind and matter, their sympathetic sensibility, what startling discoveries might we not expect? What a stupendous amount of human infelicity, ascribed to perverse temper or moral obliquity, might not be traced to the tribe of roast and boiled, of salads and of soups! A conjugal tempest may be often brewed in a psychomachic encounter grown of some abrupt dietetic deprivation. Curious to reflect that a family jar may ensconce in the leg of a chicken, or a fit of the bitterest misanthropy lie *perdu* in a devilled beef-bone.

Change of diet has its pathos, too. An ardent attachment to a favorite dish has grown into our very being; fate fulminates its fiat; the whole intensity of our affection gushes forth; our heart becomes a smitten Horeb; we would contend, but destiny mocks at our feebleness; there is a struggle and a relinquishment.[1] But we never forget; grateful are the recollections; the old saint has died in the odor of sanctity.

Nor are we, self-sufficient scoffer, essaying to bolster the subject into undue importance. We disclaim the imputative inflation. No. The study, the mart, the council chamber and the camp, each engross their portion of human attention; but the *table* is and ever has been omnipotent over all. How large a share in the world's history does it occupy! It is the veriest of extensions. From the time of the patriarchal repast, when the kid smoked upon the embers, from the time when the Athenian epicure

---

1   It may be well to recall a notable instance where there could have existed no strong personal objection to a change of diet. It was LUTHER's case. But we must remember it was of Worms.

put on a morning scowl and passed a sulky day if the wind was not fair for the fishing boats entering the Piraeus, to this era of civic feasts, when aldermanic dignity is fretted with solicitude for its turtle and its turbot; from the period of those Roman entertainments which Juvenal satirized and of which Seneca complained — although we will be sworn they never declined an invitation to dinner — from the costly dishes of Hortensius and Lucullus, to the breakfasts of Samuel Rogers, and the *recherché* feedings of Holland House, the meals of men have been the golden sands in the hourglass of their existence, and virtue and learning and valor have eaten their way through the world.

Our mess caterer had just deposited on the table a square paper package labeled, 'Steam-dried Buckwheat.' Abstractedly we had picked it up; there was the usual recommendatory appeal to the public, which we fear would not have impressed us either to partisan or purchase, but it suggested pleasant memories, and what we deemed not incurious reflections; memories, that while they eloquently touched the heart, nimbly tickled the palate, and our thoughts ran rovingly through many seasons when the winter-morning enjoyment was builded on the substantial basis of a plate of Buckwheat Cakes. 'Ah!' we exclaimed audibly and with energy, 'had it ever been the happiness of that old epicure Apicius to have known the cake of buckwheat, he would have longed for no better paradise than one eternal reminiscence.' Startled by our own volubility, we stirred uneasily in our chair and directed around a hasty glance. We were alone. From the distance outside came faintly the fluctuating chorus of a drinking song, a belated horseman clattered past the window down the street, while underneath the floor an industrious rat gnawed persistive. We listened, and relapsed.

When one undertakes a muck into the region of reverie and is likely to carry it too far, a little scribbling proves a great relief; even as your skilful leech combats a vascular turgescence by promptly tipping you the lancet. It was thus, after sitting out a pair of dreamy hours, we gathered around us the ample folds of our ancient Tweed and lounged to the inkstand. 'All this by way of explanation,' remarketh the methodic reader, 'should not have been thrown *in medias;* had you made it the frontage, we should never have waded thus far to get at your design.' Granted, most interesting censor; but get upon you a fit of gastronomic reflection, and you become perforce desultory. Logarithms, we take it, were not an after-dinner suggestion. And as to parting company, our gentle and courteous reader, why, even be complaisant for once, and go with us by easy stages to the end.

'No man,' observed Johnson, 'feels disposed for a brawl, or like a blackguard, with a clean shirt on.' But the feeling communicated by the shirt can be only skin deep. If you want to improve the moral sentiments, to elevate our common nature, you must go to the — stomach. We do not mean that your adipose men are paragons of propriety. Oh, no; the Falstaffs of this world are too fond of its Dame Quicklys and Doll Tearsheets. What we would say is, simply, all sterling philanthropists are judicious feeders. We are as thoroughly convinced that Howard, and Benezet, and Mrs. Fry were invigorated by the humanizing influence, grew up and strengthened in good works under the dispensation of buckwheat cakes, as if it were laid down by their biographers. Conversely, it may be inferred, that Swedish Charles possessed no relish for this pabulum; that Catiline would have abhorred it; and that the sight of one fresh from the griddle would have been the death of Robespierre, and have brought the Reign of Terror to an early termination. Jeshurun indeed, we are told, 'waxed fat and kicked,' (the first notable example of spiteful obesity;) nothing more evident than that Jeshurun, unhappy Jeshurun, was utterly unacquainted with the *Polygonum fagopyrum.*

Peace societies are very well in their way, but inefficient, inadequate to the end they propose. Instead of anti-belligerent congresses at Paris and Brussels for the pacification of the world, we would cultivate an appetite for buckwheat cakes. 'Then,' in the language of the Constable of France, 'we should find, they have only stomachs to eat, and none to fight.'[2] Elihu Burritt, when he went upon his European mission of goodwill, seemed to possess

---

2   Henry V.

an inkling of this improvement in ethical tactics. While with the one hand he distributed peace publications, with the other he scattered far and wide corn meal, with recipes for making pone and Indian dumplings. Elihu walked and worked according to the light he had; but it was an imperfect light, a mere glimpse, a pan-flash. Elihu was yet but in the outer porch of the temple. He did not anticipate the full fruition to come, when buckwheat is to stalk forth over the whole earth.

We believe the anthropophagi are nearly extinct; no cannibals now except in the Feejees, New Zealand, and a few other ealondie localities: still who can say but that the last horrid vestiges of man-eating are destined to melt away before the civilizing encroachments of the batter-pot, that most persuasive of missionaries?

There is no hypocrisy in buckwheat cakes; they are embodied frankness; better than full cups to unmask the soul. Your eaters of them are free, open, jovial men. They would have played the very devil with the digestion of Machiavelli. We have often thought, too, how important a part they might be made to take in the political world. Skillfully employed, what a lever in the hands of a demagogue! The Roman patron, that he might be sure of the voices of his clients, was never neglectful of their paunches. Hath not the history of the day exhibited to us an aspiring cadet of the house of the great Corsican coaxing to his purpose the bayonets of the regiments of Paris by luncheons of champagne and sausage? Is Wexford turbulent when the tubers abound? Instead of mass meetings, and partisan pamphlets, and newspaper squibs, give public breakfasts and provide plentifully buckwheat cakes. Ye suitors of power! Ye humble petitioners ever piously praying! If ye would get grant, or acquiescence, or reprieve, enter into an alliance with the kitchen, keep your eye upon the overnight buckwheat pot, and as the great man next morning rolleth deliberately in grateful prolongation the last unctuous morsel, catch his complaisant ear, and be comforted by the generous promptings of a full stomach and a feeling heart.

How finely might Ben Jonson have rounded a period, and

given the climacteric to towering sensuality in the mouth of his Mammon:

> —'I WILL have
> The tongues of carps, dormice, and camels' heels,
> Boil'd in the spirit of SOL: pheasants,
> Calver'd salmon, knots, godwits,
> Lampreys. 1 will have
> The beards of barbels served instead of salads,
> Oil'd mushrooms, *and, bliss most*
> *Exquisite* and *poignant! Buckwheat cakes.'*

We do remember a cosy, ease-dispensing tavern, one of the ancient sort, nestled in the midst of a brick-and-mortar wilderness of warehouses. There it stood, with unpretending proportions and somber front, looking out upon the hard, stony street and its pedestrians, care-visaged men of barter. There it stood, with causeway-like hall hospitably wide, projecting eaves where pigeons builded without fear of molestation, and quaint old dormers. One room we loved to frequent when unoccupied, as it almost always was. We could find great pleasure in the carved woodwork, and a hearty, pious solace in the figured tiles encircling the capacious fireplace. The pictures, incidents from Scripture history, (here and there a fabulous grouping profanely had crept in,) had so much of life mingled with oddity, that they drew you on unconsciously into a train of sprightly although subdued reflection. Here was the gentle Ruth among the gleaners; Joseph being sold by his brethren into Egypt; Pharaoh's host struggling amid the whelming waters; the omnivorous serpent of Aaron; and next to it — even now we see the fiery Cappadocian plunging to the onslaught — St. George encountering the Dragon. Ensconced in antique, leather-cushioned chair, with arms invitingly extended, we have lingered over nerving cup decocted of Arabian berry, and you, delicious 'firstlings of our heart!' brown and crisp, and hot and buttered. And then the morning papers. Talk of pleasurable sensations! Eating and reading; playing at hide-and-seek among the columns; now a morsel of cake, and now a news item.

As we write, what dear domestic memories throng upon us!

It is a dark and sleety winter's morning, when, after a shivering toilet, we descend to the dining room. The breakfast table is set in comfortable array, the viands all on, except — but cook says, 'Wait a moment; the cakes will soon be done.' A rousing fire rattles and roars away in the voluminous grate. The breath of our old dining room is warmth indeed: may God bless all who breathe it! There is a moment to spare, and we look into the street, ice-glazed and slippery. Very few are yet abroad. There goes, indeed, a thrifty citizen, muffled to the throat, with stocking feet drawn over heavy boots. Clatters along the milkman's wagon with its chilly-looking cans. Opposite, the baker stops a moment to chatter with the house-girl, who lingers with the morning's bread: some people *will* persist in French rolls, although it is the middle of December. Nothing else is visible but icicled spouts, a broad band of lowering sky, and a melancholy cat peeping through a half-opened cellar-door. A family movement toward the table, and we turn from our place of espial just in time to see enter the faithful old servitor, of placid mien and air, self-satisfied, with the plate of cakes. And such they are in truth and verity: hot, piping hot, like the coffee that hisses from the urn; mantled with a brown so rich and delicate it would excite the envy of a whole academy of painters; and then the odor! more exquisite than ever rose from perfumed censers.

Buckwheat cakes, to be enjoyed, must be in season. To appreciate them, you must respect the unities: they are among the edibles illustrative of the calendar. The juicy peach, or delicately acidulated berry, would provoke no zest at a December dinner table. Buckwheat cakes in the dog days would equally outrage propriety. They spring gently and naturally upon you when the cold November mists lean against the windowpanes; when after a season of repose the poker is again withdrawn from its swathings, and you condescend to interest yourself in the price of coal. They are with you through the 'melancholy days;' they linger until

> — 'the effusive south
> Warms the wide air,'

119

and bringeth thaw, lethargy, sunny hours, and the alosal advent, when the shad, which but a little space before was floundered in the seine, now fastened to a plank, drippeth its basting into the eager fire.

Many people nice upon the point consider sausages indispensable accompaniments. We take no exception; indeed, we rather like them, with — be bold, our pen, to write it — with a dash of garlic. O most abused, most ire inciting of the genus *allium!*

'The world is not thy friend.'

Horace railed at thee; Shakespeare put thee into the mouths of his wenches; even the kindly 'Elia' was dehortatory. But, reader, between us two, a gentle impregnation; then indeed do they become

'Of linked sweetness, long drawn out.'

How many good-natured jests did we indulge at these glorious matutinal meals! With what amiable forbearance would we listen for the fortieth time to that old conundrum, which demandeth in what respect a buckwheat cake resembleth a caterpillar? Our maiden aunt would answer in a spirit of illustrative pleasantry, taking a canticle of golden Chester county, which must have smiled in its very churn-birth, 'Because it makes the butter — fly.' But when by some inexplicable accident the cakes had not been 'stirred,' or the batter had soured overnight, would follow what a thundercloud of scowls, and cataract of mutterings! A gloomy taciturnity prevailed.

That old red earthen batter-pot! We see it now, as of yore it sat upon the kitchen hearth, capped with a pie-plate, two or three little streamlets dried in the trickling fastened to its portly sides. With what keen relish of delight have we lifted, lovingly lifted its surmounting, and gazed into the tranquil depth. Then did our mouth water, then were the salivaries pushed to action, then yearned the stomach, and leapt the blood exultingly; for we saw in the tiny bubbles, as one by one they slowly raised their heads, harbingers of bliss and breakfast.

It would be hard to say how much of lovemaking on long winter evenings, the fleecy snow falling fast outside, thou hast witnessed. How thy presence hath grown into the enamored soul, making dear in anticipation the hearth of home. How that sly romping Cupid has confessed thee more potent than all his quiver. And, oh, with what earnestness came upon the ear the returning footsteps of the bedbound good wife, as her voice, modulated to the pathos of deep entreaty, rolled down the kitchen stairs. Startling was it in its impressiveness. We hear it now: 'Betsy, don't forget the cakes!'

It is over. We are brick making in the land of Egypt, and like persecuted Israel, driven to furnish our own straw. Farewell, dear household god, venerable old friend, farewell! May it be long ere thou goest the way of all pottery; mayest thou continue in a beatitude of buckwheat, and from thy capacious maw dispense whole family generations of cakes.

YADESSAC.
San Francisco, (Cal.)

XII

September and Oysters

BY JOHN W.S. HOWE

SEPTEMBER 1842

WHAT A host of delightful associations will incontinently rush on the mind of the man of *taste,* at sight of the conjunctive title which heads this article! To the true lover of the delicious bivalve I have selected for my disquisition, September is the orthodox month when his dearly cherished edible becomes once more a legitimate object of his masticatory devotion. He has passed four anxious months not graced by the cabalistic R, which alone sanctions with your true oyster-loving devotee the unrestrained use and enjoyment of his delight. He has witnessed with virtuous indignation and horror the heresies of those demi-savages who luxuriate on his darling condiment during the months his well-tutored mind deems to be *uncanonical;* and albeit he may have 'abhorred the sin,' yet truth reluctantly compels us to admit that he has envied 'the sinners.' But September has arrived! Again visions of roasts and fries, stews and soups, patés and *huitres au naturel,* come vividly, like thick-crowding fancies, all laden with delights substantial, palpable, and lasting!

Yes, oysters are indeed the things which may be classed among 'man's chiefest good.' Unlike other 'eatables,' whose merits lie most in the adornments of art, this testaceous animal, like Beauty,

'When unadorned is adorned the most.'

Who that has revelled in the luscious delights of oysters 'RAW,'

123

fresh from their pearly shell, with Nature's sauce alone to give them zest, but will avow that even the science of a UDE would fail in conveying one charm superior to this pure and unadulterated *taste?* It is indeed 'the triumph of Nature over Art!'

I have watched with instinctive reverence an old and valued friend, whose frequent attendance at those orgies y'clept oyster suppers is worthy of all praise; I have watched him I say with his rubicund and benevolent countenance, advancing in his accustomed devotions, through the legitimate stages of soup, fried, and roasted, and mayhap coquetting with the luscious paté. But when in the 'due order of the feast' he has come to the crowning gem of the evening — the rich, the unequalled 'RAW' — how have the benevolent features expanded, and every sentient organ beamed with a more expressive force, as one by one the savory bivalves have passed gently down the aperture to that sacred sepulchre where he had already entombed their more ambitious predecessors! It was indeed the very embodiment of perfect enjoyment.

'The complete art of cookery,' however, affords a charming variety in preparing the oyster for its 'numerous admirers.' There is the delicious *soup,* so grateful to the invalid, so eagerly relished by even the uninitiated in the true enjoyment of gastronomic excellence. Your *gourmêt,* (a delightful contradistinction to your *gourmand,* which the never-to-be-forgotten JOHN RANDOLPH, in my days of juvenility, once took especial pains to make me comprehend meant, an amateur of *true taste* in the 'divine art' of 'feeding;') your *gourmêt* never violently affects the soup. It may be used as the light skirmish preparatory to the grand attack; the flourish of the leader before the full swell of the orchestra bursts upon the ear; 'the prologue to the merry play;' or the light preface to the more interesting work. But never, oh never let it take the sole place in a meal; unless it be for lunch in a December morning, when the fleecy flakes are 'falling thick as leaves in Vallombrosa.' *Then* it is omnipotent, and purely *'selon de règle.'*

Your *fried oysters* offer pretensions to sole supremacy of a higher order. Aided by their usual accompaniments of salad, or as we Gothamites facetiously term them, *'trimmings,'* your oyster fried is no contemptible 'finish' to the protracted evening sitting. Unctuous and juicy, crisp and delicate, clothed in its livery of slightly tinted brown, or, 'by our Lady!' a dark straw color, it presents charms which are irresistible. *Art* here is triumphant; for oh! the depths of science between the gradations of fried oysters, such as we have seen, ay, and to our sorrow tasted, too, and the delicious preparations we have attempted to describe! It is 'like Hyperion to a satyr,' or the antipodes to the poles. The paté also is a gem of the culinary art. Its melting crust, trembling like the first breathings of an early love — tender as the snow-drift in the opening spring — encasing the *piquant* treasures it is so worthy of enshrining, and which yields to the taste, casket and treasure united, a *morçeau,* unapproachable by any other combination of paste and its numerous auxiliaries.

But how, *how* shall we describe thee, most succulent roast! Homeric fire is too cold to portray thy virtues — Shakespearean measures too tame to celebrate thy charms! Thou solace of 'unnumbered woes!' Thou choicest morsel in life's 'fitful feast!' Yes! embedded in thy native shell, fizzing, whizzing, and steaming with odors more fragrant than those from 'Araby the Blest,' thou comest before my mind's eye as the veritable personification of all that is perfect in taste and unique in *vertu.* And here let me digress with a caution to all true lovers of the 'Oyster Roast:' 'Never, as you value the delights of pure and unalloyed flavor, *never* separate the succulent morsel from its native covering, but prepare it in its steaming prison-house, agreeably to your taste, and take it reeking from its savory sea, uncontaminated by vile contact with plate or dish, that absorbs its flavor and its aroma, and desecrates by the collision 'food worthy of the gods.'

But time would fail me were I to dilate at large upon all the enjoyments conjured up by the words I have selected as a heading to this paper — 'SEPTEMBER AND OYSTERS.' There is the list of piquant dishes rendered more savory by this 'king of bivalves;' the long array of 'bright and rosy hours' that are heralded by this indivisible conjunction. Speak for me, ye long tenantless seats in those cellars or caves where most of our oyster-loving devotees do congregate! Tell of the cheerful cry of 'Oysters for two!' 'Three plates, Raw!' 'One dozen, fried!' 'Two dozen in the shell!' which issue from your murky precincts when September comes again to cheer and brighten your late desolate and forsaken region! Aid me, ye thrifty matrons who often 'ply your evening cares' to delight the taste of admiring 'oyster parties;' when care forgetting and 'hard times' forgot, you are cased up in 'measureless content,' enjoying the feast your bounty and your skill provide for the honored guests, who repay your toils by the jest, the laugh, the song, the merry tale, that cheat this frail existence of its care, and bring man closer to his kindred man; knitting the bonds of our erring humanity, and calming asperities which are alike unworthy of and debasing to our better natures. Yes! All these delights are 'Siamese Twins;' all inseparably linked with SEPTEMBER AND OYSTERS.

XIII

The Dinner of the Months

ONCE UPON a time, the Months determined to dine together. They were a long while deciding who should have the honor of being the host upon so solemn an occasion, but the lot at length fell upon December; for although the old gentleman's manners were found to be rather cold, upon first acquaintance, yet it was well known that when once you got under his roof, there was not a merrier or more hospitable person in existence. The messenger, too, Christmas Day, whom he sent round with his cards of invitation, won the hearts of all; although he played several mad pranks, and received many a *box* in return. February begged to be excused coming to the dinner, as she was in very bad spirits, on account of the loss of her youngest child, the twenty-ninth, who had lately left her, and was not expected to return for four years. Her objection, however, was overruled; and being seated at table between the smiling May and that merry old fellow, October, she appeared to enjoy the evening's entertainment as much as any of the company.

The dinner was a superb one, all the company having contributed to furnish out the table. January thought, for the *thirtieth* time, what he should give, and then determined to give a calf's head. February, not being a very productive month, was also a little puzzled; but at length resolved to contribute an enormous cake, which she managed to manufacture in fine style, with the assistance of her servant, Valentine, who was an excellent fellow

127

at that sort of ware, but especially at bride cake. March and April agreed to furnish all the fish; May to decorate the dishes with flowers; June to supply plenty of excellent cider; July and August to present the dessert; September a magnificent course of all sorts of game, excepting pheasants; which exception was supplied by October, as well as a couple of hampers of fine home-brewed ale; and November engaged that there should be an abundance of ice. The rest of the eatables, and all the wine, were provided by the worthy host himself.

Just before sitting down to table, a squabble arose about precedence; some of the company insisting that the first in rank was January, and some that it was March. The host, however, decided in favor of January, whom he placed in the seat of honor, at his right hand. November, a prim, blue-nosed old maid, sat at his left; and June, a pleasant, good-tempered fellow, although occasionally rather too *warm*, sat opposite him, at the end of the table.

The dinner was admirably served. Christmas Day was the principal waiter; but the host had been obliged to beg the attendance of some of his guests' servants, and accordingly, Twelfth-night, Shrove Tuesday, and Michaelmas Day, officiated in various departments: though Shrove Tuesday was speedily turned out, for making rather too free with a prim, demure servant maid, called Good Friday, while she was toasting some buns for the tea table.

A short, squab little fellow, called Saint Thomas's Day, stood behind December's chair, and officiated as toast-master; and much merriment was excited by the contrast between the diminutive appearance of this man, and the longest day, who stood behind June, at the other end of the table. Master Thomas, however, was a very useful fellow; and beside performing the high official duty which we have mentioned, he drew the curtains, stirred the fire, lighted and. snuffed the candles, and like all other little men, seemed to think himself of more importance than anybody else.

The pretty blushing May was the general toast of the company; and many compliments were passed upon the elegant manner in which she had ornamented the dishes. Old January tried to be very sweet upon her, but she received him coldly. January at length ceased to persecute her with his attentions, and transferred them to November, who was of the same politics as himself, although she had not been quite so successful in supporting them. Poor May had scarcely got rid of her venerable lover, before that sentimental swain, April, began to tell her that he was absolutely dying for her. This youth was one moment all sunshine, and smiles, and rapture, and the next he dissolved in tears, clouds gathered upon his brow, and he looked a fitter suitor for November than for May; who, having at last hinted as much to him, he left her in a huff, and entered into close conversation with September, who, although much his senior, resembled him in many particulars.

July, who was of a desperately hot temper, was every now and then a good deal irritated by March, a *dry* old fellow, as cool as a cucumber, who was continually passing his jokes upon him. At one time, July went so far as to threaten him with a prosecution for something he had said; but March, knowing what he was about, managed to keep on the windy side of the law, and to throw dust in the eyes of his accusers. July, however, contrived to have his revenge; for being called upon for a song, he gave 'The Dashing White Sergeant' in great style, and laid a peculiar emphasis upon the words '*March, March away*' at the same time motioning to his antagonist to leave the room.

April having announced that it was raining hard, January was much perplexed as to how he should get home, as he had not brought his carriage. At one time, when he was looking very anxiously out of the window, to discover if there were any stars visible, October, at the suggestion of May, asked him if he thought of borrowing *Charles's wain* to carry him, as he had done so great a kindness to its proprietor? This put the old fellow into such a passion, that he hastily seized his head gear, a red cap, sallied out through the rain, and would most likely have broken his neck in the dark, had not February sent her footman, Candlemas Day, after him, with a lantern, by whom he was guided in safety to his lodgings in Fog Alley.

On the retirement of the ladies, February, May, August, and November, the host proposed their healths, which were drunk with the usual honors; when April, being a soft-spoken youth, and ambitious of distinction as an orator, began to return thanks for them, in a very flowery speech; but was soon coughed down by December and March; and March, by the by, at length got into such high favor with his old enemy, July, that the latter was heard to give him an invitation, saying, that if ever he came to his side of the zodiac, he should be most happy to see him. October told the host that, with his leave, he would drink no more wine, but that he should be glad of some good home-brewed, and a pipe. To this December acceded, and said he should be happy to join him, and he thought his friend March would do the same. March having nodded assent, they set to, and a pretty *puffing* and *blowing* they made. April, however, continued to drink Madeira, while June, July, and September stuck with exemplary constancy to the Burgundy.

After repeated summonses to the drawing room, they joined the ladies at the tea table. November drew herself up, and affected to be quite overpowered by the smell of smoke, which March, October, and December had brought in with them; although it was well known that the old lady herself could *blow a cloud* as well as any of them. August, a grave, stately matron, of extraordinary beauty, although perhaps *un peu passée*, officiated as tea-maker. Good Friday, who by this time had recovered the fright into which Shrove Tuesday had thrown her, handed about the toasted buns; and Swithin, a servant of July, was employed to keep the tea-pot supplied with water, which he too often did to overflowing.

Tea being over, the old folks went to cards; and the young ones, including October, who managed to hide his years very successfully, to the pianoforte. May was the prima donna, and delighted everyone, especially poor April, who was alternately smiles and tears during the whole of her performance. October gave them a hunting song, which caused even the card tables to be deserted; and August sang a sweet, melancholy canzonet, which was rapturously encored.

At length, Candlemas Day having returned from seeing old

January home, his mistress, February, took leave of the company. April, who was a little the worse for the wine he had drunk, insisted on escorting November; although she had several servants in waiting, and her road was in an opposite direction to his own. May went away in her own carriage, and undertook to set June down, who lived very near her. The road was hilly and steep, but her coachman, Ascension Day, got the horses very well to the top; and July and August both walked home, each preceded by a dog-day, with a lighted torch. September and October, who were next door neighbors, went away in the same hackney coach; and March departed as he came, on the back of a rough Shetland pony.

XIV

Something About Wine

BY HENRY T. TUCKERMAN

AUGUST 1858

PART ONE

'OH! that men should put an enemy in their mouths to steal
away their brains.'

— SHAKESPEARE.

'AND wine that maketh glad the heart of man.'

— PSALM CIV.

THE extraordinary revelations of chemistry, which indicate the
mineral nutriment of animal life obtained through plants, have no
illustration so delicate and marvelous as that of the grape. That
magnesia is a constituent of oats, and was made by a speculative Scot
to account for the local genius of his nation fed on oat-cake: that the
phosphorus abounding in fish is a cerebral stimulant, whence a minute
philosopher might infer the frequent coincidence of piscatorial and
meditative tastes; are facts of physiological science curious indeed,
but not so refined and complex marvels as may be found in those
exquisite distillations of the soil conserved in a grape-skin. When
it is remembered how the peculiar flavor, strength, and quality
of wine is identified with distinct parts of the globe, derived
from special traits of soil, season, and atmosphere; and how,

through ages, this individuality has remained intact, we realize the aristocracy of vegetable race, the law of blood in the vine. Grains, grasses, and fruit trees — the commonalty of agriculture — are reproduced identical in various countries. The French *émigré* tastes the pear of his native province in an orchard of New England; the Italian finds in the aboriginal maize of this continent the *'gran Turco'* of Lombardy; and Clinton discovered in a wild cereal of Western New York, a farinaceous product indigenous on the shores of the Caspian. But there are varieties of the grape, not only confined to a certain latitude or island, but to a few acres of favored earth, whose qualities alone, by an inscrutable and inimitable combination of elements, produce an unique vinous result. Sometimes a worldwide fame and value, as in the case of Madeira and Champagne, and Chateau Margaux, is the evidence of this local superiority and character; and in others, the merit is known only to a neighborhood, and the privilege monopolized by a single family. The famous poem of 'Bacchus in Tuscany' celebrates two villas thus favored:

> 'Ma Iodato
> Celebrato
> Coronato
> Sia l'eroe, che nelle vigne
> Di Petraja e di Castello
> Pianti prima il Moscadello.'

In volcanic countries, these isolated gems of vineyards are of frequent occurrence; and their secret treasure guarded with jealous care. Out of Sicily, the wine universally known as the characteristic product of that fertile island is Marsala: only the long resident, or favored traveler is aware that a small fraternity of monks boast a row of vines springing from a few roods of decomposed lava, which yield annually fifty gallons of a nectar, which seems to unite the vital salubrity of Etna's salts with the prolific glow of her hidden fires and the cool purity of her virgin snow; these varied elements, 'so mixed' into a rich yet delicate vintage, that no one who has shared can ever forget the special flavor of the hospitality enjoyed at the convent of San Placido. The

Garonne's rushing tributaries have, during centuries, brought from the Pyrenees deposits that form a soil whence spring some of the choicest wines; so hard is it two or three feet beneath, that it must be broken before the vines will grow; and the best Medoc is born on a pebbly ground of quartz; the vine, indeed, requires what is called stony soil, because it is more retentive of heat by night.

There is an analogy between the customary beverage and the character of a people, which suggests many philosophical inferences. All travelers have noted the infrequency of ebriety, and the cheerful, vivacious disposition of the peasantry in wine countries; the social degradation incident to excess in alcoholical drinks, and the heavy dogmatism and stolid temper observable among the working class of Great Britain, whose habitual drink is malt liquor. There is an intimate relation between German metaphysics and beer. 'It is little wonder,' says an acute writer, 'that the German nation should remain subject to the rule of thirty-six petty tyrants, when, in fact, beer, by its, properties, destroys all the distinctions, and its habitual use grinds the edge from our critical faculties.' But there is also a singular adaptation in these to the climate. Englishmen, who daily imbibe their 'Brown Stout' with impunity at home, find it productive of vertigo and plethora in the United States, where the sunshine and alternations of temperature develop such a degree of nervous excitability, as to make solid stimulants unwholesome. In Russia, a man exposed to the elements, and accustomed to labor, would find claret an ineffective substitute for brandy. The latter is seldom palatable in Southern Europe, except in the diminutive cordial glass, and after a meal; while the common wine, all things being equal, produces a glow and exhilaration which only a water-drinker would realize in northern latitudes. We wonder, in France, how a glass of old Madeira could have ever seemed otherwise than fiery; and, while amid the fogs of London, Port has the taste of a seasonable restorative, in Italy its body and warmth are oppressive and heating. It needs an ascent of the Highlands and a Scotch mist, or a January night in America, to develop the innate virtue of Mountain Dew. Orvieto tastes flat away from Rome, and

Vino d'Astí is a homely draught, except in the temperate latitude of Lombardy. Old Rum, we are assured by Creole planters, can never be fully appreciated except in the West-Indies; and to duly estimate the excellence of *Schnapps*, one should be in Java or Holland. This sense of the appropriate in dietetics is felt when we first imbibe wine in the country of its growth. Panting with the ascent of Vesuvius, we subscribe heartily to the extravagant laudation of *Lachyrma-Christi*:

> 'WHAT undiscerning clown was he
>   Who first applied that doleful name,
> A bugbear to good companie,
>   To wine which warms the heart like flame?
> A smile were fitter word than tear
>   For what our generous grapes give here.'

Dining at Bordeaux, we respond to the inspiration of her vintages; gazing on the picturesque scenery of Heidelberg, we think Rhenish the best of vinous entertainment; the saccharine Malaga and Muscatel are delicious in Spain, and the strength of Sherry is a happy medium to brain and nerves at Cadiz. Tokay has its imperial sway undisputed in Hungary; and Sitka, if our explorers are to be credited, is the best of toddies at Japan. The relish of wines especially is dependent upon time and place; they seem to have a local and untranslatable virtue, except in those species which, from inherent power, improve, like great souls, by transit and range. It adds to the mellow rareness of the strong wines, as it does to the manly energy of the generous seaman, to 'double the Cape;' but the more delicate varieties, like the graces of feminine character, keep and impart their choicest zest in the atmosphere of home.

In the history of modem reforms, should such a work be ever written by a philosopher, no chapter will yield more remarkable facts than that devoted to Temperance. The reaction inevitable to all social revolutions and extremes of opinion, now throws an apathetic spell over the subject: but the simultaneous crusade against stimulating drinks undertaken in England and America; the means resorted to; the eloquence and the treasure; the banded fraternities and the single apostles; the tragic confessions and the extraordinary reformations; the intensity of the public zeal and the abnegation of private rights of judgment and action, which were dedicated to this movement, have no parallel in the social annals of modern civilization. Probably the extent and demoralization of intemperance in the use of alcohol, were not exaggerated by the most fiery advocates of this reform; probably the most ultra measures adopted were requisite to the moral exigency; and doubtless a radical and permanent good has been effected. The spectacle of domestic misery and personal degradation incident to this vice, once so common, is now comparatively rare; a better habit has been initiated, and a more healthy public sentiment established; so that, although the statistics of intemperance are and will be appalling, the evils — moral, physical, social, and individual—are as clearly defined, and as generally recognized, as those of war, pestilence, improvidence, or any other human misery. The insidious nature of this scourge has been disclosed, the warning has been proclaimed, and society awakened thoroughly to the perception and consciousness of a foe which once desolated its ranks, unchallenged and unopposed, save by isolated and ineffective protest.

The grand primary fact to be recognized by the philosopher, is that instinctive love of excitement, based on the very laws of human organization, whereby the nerves and brain are susceptible of an exhilaration that intensifies and sometimes absorbs consciousness, wraps the intellectual in exalted dreams, bathes the voluptuous in pleasurable sensations, and fills the ignorant and debased with animal complacency. And the next consideration is, the degradation and brutalization incident to the habitual indulgence of this possibility. Brain, appetite, and reason, to say nothing of conscience and religion, have a subtle battle, and one the issue of which, experience proves, cannot be foretold from the comparative intelligence or will of individuals. Perhaps no temptation has excited so little sympathy, from the fact that it is so modified, both in degree and frequency, by peculiarities of constitution and of consciousness. When such a man as Robert Hall descends from the pulpit, which his pious eloquence has made a holy throne to millions, to eagerly seek the relief which tobacco and laudanum afford to corporeal anguish; when such a vivid intelligence as kindled the brain of Heine was voluntarily clouded by narcotics, as a respite from nervous torment; and the sensibility of Charles Lamb, which trembled on the verge of sanity, made the artificial excitement of alcohol a welcome though dreaded resource, we can scarcely wonder that the unfurnished mind of a Japanese should yield to the feverish charm of his rice-distillation; the limited understanding of a Chinaman dwindle to imbecility amid the sedative vapor of opium; the American Indian forget his woes in fire-water; and the idler in the gardens of Damascus fall an unresisting victim to the enchantments of Hasheesh. Ignorant, care-worn, anxious, disappointed humanity, so often quelled by the fragile temple it inhabits, or baffled by unrecognized aspirations, corrosive want, vain sacrifice — isolated, weary, discouraged, unbelieving, hopeless — how natural, while imprisoned in blind instinct, unsustained by faith, wisdom, or love, that it should rush to the most available delusion and the nearest Lethe!

The woes of Intemperance have been said and sung; but the graces and the blessings of Temperance have yet to be appreciated in northern lands. Science gradually but surely lights up the arcanas of social economy; she vindicates the use, while reproaching the abuse of whatever created thing is obviously related to human wants and welfare.

The author of 'Margaret,' that most authentic and profound, as well as best illustrated story of New England primitive life, attributes the prevalence of intemperance among the descendants of the Puritans, to the lack of amusements, gross physical being substituted, according to the law of compensation, for harmless and intellectual or artistic recreation; and in confirmation of this theory, in the exact ratio that music, painting, the lyceum, the theatre, the dance, regatta, horsemanship, rural taste, and other enjoyments, once sternly proscribed, have been cultivated, addiction to intoxicating liquors has become less a social habit. The once universal punch bowl at noon, sitting over wine after dinner, and array of decanters at funerals, have grown obsolete; light wines have taken the place of strong potations, a delicate flavor is appreciated beyond alcoholic strength; excess is deemed not less vulgar than immoral; taste in beverage is as potent as in art and dress; and the tippler is ostracized from good society.

On the other hand, the fanaticism of temperance has chilled the glow of hospitality, and checked the frankness of intercourse; if there is less conviviality, there is more calculation, avarice holds Carnival where appetite keeps Lent; colic instead of inebriety is the penance of festivals, cynicism too often is the substitute for headache; and instead of 'sermons and soda water,' as the antidote for indulgence, there is wanted charity and fellowship to hallow the banquet.

There is no greater fallacy than the popular notion which identifies wine and animal spirits. The cordial that reinvigorates the exhausted frame and cheers the fainting heart, when neither are in need of such artificial refreshment, confirms rather than changes the existent mood; melancholy grows deeper, irritation is aggravated, and heaviness increased, by more heat in the blood, and excitement to the nerves already over-burdened by moral depression. All the praise of wine is involved in conditions: only to the temperate is it a genial stimulant. The man unfamiliar with the remedy most certainly responds to its application. They who, like the hale, faithful servitor in 'As You Like It,' have not in youth habitually known 'hot and rebellious liquors,' feel the sanative power of which they are capable, in the prostration of fever, or the loss of vital energy through exposure, fatigue, and infirmity. Ale and apoplexy, port and gout, cider and rheumatism, punch and bile, have an intimate relation. Yet we are assured, that in the cities of the Rhine, the apothecaries have a poor business, because of the wine — there a general commodity; and in point of physical development, the bravest knights and monks of old, who achieved wonders with muscle and brain, that make us their everlasting debtors; and the prosperous English of today, excel the average of the race, by virtue of alternate exercise of their vital force, and its sustainment by generous viands and draughts. The oracles of

Temperance, when they bade men swear to taste only water, and, as in the case of seventy Boston physicians, signed a declaration, that the use of stimulants *invariably* led to increase in quantity, and was *never otherwise* than an injury to health, exceeded their commission and misstated the science of life. French people, from childhood to age, are content with their *petit verre* of *eau de vie* after the *demi-tasse* of coffee which closes the dinner; and to reach intoxication, an amount of the common wine of countries where the grape is a harvest must be drunk, at which the capacity of the stomach revolts. Beer and pipes are said to have obfuscated the modern German brain; yet the parsons meet in the public gardens, and without conscious wrong, empty their frugal glasses and send abroad lusty whiffs, with a quiet zest that disarms theological strife; and the artists in Italy eke out their economical repast with *un poco de vino*, as free from any sign of unspiritual hardihood, as the peasant over his coarse bread, or the dowager at her tea. The gin-palace in London, and the drinking saloon in New York, tell quite a different story: abuse and use, motive and act, the individual and the indulgence, are only confounded by the bigot and the fanatic; and the idiosyncrasy which leads a few, through the mere taste of a drug or a drink, to rush into intoxication, is no more a precedent for mankind than the recoil from water in the victim of hydrophobia. Any natural appetite may become morbid, and the most unrecognized intemperance in America is that of eating, and unscrupulous gain and ambition.

All legitimate praise of wine, therefore, presupposes temperance. To the toper it is an impossible luxury; those refinements of palate, of nerve, of sensation and of sentiment, to which the quality, virtue, and significance of wine alone appeal, are incompatible with other than an unperverted body, and a discriminating taste: conditions impossible, not only to the intemperate, but to the hackneyed devotee of Bacchus. There is something manly and quaint, as well as eloquent, in the following defense of wine, by a late writer, classed by Emerson among the modern original minds of England:

'And if wine is good to drink, it need not be drunk on pretexts. Men have drunk it from the beginning for that which is the best and the worst of reasons — because they like it. 'Wine maketh glad the heart of man:' there lies the fortress of its usage. To the wise, it is the adjunct of society; the launch of the mind from the care and hindrance of the day; the wheel of emotion; the preparator of inventive idea; the blandness of every sense obedient to the best impulses of the hours when labor is done. Its use is to deepen ease and pleasure on high tides and at harvest homes, when endurance is not required; for delight has important functions, and originates life, as it were, afresh from a childhood of sportive feeling, which must recur at seasons for the most of men, or motive itself would stop. A second use is to enable us to surmount seasons of physical and moral depression, and to keep up the life-mark to a constant level, influenced as little as possible by the circumstances of the hour. Also, to show to age by occasions, that its youth lies still within it, and may be found like a spring in a dry land, with the thyrsus for a divining rod. A third use is, to soften us; to make us kinder than our reason, and more admissive than our candor, and to enable us to begin larger sympathies and associations from a state in which the feelings are warm and plastic. A fourth use is, to save the resources of mental excitement by a succedaneous excitement of another kind, or to balance the animation of the soul by the animation of the body, so that life may be pleasant as well as profitable, and the pleasure be reckoned among the profits. A fifth use is, to stimulate thoughts, and to reveal men's powers to themselves and their fellows, for *in vino veritas*, and intimacy is born of the blood of the grape. But is it not unworthy of us to pour joy's aid from a decanter, or to count upon 'circumstances' for a delight which the soul alone should furnish? Oh! no; for by GOD's blessing, the world is a circumstance; our friends are circumstances; our wax-lights and gayeties likewise; and all these are stimuli, and touch the being within us; and where, then, is the limit to the application of Art and Nature to the soul? At least, however, our doctrine is dangerous; but then fire is dangerous, and love is dangerous, and life with its responsibilities, is very dangerous. All strong things are perils to one whose honor's path is over hairbreadth bridges and along giddy precipices. A sixth use is, to make the body more easily industrious in work times. This is the test of temperance and the proof of the other uses. That wine is good for us which has no fumes, but which leaves us to sing over our daily labors with ruddier The seventh use is, in this highest form of assimilation, to symbolize the highest form of communion, according to the Testament which our Savior left, and to stand on the altar as the representative of spiritual truth. All foods, as we have shown before, feed the soul, and this on the principles of a universal symbolism; this, then, is the highest use of bread and wine — to be taken and assimilated in the ever-new spirit of the kingdom of heaven.' [The Human Body and its Connection with Man, Illustrated by the Principal Organs. By James John Garth Wilkinson.]

From the standpoint of political economy, grape culture is a vital interest; in France, Germany, Italy, Switzerland, Madeira, and elsewhere, the 'vine-rot' and 'grape disease' are national calamities. Not only is wine the beverage of the peasant, and often its most nutritious element, but the cultivation of the vine and the manufacture of its fruit into wine, is their most profitable labor, while the income derived from its sale is the chief resource of the landed proprietors. In seventy-seven of the eighty-six French departments, the vine is cultivated; and in whole districts it is the sole dependence. It has been estimated that it forms one-seventh part of the net product of the soil. A thousand million of francs has been computed as the result of the annual sale, in prosperous years, of the wines sold in France and abroad. During the last ten years a great diminution has occurred; the mysterious scourge, apparently unknown in ancient times, has bred a famine in many parts of Southern Europe. Every season in France and Hungary, along the Rhine; in Spain, Sicily, and Asia Minor; on the lower Moselle; in Wurtemburg, Baden, and Alsatia; throughout Italy; in Switzerland, the Canary Islands, Portugal, and on the Ohio, the prospects of the grape crop are watched, discussed, and proclaimed as the most important economical interest of prince and peasant; and this the more anxiously, since the advent of the 'vegetable cholera,' as the vine-rot has been aptly called.

'The vine occupies two belts on the earth's surface, both of which lie in the warm regions of the temperate zones, the higher the latitude the more inclined to acidity is the grape, hence the difference between Sicilian and Rhenish; its strength is manifested by proximity to the equator, hence Madeira. In the fifth year only vineyards begin to produce. The must or juice ferments at 65° Fahrenheit; spontaneously abates, when clear and exhaling a vinous odor. Analysis discovers water, sugar, mucilage, tannin, tartrate of potash and of lime, phosphate of magnesia, muriate of soda, sulphate of potash. The saccharine principle, affinity with oxygen and tartar are predominant characteristics. The grape is susceptible of modification from quality of soil, exposure, inclination of ground, seasons, etc. The color of wine is derived from the skin of the grape; this and astringency and aroma identify the species. The ancients thought the vine should grow high upon trees, and the Greeks added salt-water to their wine.

In proportion as wine became a luxury and material of commerce, the best was exported, and adulteration increased, so that it is proverbial that there is no good Sherry in Spain. Burgundy produces the Constantium of the Cape. In England an innkeeper was detected in an habitual process of manufacturing impromptu from two kinds, every variety of strong wines; and wine tasting is a profession in France. The only way to secure even an average quality at Paris is to obtain specimens from various dealers, under pretence of a large investment. One of the Düsseldorf painters made a famous picture of connoisseurs testing the contents of a wine cellar. In France, 'God's Field' is a vineyard, in Germany a graveyard. Wine, however, is of Eastern origin; its simplest form is the juice of the palm; hence the significance of the parable in the New Testament: 'I am the vine,' etc. Pliny wrote its history; Pliny describes its culture; Horace glorifies its mellowed product in his beloved Falerian; and a more recent authority says:

'ONE drop of this
'Will bathe the drooping spirit in delight
Beyond the bliss of dreams. Be wise and taste!'

It has been asserted that of the four-score most generous wines, more than two-thirds were produced on the soil of Italy. The grape grew wild in Sicily, and brought no luxury to the savage inhabitants.

The sweet and dry sherries are the product of the same grape, although so diverse in color, odor, and taste; the process of manufacture is also the same. The causes which modify what is called natural Sherry, and make Amontillado, are mysterious. The secret is hidden in the course of fermentation; sometimes but a limited portion of the juice will be thus affected. What adds to the charm of the enigma is, that it is indicated by a fine vegetable fiber germinated after the wine is placed in casks, which bears a minute white flower, that soon dies and leaves behind this peculiar flavor.

Proved methods of grape culture are now recorded in manuals; the choice of ground, pruning, manuring, staking, etc., are detailed by experienced writers; and then they declare, that 'to make good wine, you must catch Jean Raisin at the exact point of ripeness, concoct with celerity and decision, watch cask and bottle, and in short, go through a process, each step of which is clearly defined by science and custom.' Yet is there a secret in wine as in genius, 'beyond the reach of art.' Vintages, like stars, differ mysteriously from one another in glory. You may pass months at Troyes and keep vigil in the cellars where Champagne is fermented in darkness, or haunt the vineyards of Burgundy, and yet the sun and soil, the felicitous combination of agencies in nature's laboratory, which achieve a miracle of wine one year and a commonplace product the next, shall baffle your insight. The vicissitudes of the wine culture, all over the world, have indeed so multiplied, that it has been prophesied some familiar wines will become a tradition, and that new species and new latitudes must supply the demands of future generations. Dolorous for years have been the accounts of the grape disease in Madeira, Spain, and France; and although the microscope has detected an insect origin, no effectual remedy has yet been devised against the blight.

'The first symptoms of it,' remarks an intelligent writer, 'were observed in England, on the warm coast of Margate, by Mr. Tucker, a gardener, after whom the disease is called 'oïdium Tuckeri.' It is to be noted that the vine was first attacked in a country where the grape is not obtained without artificial means, by forced culture, and in warm situations where the moist and mild temperature prevails, described by Pliny. Human art is sometimes punished for having forced nature to produce what she does not give spontaneously. At first this phenomenon was only an object of curiosity. Rev. Mr. Berkeley, a learned botanist, studied this particular affection of the vine, marked its characteristics, and gave a faithful description of it.

'Soon proceeding from the coast of Margate, the evil spread into other countries. The atoms or small weeds of this parasite and destructive vegetable, borne by the winds, crossed the sea in 1847, and the oïdium was found in the neighborhood of Paris. In 1848 the disease began to extend to Versailles, to Suresnes, in Belgium, and elsewhere. But our Southern provinces were still spared. In France, as in England, the scourge first appeared in warm spots, and in greenhouses, and not where the grape ripened in the open field. Is not this a proof that the vine-rot would have been avoided, if man had not tried to force the natural products of the ground?

'In 1851 the evil increased prodigiously, and awakened proper anxiety. Many vine-growers, reduced to extremities, had to abandon their fields, which were become unproductive, and resort to other occupations for subsistence. The Bishop of Montpellier and other prelates ordered public prayers in the churches of their dioceses, to supplicate the LORD to stay the calamity. Agricultural societies, seconded by the French, German, and Italian governments, appointed committees to inquire into the state of the vines, the cause of the disease, and the measures proper to stop it. But human knowledge, alas! was found here, as elsewhere, to be limited.

'The marks of the disease are everywhere the same. The leaves and grapes are suddenly covered with small fibers, of a pale white color; a sort of vegetable or mushroom which creeps to the surface, attacks and surrounds the skin of the fruit. Soon the grape becomes black, wilts, dies, and drops off. The same with the leaves, which become yellow or brown, and fall off. The twig even is attacked, and becomes dry.

'Different causes are assigned for this evil. The peasants, ever inclined to superstition, attribute it to the progress of science, and fancy that the air has been corrupted by the steam engine in railroad cars and manufactories! For the vine is not affected in countries where there are no railroads. Others pretend that the disease is an *organic* weakness, a *degeneracy*, as if the plants which are constantly renewed, partook of the fate of human beings, who decline, grow old, and die! The only thing certain is, I repeat it, that the evil begins in warm localities, or under artificial culture.

'As to the means of cure, various processes have been tried, without satisfactory success. It is said, however, that sulphur, applied at the right time, stops the progress of the oïdium, and enables the grape to ripen. Some planters sprinkle sulphur powder early in the spring, others mix sulphur and water, and water their whole vineyards. After some days the leaves resume their green color, and the grapes look better.

'But this remedy is inconvenient. First, it does not always succeed, and many vine-growers, either not applying the means rightly, or from some other cause, have lost their time and money. Next, the use of sulphur is very expensive, and requires great care: it is good for tender plants, but for large vines, is impracticable. Lastly, the sulphur communicates to the wine a disagreeable odor, at least when drank immediately after the vintage. Hence sulphur is not generally used. The true remedy, if there is one, is not yet found. Some regard drainage as a good preservative.'

XV

Something About Wine

BY HENRY T. TUCKERMAN

AUGUST 1858

PART TWO

WITHOUT BEING a *bon vivant*, and simply by virtue of the association of ideas in which sensation and sentiment bear an equal part, the places of a traveler's sojourn are identified with certain wines, so that a special vinous flavor in after-days, conjures up the image of a favorite companion and the scenery of a picturesque locality. The very name of Orvieto revives the artistic companionship of the *trattoria* Lepri at Rome, or the picnic at Albano or Tivoli; *Vino d'Asti*, in its golden effervescence, whispers of the enchantments of Lake Como and the battlefield of Marengo; the glow of old Marsala is warm with memories of Ætna, or breezy evenings on the Marina at Palermo, whence we retired to a hospitable palazzo where, on a marble table, stood the decanters immersed in the old volcano's snow;

> 'Son le nevi il quinto elemento
> Che compargono il verro bevere.'

Whoso has studied in Germany, will greet the sight of an old emerald glass sacred to Johannisberg, and hear in fancy the Rhine song; the twang of choice Claret transports another to the *Trois Frères* or *Café de Paris*, or makes him respond to the poet's benediction:

'Benedetto
Quel Claretto
Che si spilla in Avignone.'

Old Port beams with the reflected tints of London mahogany and coal fires; Metternich and old castles reappear in the mirror of a dusty bottle of Hock; Burgundy inspires dreams of Southern France, the day at Nismes, or the quays at Bordeaux; Malaga is sweet with Spanish memories, and the nabob at home regrets the zest of his Sherry at Calcutta. A vinous amateur could indeed designate eras by vintages, make landmarks of vineyards, and most vividly keep alive local memories by the diversified flavor of the grape. Lebanon wine would hallow Bethlehem to his imagination more than monastic relics; his London banker's Port, the Duke of Nassau's Steinberg, the bottle of St. Peray hastily purchased while the steamboat tarries on the Rhone, the Brousa of Stamboul grown under the snows of Olympus, blend with and identify these scenes forever to his epicurean reminiscence; and Beaume and Chambertin are names as classic in his estimation as Racine and La Fontaine; he knows the Dukes of Burgundy only as the Princes des bons Vins; and honors Madam Cliquot more than the Maid of Orleans, because she is the largest Champagne grower of Rheims; the amber of Muscat is more precious in his eyes than that found in the torrent's bed; and he descends into a crypt of Nazareth to choose a jar, escorted by some modern Miriam or Ruth, with more zestful expectancy than Belzoni an unexplored catacomb.

The French speak of a Bordeaux which talks; the ruins of the Rhine are, as it were, set in an ever-renewed garland of vineyards and mellowed, in the retrospect, by the song, the flavor and cheer of the wine. Burns' John Barleycorn; Faust in the cave; the Dutchman's Schnapps; the Englishman's 'Old Particular;' the Jerseyman's Cider; the Buckeye's Catawba, and the Bavarian's Beer; all places and poets, all nationalities and literature exhale this convivial element, more or less refined and characteristic. From the wine stain yet visible on a Pompeii slab to the silver punch bowl which in some of our few remaining country mansions is the heir-loom of families; from Cleopatra's pearl dissolved, to Clarence drowned in wine; from Horace to Tennyson; from Noah to Metternich — history and humanity are reflected in wine. How *apropos* to these two last *convives* are Müller's quaint verses: [Translated by C.T. Brooks.]

'We forfeited by eating —
    Not drinking — Paradise:
What once we lost through Adam,
    And his confounded vice,
Good wine and jovial chorus
Abundantly restore us.

'And when again, in vileness,
    The world corrupted sank,
And every earthly creature
    Death in the deluge drank,
To Noah life was granted,
'Cause he the grape had planted.

'Within his biggest cask he
    With wife and children did get:
It floated on the waters,
    And not a soul was wet;
All saved by wine so oddly
From watery graves, the godly.

'And when the flood abated,
    There stood the round house then,
High and dry on the top of a mountain,
    And all came out again,

Thanks for deliverance chanted
And straight new grapevines planted.

'The cask for a memento,
    Stood on the mountain's brow;
At Heidelberg on the Neckar,
    You all can see it now;
It needs no further guessing
Who gave us the Rhine-wine's blessing.

149

'And whoso dares disparage
   The sacred wine we drink,
He in a watery deluge
   Shall miserably sink!
Sing, brothers, 'tis before us,
Brave wine and jovial chorus.'

Noah planted a vineyard; Solomon and David praise wine; and in Job it is prescribed for the weary. The grape is the most ancient of Egyptian symbols; Montaigne calls its juice the 'last pleasure of life,' and says 'it takes the place of natural heat;' while Liebig declares it the 'milk of the aged.' Heard Redi:

'Se dell 'uve il sangue amabile
Non rinfranca ognor le vene,
Questa vita é troppe rabile
Troppo breve é sempre in pene.'

The Tuscan proverb says:

'Il vino é la poppa de vecchi.'

There is a curious analogy between the process whereby wine reaches its perfection, the vicissitudes to which it is liable therein, and human life; a mysterious blending of original elements, the pure but crude juice, when new, like childhood's unadulterated aspect; then the hazardous fermentation, parallel with the impassioned development of youth; the product, if weak, liable to become sour and vapid, and if strong, reaching through time and change, a mellow richness, like the genial force of a noble character, or the mature grace of a vigorous mind.

Within a few years those indigestible mixtures which, under the name of punch, made our ancestors dyspeptic and bilious, and the strong wines that detained gentlemen so long from the drawing room after dinner, have given place to the more salutary hygiene, long prevalent in Europe, that makes the light and pure wines of France and Germany the accompaniment instead of the *finale* of the chief diurnal banquet. As nervous stimulants, tonics, and aids to digestion, the milder and least adulterated juices of the grape are sanctioned by adaptation to climate, individual constitution and states of health, under the best medical counsel. In France especially, the science of nutrition in this regard has reached a bright point of discrimination; the best quality of cheap red wine, blended with mineral waters, has been prescribed with excellent effect. Alsatico and biscuits prove a salubrious regimen for invalids in Tuscany; and a popular writer of Paris remarks that 'Le vin Champagne frappe, non point aprés, mais pendant le repos, serait, pour la plupart des estomacs un precieux auxiliare de digestion.' The arbitrary succession of wines ordained by custom at American dinners, is a serious interference with the personal hygiene so desirable in a luxury which should be used according to the taste and requirements of each guest; limited quantities of various species is the rule; whereas those who consult health and inclination prefer adequate supplies of one kind, a privilege which is often unattainable under the present code of prandial entertainments. An American traveler entertained at the grand ducal table of Weimar, records the custom dictated by enlightened hospitality in this regard: 'No sooner was a glass emptied than it was replenished by the watchful attendant. Through this silent savory sign your preference, if you had one, was learned and hospitably indulged. You had, for instance, but to leave your Claret and Rhenish and Champagne unfinished, and to drain your Burgundy glass; so often as it was found empty it was re-filled with Chambertin or Clos Vougot, to the number of a dozen or more fillings, should any guest be rash enough to trust his head with so many.'

It is with wine as with other luxuries of life, association has more to do with relish than either quality or quantity. The poor artist with whom I used to clink glasses of vino nostrale at Florence, which cost five-pence a pint, when he had risen to fame and married a fortune, slyly indicated to me across the table at his first banquet, his little flask of our frugal beverage, concealed behind a splendid array of aristocratic wines. The taste acquired in those days of self-denial survived the advent of prosperity. Few casual visitors at the Tuscan capital, however, understand how to procure even the cheap common wine in perfection; the wine shop and the restaurant are not to be trusted; but the good graces of some Principe's steward must be won, and he will furnish from his perquisite of the family vintage cobwebbed flasks, parsed mysteriously through the stone loophole of the cellar; and when you have pulled out of its slender neck the wisp of tow, and dashed away the thimble-full of oil that has kept it from the air, you taste that pure juice of the purple grape of whose virtues Redi has sung with a melodious eloquence, that links its remembrance with the hills around Florence, the winding Arno, and the handsome peasants, in one harmonious picture of rustic plenty, grace, and cheer.

> 'IL Dio del vino
> Fermato avea l'allegro suo soggiorrno
> A í calli Etruschi intorno.'

Gensano gives a 'local habitation and a name' to a wine that your Roman padrone believes, when taken warm with roast apple, is an infallible remedy for the *forestiere's* catarrh. The bard of Italian wines calls Montepulciano *manna*, and of Chianti sings:

> 'MUESTOSO
> Imperioso,
> Mi passeggia denteo il cuore,
> E ne scaccia senza strepito
> Ogni affano e ogni dolore.'

One of our countrymen has sung the praises of a wine encountered at a little town in Provence, and a sagacious wine merchant of Gotham has made the cordial stanzas a matter for the arabesque label of his favorite brand:

> 'WHEN to any saint I pray,
> It shall be to Saint PERAY;
> He alone of all the brood
> Ever did me any good.' [T.W. PARSONS.]

The social relations of wine have an interest for the conservative as well as the jovial. The cobwebbed bottle produced on rare occasions and in honor of a favored guest, or household festival; the 'dozen' preserved as a birthday deposit against the bridal feast; the ancestral relic of mellow wine with the memories of the loved and noble who quaffed its virgin juice, appeal to something beyond the mere gusto of the palate. I once heard an honest and benevolent veteran declare that, could he dictate a tribute to his memory, his friends, instead of useless tears and idle regrets, should talk cheerfully of him over a bottle of his choice old wine, and thus consecrate a genial and hospitable hour to pleasant recollections. The peculiar intellectual flavor of those admirable criticisms which insured its dawning fame to 'Old Ebony,' sprang from the *abandon*, freedom, and conviviality of the intercourse over which Kit North and the Ettrick Shepherd so memorably presided. As we read them, despite of modern temperance fanaticism, we recall with zest Plato's extravagant declaration, that a sober man to no purpose knocks at the door of the Muses; and, with another philosopher of antiquity, recognize Bacchus as the good deity who mollifies the passions of the soul, restores to young men their good humor, and to old men their youth.

Therefore has art and literature celebrated the vine. From Anacreon and Virgil to Tom Moore and Béranger, its praises have been memorably sung; Bacchus, when he ceased to be a recognized divinity, became the myth which statuaries loved to embody and poets to revive. The convivial is an essential element of modern romance and old English dramas, as exhibiting the convivial side of genius, the freaks of imagination and outbreaks of heart otherwise inconceivable to our restrained civilization. What were Horace uncheered by Falernian; Falstaff's wit bereft of his sack; Don Quixote without the adventure of the wineskins; the Vicar of Wakefield's hospitality devoid of Mr. Primrose's gooseberry wine; Ivanhoe without Friar Tuck's flagon? *'La vigne,'* says a French writer, *'a surtout, depuis bien des siecks, fait fleurir en France, la chanson. Le vin et la chanson sont conime frére et soeur.'* Among the acknowledged hygienic properties of ripe grapes are, to cool the blood, facilitate its circulation, remove obstructions from the liver and kidneys, and impart vigor, tone, purity, and freshness to the vital principle.

The act of taking wine together, like the Eastern superstitions regarding salt, hath in it a domestic significance, and, as it were, a challenge of love and loyalty. 'If Bacchus often leads men into quagmires deep as his vats,' says Douglas Jerrold, 'let us yet do him this justice — he sometimes leads them out. Ask your opponent to take another glass of wine.' 'Un poco de vino?' mellifluously asks your Italian neighbor, and then he wishes you a life of a thousand years and figli maschi — a sentiment born of the old feudal primogeniture; the viva which precedes the draught is responded to by its own vital glow: how perfectly has Donizetti embodied in music the festive idea of abrindisi, in the famous song of 'Lucrezia Borgia!' Ben Jonson's yet current ditty, 'To Ladies' eyes around, boys,' is instinct with sentimental joviality; and of American lyrics, few have been greater favorites than the 'Health of Pinkney.' 'Port, if you please,' says the English girl, when you ask her to join in a glass of wine; how long the draught of the Catalonian peasant, as he keeps poised, in silent content, the collapsing wineskin! and what a picture of animal epicurism is a venerable English squire, seated in his comfortable parlor, with a boon companion, holding up to the light, and then to his lingering lips, the glass of Madeira, whereof, between the sips, he tells the 'adventurous tale.' Not less enjoyable, and far more generous, is the sight of a group of Tuscan peasants at their noon repast beneath a tree, passing round the red vino, with ready carol and greeting.

It is with wine as with scenery, pictures, and love, as with all the rare elements of human pleasure — the best, or at least the most enjoyed, is often encountered unawares, and, as it were, by some happy accident. At a pension initiated by the first Italian opera company that visited New York, for years could be found the most pure and cheapest claret, annually exported in the wood, by an old friend of the house. Who does not remember the agreeable surprise given him in his travels, by some complacent native, who, in out-of-the-way nooks, has caused to appear the choicest vintage? Almost all statesmen have been connoisseurs of wine: Fox and Webster, Sheridan and Talleyrand knew the twang or recognized the age at a sip. 'The wretchedness of human life,' said Sydney Smith, 'is only to be encountered on a basis of beef and wine' — an unspiritual precept, born of a national instinct. Addison's constitutional reserve, we are told, could only be thawed by wine. One of the relics of Washington's campaigns, presented by a member of the family to Leutze, in honor of his noble painting of the 'Passage of the Delaware,' is a silver can, bound with leather — the drinking cup of the rare and moderate official entertainment; the bottom is scratched with the sword-points used to mash the sugar: it is probably the only trophy of those men and times unassociated with privation. There is an effervescent Hock identified with the banks of the 'Blue Moselle,' as much as the pensive-eyed and gray oxen are with the Tuscan vintage, St. Julien with Paris suburban cabarets, or Steinburg with a Rhine estate. The favorite lunch of one of our most gifted and genial artists, was Chablis and oysters; no one who ever shared it with him failed thenceforth to associate the wine with intellectual fellowship. Dr. Franklin philosophized over a fly found in a bottle of old wine; and that kindly bard, John Kenyon, says:

> 'Lily on liquid roses floating,
>   So floats yon foam o'er pink Champagne:
> Fain would I join such pleasant boating
>   And prove that ruby main,
>   and float away on wine!'

Of native Anacreontics, none is comparable with 'Sparkling and Bright' — a song, which to hear from the author's lips on a moonlight night by the Hudson, with a chorus of good fellows, is memorable, and is now endeared as the eclipsed hilarity of a shattered harp. Tennyson indicates with a line the hour of thorough English self-content and 'breathing-time of day,' of retrospect and ideal comfort, as 'over the walnuts and the wine.' Modern science has detected, and popular journalism exposed, the adulteration of wine: the Greeks mixed with it resin, tar, cypress, and almonds; chalk, alcohol, sugar, and sulphur are modern expedients, and to destroy the taste of the latter; cloves, thyme, cinnamon, and other spices are added; putrescence and acidity are the conditions it is thus attempted to neutralize or avert. Chemistry has analyzed the normal qualities of wine, only to demonstrate that there is scarcely such a thing in commerce as pure grape juice.

From the calcined leaves of the vine is made the ink wherewith bank notes are printed. Franklin was assiduous in his endeavors to introduce the Rhenish grape into our nascent horticulture, doubtless anticipating, from his experience in France, the temperance and invaluable economy involved in successful vine-culture. The accounts of the early colonists agree in representing the wild grape as abounding in our forests; Bishop Berkeley, in his letters from Rhode Island, alludes to its luxuriant growth in that region; the French colonists cultivated the vine in Carolina before the Puritans came to New England; there were flourishing Jesuit vineyards among the first settlers, and vignerons were imported into Virginia as early as 1630; Penn attempted wine manufacture in his province fifty years after; and about a century ago, it is recorded that a band of *émigrés* made a hundred hogsheads of wine in Illinois. Numerous experiments, in widely distant localities throughout the country, have resulted in producing it on a small scale, and as a matter of curiosity rather than luxury and profit. The great desideratum was to fix upon the best quality of grape which could attain perfection in the open air, and then to invest enough in land and labor to warrant liberal and successive vintages. Thus far the enterprise has been adequately realized only on the banks of the Ohio; statistics there indicate a regular staple, and profitable as well as very extensive interest in the wine manufacture of Cincinnati. 'At last,' says a genial authority, [Cozzens' *'Wine-Press.'*] 'our national vines have become so far popularized, that the value of the home production exceeds that of the consumption of foreign wines in the proportion of nearly two to one, and that with a constant increase in the home market:'

'For the richest and best
Is the wine of the West,
That grows by the Beautiful River.'

Crabbe eulogizes Port, Prior Claret, Moore Champagne, Boileau Burgundy, and Redi Multepulciano: how analogous these preferences with their respective genius! The comic writers of Charles the Second's time, we are told, 'worked on Claret;' and a cask of this wine always stood in the hospitable halls of old Scotland. Sack, Canary, Sherris, Malmsey, are the familiar drinks in the old English plays: 'Set a deep glass of Rhenish wine' is a phrase in Shakespeare; and coffee has been lately called 'the *coup d'état* to drinking after dinner;' Sherry, ginger and biscuit is a favorite lunch in British India, and Chablis and oysters in France; thus universally is wine identified with places and periods. Byron, although he sang of the Samian wine, and spurred his flagging muse with gin, declared that the most exhilarating of draughts to him was a dose of salts; Dr. Johnson's favorite stimulus was tea, and so was Cowper's; De Quincey has made opium and its effects the subject of memorable psychological revelations; Schiller wrote under the inspiration of Champagne; and Malibran gained spasmodic voice and heart by means of porter and Cologne-water; while the most affecting of homilies is Lamb's 'Confessions of a Drunkard.' These and countless other 'infirmities of genius' indicate, on the one hand, the exhaustive conditions of intense mental life, and on the other, point a moral in regard to the weakness inherent and inalienable, of the most nobly endowed human beings, appealing both to sympathy and to science; for the latter has interpreted the physiology of man in its relation to that craving for and addiction to these means of renovation and excitement, common alike to the savage and the most highly endowed of the species. Perhaps no writer has more fully brought out the philosophy of the subject than Shakespeare: Rodrigo's self-reproach and reprobation of that invisible spirit of wine; the effects of that cask that came unbroken to shore in the 'Tempest;' Falstaff's excess; Bardolph's nose; and especially the incidental allusions of the great poet, as when he speaks of treachery 'false as vows made in wine,' and while he calls wine 'a good familiar creature, if it be used well,' explains a quarrel by, 'it was excess of wine that set him on,' and makes disenchanted and forlorn Macbeth exclaim: 'The wine of life is drawn.'

It is owing to these charming though, often vague associations, that the vine is so pleasing an object in rural scenery, whether it covers rude angles on the stone cottage, twines as the emblem of conjugal devotion around the stately elm, spreads its leaves of lucent emerald between the sunshine and the lattice, wreathes the hospitable porch with graceful ornaments, whence the finest of architectural devices is borrowed, rears itself on stakes, as in France, as if to assert its capacity for homely productiveness, festoons 'from tree to tree' in scenic beauty amid the mulberry orchards of Italy, or twines in gigantic convolutions around the prone and massive temples of Central America, it is always in the exuberant flexibility of its growth, in the exquisite contour of its leaf, as well as in the poetic and recreative ideas it suggests, one of the loveliest and most endeared phases of vegetable life. What ornament for the brow of the fair, or the arabesque of an urn, or the crowning of a column — for wreaths, sculpture, robe-pattern or dish excels the vine leaf? With what more beautiful emblematic token do the *pietra-dura* artists of Tuscany inlay their marble than amethystine grapes? The very dying foliage of the vine detached by autumn's breath is golden; and the shadow of a fluttering vine, its picturesque stalk, finely outlined leaf, and curling tendril is the perfection of evanescent phot

XV

General Washington's Wine-Glass

ADDRESSED TO MRS. B.G.W. BUTLER,
OF DUNBOTHE, LA., ON RECEIVING FROM HER
A CHAMPAGNE-GLASS FORMERLY BELONGING
TO GENERAL WASHINGTON.

SEPTEMBER 1845

AMID my choicest treasures why retain
This simple glass of fragile antique ware?
Why guard it with a fond and reverent care,
Which goblets costlier far may crave in vain?
Why is it that in it the bright champagne
With fresher brilliance sparkles, than rich cups
With wreathen silver sides and burnished tops,
Or bowls of gem-bestudded gold, can gain?
The hand of WASHINGTON, in times of yore,
Hath touched, and given it immorality!
Age after age the relique dear shall see:
While, with the name of thy great ancestor,
Thine, too, shall be remembered, lady fair,
With warmest gratitude for gift so rich, so rare.

J.H.H.
Bayou Goula, La.

Part Two

Part Two

I

Impromptu Invitations To Dinner

BY JOHN WATERS

JANUARY 1846

It storms overhead—
It storms underfoot—
Gutters to Rivers spread—
Nowhere stands a dry boot.
Yet cheerful is my fireside
As youthful groom, or laughing bride.
Thus welcome were the sight
Of friend, with visage bright,
Who on a single crambo line
Like this, will come, at *five*, to dine.
My punch is mix'd and brew'd with care,
My soup and fish in order are,
And every word of praise is tame
To this, that CYNTHIA cooks the game.

Come then, my friend, and let the storm
That reigns without, make doubly warm
The heart within. Life's purest tide
Is spent along the fireside.

JOHN WATERS.

II

A Dish of Tea

FEBRUARY 1839

PART ONE

'DIABOLICAL Envy, and its brother Malice, with all their accursed company, sly whispering, cruel backbiting, spiteful detraction, and the rest of that hideous crew, which I hope are very falsely said to attend the tea-table, being more apt to think they frequent those public palces where virtuous women never come.'

THIS VINDICATION, from the very clever preface to the letters of LADY MARY WORTLEY MONTAGU, will be confirmed by the 'wisdom of ages.' The dignity of the tea table will be maintained, in spite of the insane ravings of 'the Graham.' Let the reader call to mind the circles of his own tea-drinking acquaintance, who are confirmed in that practice, and seriously answer to his own heart, whether 'diabolical envy and its *brother* malice, with all their accursed company, sly whispering, cruel backbiting, spiteful detraction, and the rest of that hideous crew,' are not *very falsely* said to attend the tea-table.

I recollect a knot of antique sociables, of whom Miss Patty was the presiding deity, who held their assemblies all the year round at the Honeysuckle Cottage. Not that any formal invitation was given out, but there seemed to be a tacit understanding betwixt them that they should come together weekly, to enjoy each other's society, and to drink tea, 'sociably.' Nor was there any grudging of hospitality on the part of my aunt, who was knit to these 'good souls' by bonds of the tenderest affection. And it can be with truth averred, that these pious women indulged only in virtuous discourses; and the only inroads which they made upon anything, were upon my Aunt Patty's best souchong tea. Oh, they loved their tea! It was their nectar, their 'chief good,' their ambrosial food. To this delicious beverage, all other viands yielded up the palm.

How well do I remember them, grouped about the tea table, on a winter's evening, starched and prim, waiting for the 'moving of the waters.' A genial fire burnt brightly on the hearth; the tidy bricks were painted of a flaming redness; the brazen andirons were like refined gold. In those days, grates, Franklins, and other paraphernalia, had not possessed the ample jambs, nor dissipated those feelings of greater sociability, which rallied around the ancient hearth, like an altar. There was no intense and sulphur-breathing coal, to clog the free atmosphere of the apartment; but gay and brilliant flames shot upward, with an agreeable crackling, diffusing the double luxury of light and heat. A tabby-cat, that requisite appendage to a picture of domestic comfort, lay wrapped up in perfect quiescence on the rug. She was a beautifully tortoised creature, and would have graced a painter's canvas. The mantel was not crowded with shell temples, and other gimcrackry of a vulgar school, but with four substantial brazen candlesticks, with china vases between, and at the ends two polished conch-shells, which made a dreary sound when applied to the ear, like the distant roaring of the surge. The family Bible occupied a conspicuous place in the apartment, and was reverentially supported by a polished walnut stand. The walls were adorned with needlework, in excellent preservation, enclosed in narrow gilded frames, and protected from dust, dirt, and close inspection; the enduring monuments of Miss Patty's early taste and ingenuity. In order to save the trouble of answering questions, they were severally inscribed, 'basket of flowers,' 'fruit,' 'robin red breast,' etc., etc., and underneath, in legible characters, 'PATTY JONES.'

In fact, everything about the apartment looked 'so nice.' The carpet was most cleanly swept; the sideboard was polished to the last degree; the mahogany table in the center reflected a plate of very desirable toast. The tea-urn, that honored receptacle, was worthy of its pure ambrosia. '*Non cedebat honori.*' It raised itself in silvery whiteness, above all the minor utensils of the table, while the steam ascending from it, like rich incense, made a shadowy undulation on the wall. Around its circumference was an embossed representation of a fox chase. Reynard was flying for his life; the huntsmen were winding their horns; the horses were dashing over the hedge; the hounds were in full cry, over 'bush, brake, and scaur,' and pursuing the game unto the death. The milk-pot was a little model of classic elegance. The cream reposed in it like double refined snow of the Appenines. It seemed as pure as purity itself. It looked a cordial, as if it might be 'parmaceti for an inward bruise,' a balsam for the most deadly wound. And then the sugar! — rivaling the milk in whiteness! — glistening in the bright light; cracked into the most convenient lumps, and ready to be conveyed with tongs of silver for the grand amalgamation!

Is not your mouth moistened, my reader? Does not a tear-like drop struggle and gush from its corners, and your inmost stomach yearn? The lip has its tears of sympathy from a yearning stomach, as well as the eye from the 'burning crucible of the brain.' Oh, delightful banquets, '*noctes cenoeque Deûm!*' — superior to all other banquets, and worthy the sweetest inspiration of the muse. Dinner, with its viands, is a gross, brutish, animal enjoyment. Teeth, muscles, eyes, heart, soul, must be engrossed in despatching its solid masses. But tea is a divine, ethereal, subtle symposium. It distills into the brain, it enliveneth the soul, it sharpeneth the tongue, it brighteneth the eyes, it smoothes down wrinkles and cares; it is worthy of a god above the purple god Bacchus; worthier far of chased goblets, and to be crowned with flowers. Tea bringeth no redness of eyes, no defection of the wits, no groveling obeisance to the earth, no mockery of the world, no melancholy abstractions. Tea clothes none with raggedness, shakes no man's credit, forfeits no friends, brings no 'gray hairs in sorrow to the grave,' makes no wives broken-hearted, no children beggars, no houses desolate. And can the bacchanal say as much, who steeps his soul in forgetfulness, and riots on the juice of the grape? Come with me to the garden of Rollo. He is a raving votary of the god. He revels in nocturnal orgies. Look around you, and behold the garden of the sluggard. How are these walks clogged with rubbish. These beds, once so redolent of fragrance, how vainly do they struggle against the dominion of weeds. How doth this tender plant droop for shelter. How doth that sweet flower struggle to bloom. How doth the bruised and trampled vine beg for thy training hand, heart-broken wife of his bosom! How even the birds do not pause upon the wing which once descended, and made these alleys vocal. Behold here a ruined arbor, a neglected grotto; there a fallen statue, and a fountain choked with leaves. The train of the serpent is over the 'flowers of loveliness;' the wild grass grows long and unheeded, and I gaze upon a waste and desert spot, which might have been a garden of paradise.

Direct your eyes to the old mansion, at the end of the avenue. The moss grows on the roof, the bricks drop from the chimney, the windows hang by a hinge, and the lintels are decayed. Does it bear about it any appearance of a HOME? Are there any altars around which the affections may gather in holy sacrifice? Alas, the golden censers have been broken, the sweet incense goeth up no more. And are these thy fruits, oh Bacchus, giver of joy? And is the danger sweet to follow the god whose temples are encircled with verdant leaves? Away with thee! I contemn thee, thou crowned god! We will tear down thy altars, and build others, even to new divinities. Behold a contrast. Come to the cheerful mansion of Miss Patty, and to her 'small domains.' Nightly she sips of her nectarean TEA. Do you see there aught of the elements of disorder? Is anything apart from its own peculiar place? Are the walls unbrushed of cobwebs? Does the mantle harbor dust? The gauzy robe of Queen Mab might be trailed over those floors, and yet contract no soil. The spirit of comfort reigns within and without. The courtyard is blooming with *prim* roses, the weeded garden is sweet with herbs. This then is the spirit of tea!

Yet are there cavilers without number, despisers of God's blessings, setters forth of strange doctrines, who declare that

even this harmless beverage is a poison. I abhor them — I detest
them! Keep your 'Journals of Health,' gentlemen, your inane
scribblings. More life has been sipped from a teaspoon, than
will ever be sucked through your quill. I wonder what next will
be asserted; what new device to torture patience, or what new
pledges will be required. Is tea a poison? Then is there ratsbane
in a peach. Then call all things poison. Write poison on the flood
of the rock, destruction in the air we breathe, or death upon the
heavenly manna. Point me to the wretch who, being weary of life,
seeks not the ordinary method of departure, and neither blows
his brains out, nor leaps from the fourth story, and gasps out his
life on an iron pale, nor tosses himself from some Milvian bridge
into the sea, nor hangs like a dog in his own garret, nor draws
his razor at right angles with his throat, and severs the vein
jugular, but resorts to a more simple operation, and with all the
coolness imaginable, tells cook to put the tea-kettle on a simmer,
and mixing cream and sugar, drinks down the deadly hemlock,
and departs to his fathers. Or have you ever known a coroner or
a jury render a verdict in the words following, to wit: '*Poisoned
by a cup of tea?*'

'Ay, Sir, we grant you; but cause and effect are not always
simultaneous. There be some things which loiter and lurk in the
system, and the end of them is death. 'It is a slow poison.' Slow
as a snail's pace, doubtless. It is a potion to be taken every day,
and 'warranted to take effect' at the end of three-score years and
ten. Then, when the aged gentleman, with head like an almond
tree, and well contented, goes to his long home, ye say, 'Behold
the victim!'

It were a mockery to measure the depths of such shallow
reasonings. Give me none of your 'TEA-total pledges.' I shall stand
up for this 'ardent liquor,' be it green or be it black, 'without
distinction of color.'

Is it not enough to cast away so many of God's 'good creatures,'
and would you dry up this last drop of comfort also? Shall every
upstart reformer be thrusting his pledge and statistics in the
face of my conviction, and attenuate my already slender 'bill

of fare,' dictating to me what I shall eat, and what I shall drink, and wherewithal I shall be clothed? Reining me within bounds, and saying 'hitherto shalt thou come, and no farther?' Shall my stomach never 'vaunt itself?' Shall it never be 'puffed up?' Truly, my poor judgment will have little to exercise itself upon, if it thus yields up its prerogative, but will be warped and twisted to suit the will of these moral charlatans. There is 'the Graham,' on the one hand, would starve me into a 'walking shadow,' and deprive me of those nutritious solids which make the man, substituting his own bran, worse than the broth of the Spartans. There is a host of zealots on the other, of whom we would not grumble a monosyllable, so long as they kept within modest bounds, and did not wax insolent in their might, but who, not contented with their 'inch,' but they must take an 'ell,' would banish from high days, and holidays 'all that can intoxicate,' pledging insipid healths in brimmers of water—*risum teneatis amid!* Ye vaunting philanthropists! Have ye yet to learn that it is not wine alone which can intoxicate? That there are other draughts, more delicious in the quaffing, and which make the brain reel and madden; love, beauty, flattery?

But your senseless code would banish all that comes in 'questionable shape.' It would ostracize the most precious gifts of our good God, and forbid their use, because he trusted that his creatures would not abuse them. The bright scenes of pleasure should never expand, because they may be too much indulged in; and the breath of music should never be heard, for its tones are too seductive; and the rose should be banished forever from the garden, because it has a thorn.

But worse than all, the ghost of the Boston conspiracy is stalking. At midnight it again moves, which is best suited for unhallowed deeds. In the guise of savages, a tumultuous crowd rushes whither the sea-crossing ships are riding at anchor. Listen to their infernal yells! Chest by chest they throw over the precious weed into the waves. Did ever the greedy sea receive such a treasure?

We are then to be reduced to the original element of water,

as our father Adam drank it, sparkling. Is not this retrograding with a vengeance? Is not this 'rolling back the tide of time,' and throwing the world into infancy? What advantage then hath it of all its discoveries, at which it has arrived by no sudden flash of intelligence, but slowly and painfully? But, no, no; we will oppose this deep-rooted conspiracy; by the powers of Souchong! We will oppose it. We will not be reduced to the extremity of water. Flow on then, thou generous liquor! — flow on like a river:

'Mingle, mingle, mingle.
Ye that mingle may.

Water is decidedly good 'in its own place;' and a manly tar once stutteringly declared, that 'no one thing has done so much for navigation.' But to return to that alone, is too much like returning to the dead weight of metallic currency; like discarding the superior light and discoveries of the age, and going back to the land of Egypt. I say again, I love water. It is delicious; and when the tongue is parched, and fever rages, would willingly plunge into its refreshing depths. But it is too cold, and not pungent enough for the social board, or for occasions of extraordinary rejoicing. Water is tasteless, as air is colorless, and as everything that is good, is unmixed and pure. I look upon other liquors, when compared with tea, with the respect of a Virginia host, who advertised his whole stock to be sold. His cider was excellent, his champagne wines were worthy of the highest consideration, but his Madeira was 'so old, as only to be mentioned very reverentially!'

Let these new-fangled pledges, the cunning inventions of a generation spiritually proud, who are perpetually discovering some new land in morals, (and who then kneel down in thanksgiving, as did Columbus, and erect their standard to the breeze, and claim it in the name of God, by right of the first discovery,) let these pledges be applied to *tobacco-chewers,* if you please. They may be driven out, we maintain, by all means, by fair or by foul, as we would bid a guilty, outlawed, garlicky wretch begone. If he departs precipitately, it is well; 'if not, we turn him out, without compunction. Oh! the filthy, nauseous weed! — and oh, ye snuffing, sniveling, sneezing, chewing, spitting, squirting votaries, who make your mouths reservoirs, and your lip corners aqueducts for foul waters to gush through; ye are the depraved subjects for the violent benevolence of this age! Let the BACCHO ABSTINERE of the present wine-pledge be modified or altered thus: ABSTINERE TO-BACCO. To expel this noxious weed, 'pledges' may be employed, or any other means, lawful or unlawful, Jesuistical or Christian; as no argument can be trumped up, which is not ingeniously absurd, to prove that it was ever intended for the human mouth. In other respects, we are opposed to the unnecessary increase of pledges; and surely it is imagining 'a vain thing,' to expect us to abstain from delicious, purifying, enlivening TEA. Are any so depraved, that they cannot use a good thing moderately, but must pledge themselves to abstain from it altogether? The more shame for them! And the command of their appetites, and the knowing where to stop, are habits which ought to be acquired. He who never faces danger or temptation, deserves little credit for his virtue; but whoso can sit down at a luxurious banquet, and, like a skillful charioteer, command the reins of his appetite, is entitled to more regard, and acquires a more important lesson in the science of self-government. It is true that most men find it *more easy* to abstain entirely — as thou, Boswell, canst adduce an illustrious example — but that will not alter, but rather strengthen, the principle which is here laid down, that temperance is better, more honorable, more praiseworthy, than abstinence.

When 1 behold a person at the cheerful board abstaining from the proffered cup of green or black, and all through fear of being carried away by an excess of love, I cannot help lamenting that he is so little able to trust himself, and that appetite must be cruelly imprisoned and confined, for fear of hurling coward reason from the throne. Instead of awarding the palm to such a one for superior self-denial, I cannot, except for his pusillanimity, give him any credit at all. When, on the other hand, I behold a person, after thankfully indulging in his 'two cups,' that Rubicon of prudence, beyond which it is unlawful to pass, yearning for a third, and yet with an easy sway, lording it over his appetite, curbing it, as it were, with a well regulated police, and coming off with a renowned victory from the conflict, I find it impossible to conceal my admiration. Surely for such a triumph it was not foolhardiness to have entered the lists; and they who can so gloriously conquer themselves, are prepared to encounter the world beside.

Who then will ingloriously relinquish his prerogative? Who will pledge himself to give up the reins of judgment, and tremble to let his appetite go forth on its lawful errands, lest it should get the better of him? Nay, rather give it its own, and then if it should set up its rampant claims, fight against it manfully, and have it distinctly to know that you are not to be bullied out of propriety. Again I say, give me none of your TEA-total pledges. Shall I not, (by way of parenthesis,) put in one good word for coffee? As I am attached to the true faith, shall not this 'article' be protected against the heretical attacks of the reformers? I shall prove myself a very HENRY in these matters, and shall be a stubborn casuist to deal with. Summon your conclave, my dear Pope Leo, and tickle my ears with the title of 'Defender of the Faith.' These levelers shall find the country too hot for them. We will bring fires and kindle around the renowned DELAVAN, and GRAHAM shall be singed like a burnt crust of his own bread. How happy and exhilarated am I after my two cups at breakfast! The world appears new and bright, after the night's refreshing slumbers, and casting aside slippers, I am ready to jump into boots, and to face the busy world. The Arab sips of it in the desert, and it imbues him with the spirit of his steed; and out of tiny and gilded cups, all spiced and fragrant, the houris of the harem drink it. IT IS GOOD. But shall I compare it with tea? As well compare the fountain, which sparkles in its vivacity, with the dull and sluggish pool. It does not claim eminence. But enough for the present. I shall be back to tea, and join the maiden drinkers in another 'dish,' anon.

III

A Dish of Tea

PART TWO

I PROMISED that I would return to tea, and join the maiden drinkers, in another dish. But first, let me remark that there is a point of some importance, connected with this subject, which I must leave to learned scholars to determine; whether the herb which we call tea, be not that same nectar, so often mentioned in classic writings. I am mainly of the opinion that it is; that this the supplanted Hebe, and the bright boy Ganymede, who was too beautiful for earth, passed in golden goblets to the gods 'having Olympian habitations.' How universal now is this soothing beverage! Not many years ago, and a few boxes, coming with pomp and circumstance from imperial Canton, were sufficient to glut the market. Once it was known to the rich and the noble; now it is as extensive as the blessed light. The humble tenants of a cabin or a hut may sip their social tea in comfort. Where is the lip that doth not sip it? Where is the cottage in which the smoke of its incense goeth not up? How nicely is it adapted, by its delicately varying shades, to every especial palate! There is your Bohea, and Congo, and Campo, and Souchong, and Pouchon, and Pekoe; there is Twankay, and Hyson, and Young Hyson, and Hysonskin, and Gunpowder, and Imperial. True, it is not all of equal excellency, or 'quality,' but still it hath the name of tea, and there is much, there is very much, in that, you know. But I am again with the drinkers.

It always truly did my heart good to see Miss Patty presiding at the tea table; there was such an irradiation of comfort from her bland yet tristful countenance. She was a fitting priestess to do the divine honors of the occasion, and to pour out libations. She performed them, not indeed with the airy grace and flourish of one who presides at a profane dinner, nor with the trivial air of a master of ceremonies; but with a placid gravity of demeanor, which was worthy of the nature of the banquet, and the starched dignity of her cap. How can I forget her ancient 'loving kindnesses,' on such occasions? How devoted was she to the interests of her guests! With what watchful assiduity she anticipated their wants, and hastened to 'nip them in the bud!' How hardly she herself fared, barely stopping to take a casual sip, at intervals, like angels' visits, 'few and far between!' With what an air of serious importance, of ministerial solemnity, went forth the questions: 'Have I made your tea right?' 'Is your tea agreeable?' 'And yours, madam, and yours?' And the no less solemn replies, 'A little more milk, if you please.' 'No milk, if you please.' 'The least bit of sugar.' And then what a stirring of spoons, and what a sipping, and tasting, and testing, before it was ascertained with certainty whether the beverage was precisely adapted to their hypercritical palates. It would go hard with it, if the temperature were either blood warm, or moderately hot. It was like molten lead, and had it been thrown upon a dog, would have scalded him to death; but to their salamander tongues, it was only genially warm. This perhaps was well, as they did not gulp it humidly into the throat. They permitted it the rather to linger and loiter, like schoolboys' candy on the tongue, and to go gradually trickling and percullating to its destination. Thus they protracted the enjoyment, until much time necessarily elapsed before that important era of the entertainment arrived, the moment for a SECOND CUP. To indulge in a second, was a mere matter of course. Some, it is true, very moderately requested a 'half a cup,' but Miss Patty, in the generosity of her heart, always poured out a whole one, at least very nearly. I never knew a half a cup to descend lower than the second rim. She was not sparing of her tea. She never did things by halves. She thought it a pity that those who 'looked upon the wine when it was red,' should pour forth their deathful brimmers, and that virtuous liquor

176

should be abstained from. She was herself a veteran, and drank the best green. Never was a taste more accurate. She was not to be deceived by an inferior weed. She knew 'what was what.' She drank none of your mild infusions; she loved to behold the milk curdling in a strong decoction of the weed. It was in such cups, that her guests were wont to pledge her. And here, instead of putting them by the heads together, to defame their neighbors unjustly, I shall vindicate my client's liquor from the vulgar charge that it is the parent and promoter of scandal, and that its sacred urn is the favorite rendezvous where spinsters hatch their treasonable schemes. This charge, from being at first jocosely made, has come to be considered a hackneyed truth. But it is a pity that two things should be associated in the mind, which have no necessary relation or connection. PINDAR COCKLOFT, Esq., in his poem on Tea, which is particularly addressed to maiden ladies, falls in with the common notion:

'In harmless chit-chat an acquaintance they roast,
And serve up a friend, as they serve up a toast;
Some gentle *faux pas,* or some female mistake,
Is like sweetmeats delicious, or relished as cake;
A bit of broad scandal is like a dry crust,
It would stick in the throat, so they butter it first
With a little affected good nature, and cry,
'Nobody regrets the thing deeper than I.
Our young ladies nibble a good name in play,
As for pastime they nibble a biscuit away;
While with shrugs and surmises, the toothless old dame,
As she mumbles a crust, she will mumble a name:
And as the fell sisters astonished the Scot,
In predicting of Banquo's descendants the lot,
Making shadows of kings, amid flashes of light,
To appear in array, and to frown in his sight,
So they conjure up spectres all hideous in hue,
Which, as shades of their neighbors, are passed in review.
The wives of our cits, of inferior degree,
Will soak up repute in a little bohea;
The potion is vulgar, and vulgar the slang
With which on their neighbors' defects they harangue;

But the scandal improves, a refinement in wrong!
As our matrons are richer, and rise to souchong:
With hyson, a beverage that's still more refined,
Our ladies of fashion enliven their mind,
And by nods, innuendoes, and hints, and what not,
Reputations and tea send together to pot.
While madam, in cambrics and laces array'd,
With her plate and her liveries in splendid parade,
Will drink, in imperial, a friend at a sup,
Or in gunpowder blow them by dozens all up!'

Ah! poesy — sweet poesy! thus to revile this newest source of all thy inspiration! What if Harold, the morose bard, when he approached the 'old poetic mountain,' instead of that fine burst and apostrophe,

'Oh! thou Parnassus, whom I now survey,
Not with the frenzy of a dreamer's eye,' etc.,

had poured forth maledictions on that hoary head? Ah! Pindar Cockloft, who knoweth but these *paullo majora* strains of thine were excited by this very tea? — poured from its own exquisite urn, by some delicate hand which thou lovest; and yet thou dost turn round ungrateful, and revile the very muse and fount of thy poetic transports. This was an unkind cut. And prose lifts up her harsh voice, too. 'What wonder,' exclaims a Grahamitish friend of mine, who describes a knot of his acquaintance, and lets out his spleen against all vile narcotics, in a playful epistolary philipic; 'what wonder that the powerful fumes of tea like theirs should ascend to the head, and tinge the whole current of conversation? The intoxication of it is indeed apparent; not such, it is true, as the wine produces, when wisdom grovels in the dust of debasement, and doffing her garments of soberness, enacts the harlequin, to excite the laughter of fools. I suppose we may rather call it a sacred rapture, such as the Delphic priestess felt, when she prophesied from the tripod of Apollo. It consists in a more vivid sense and appreciation of virtue. Their eyes flash with an unwonted fire; their tongues are like a two-edged sword. Little spots, small stains in the reputation of others, scarce visible to the eye of a blind charity, now develop themselves as distinctly as the spots of the leper, and are held forth in the clear sunlight in all their hideous colors; and to have seen this little sanctimonious band exercising the right of a stern censorship, and diligently seeking for motes in their neighbors' eyes, you would have thought that they were pure, even as an icicle is pure. I have known a flaw to be picked in the most virtuous of characters between a couple of sips of the best green tea, and the whole fabric of it to be demolished before the cup was 'out.' I have known many a 'good name,' to which the gold of Peru were but 'trash,' thus taken violently away, (for, gentle souls! they did not dream that it was a kind of robbery that they committed,) and the unhappy owners rendered 'poor indeed.' When the tea-table was cleared away, and the fumes ascended, and the lights were new-trimmed, and their feminine work drawn forth, so as to present a show of industry, the business of the evening fairly commenced. Then came the hour for the discussion of character, for the comparison of notes, for the digestion of rumors, for the propounding of delicate questions, for the development of fresh scandal, and for settling the respective places of this, that, and the other, on a graduated scale of character. Woe, woe to those who were obnoxious to such a sifting! Shadracks, Meshecs, and Abednegos, must they be, who could come out unscathed from such a fiery furnace! He that was writhing beneath on in e tongue like theirs, might not be deemed to sleep upon a bed of roses; but I pity the wretch condemned to suffer the combined attacks of all; from my soul I pity him, thus set upon, distracted, torn asunder; like Caesar at the base of Pompey's statue, stabbed with many wounds.

'It was not any of your dry crusts of scandal, that Susannah served up at these evening coteries. She brought none but dainty intelligence, tit-bits, delicate morsels, curious scraps. She brought to light things which might ever have remained hid; she exposed to view astounding derelictions from sobriety, from chastity, and from a holy life. Her developments were of so extraordinary a nature, as to cause a general rustling of caps in the apartment. They were not attended with any such provoking exclamations

179

as, '1 expected as much;' 'not to be wondered at;' 'exactly as I predicted;' and such like, which take away of a sudden the right of discovery, and show that the ground has been occupied before; but by unfeigned and gratifying ejaculations of 'Who would have thought it? 'Is it possible?' 'Lord save us! — What is the town coming to?' Then their mouths might be seen puckered into an elliptical form, such as would be produced by the utterance of the syllable *aw!* — while low, monosyllabic, guttural ejaculations escaped them. These were accompanied with a rocking motion of the body, and a munching of the mouth, and pinches of snuff, taken with a nervous trepidation.

'Of all persons whom I have ever known, I think that these spinsters had the most consummate knack of arranging circumstances so as to bring out a desired result; in putting 'this and that together, to make that.' Things which, taken separately, would not weigh the weight of a feather, when summed up, formed an irresistible evidence. They prepared, they arranged, they combined their materials. They did not permit little things to escape them. The glance of an eye, the blush of a cheek, the expression of an unguarded moment, together with what Mistress Such-an-one had 'confidentially mentioned;' all went to prove something, or as Susannah would express it, with a significant wag of the head, 'This and that put together, makes *that.*'

Thus far the disciple of the Graham. Shall I condescend to make any reply to such hackneyed phrase? I will, in as few words as possible, merely by way of blank denial. That scandalous women sometimes gather around the tea-urn, I grant you; and that their cold natures seize upon that opportunity, when others would be melted into kindness by such social intercourse, to blast their neighbors' reputation. What then? They must have been full to the brim of malice, and must soon have given it vent elsewhere; perhaps more profusely, and with redoubled bitterness. But to cast reproach on the mild spirit of tea, for setting their wagging tongues in motion, would be as impolitic as to reproach the vernal breath which released the frozen notes from the baron's horn, and sent them forth, harsh, and discordant, to torture the ear, and find an echo where they could. If indeed there be envy, malice, or any other 'roots of bitterness,' nourished by the sex, so far from their being most prevalent around the tea-urn, I am more 'apt to think that they frequent those places where virtuous women never come.' On the contrary, I assert, that tea mollifies instead of drawing out the evil passions, and that more schemes of Christian benevolence, such as feeding the hungry, clothing the naked, educating the piously disposed, and providing 'the little negroes of the West Indies with flannel drawers and moral pocket-han'kerchers,' are matured over the tea-table, than in any other place whatever. So let us hear no more about tea-total societies. Blot out every letter from the alphabet of mercies; we cannot part with T:

> O sweet exotic of the east!
> Whose praises I resound,
> Whose very fragrance is a feast,
> Come, crown my garden ground!
>
> Come rule o'er all the flowery host,
> Which decks the fragrant bed;
> The violet's odors shall be lost,
> The rose shall droop its head.
>
> Not all the herbs which dames respect,
> Will kill disease so soon;
> Not all the herbs which dames collect,
> Beneath the quiet moon.
>
> Thy virtues are supreme enough,
> To sooth each torturing pain,
> When pinch on pinch of recreant snuff
> Goes up the nose in vain!
>
> In weal or woe, at night or morn,
> I gladly fly to thee;
> 'O Molly, put the kettle on,'
> And let us drink our tea!

Welcome, thrice welcome, ye proud Indiamen, whom prosperous gales have wafted from the distant India, filled to the blue wave with antique boxes, marked with strange characters, and filled with little mystic scrolls, to be unrolled in the vapors of the tea-pot, and to be interpreted at the bottom of the cup! We will prize the treasure, which thou bringest, (what were we without it?) drink of it, be soothed by it, be thankful for it, and be as happy as a grasshopper intoxicate with dew! Yea, we will imbibe it to the very dregs, and until we have exhausted it of all its sweetness, we will not cast it 'like a noxious weed away!'

IV

Coffee

BY MISS MARY L. LAWSON

JANUARY 1853

ALL sing the praise of ruby wine
   Through crystal goblets flowing,
And murmur of the purple vine
   'Neath endless summer glowing;
How well it charms, the heart it warms,
   The soul in sunshine steeping,
As beauty, mirth, and hope's bright birth
   Lay chained within its keeping.

But wherefore gild the tempting draught,
   Which stains the lip that praises?
A nectar far more pure and sweet,
   The wearied spirit raises:
'Twill tinge with light care's darkest night,
   Like some divine libation;
Joy fills the eye and hearts beat high
   Beneath its inspiration.

It ripples through the silver spout,
   In clear transparent china,
Brought freshly from the sparkling hearth
   By PHILLIS or by DINAH.
How rich the scent when softly blent
   With cream, rich, thick and yellow,
Whose currents glide in mingled tide
   Its pungent strength to mellow!

COFFEE

It stirs the flash of soul and sense,
    Till wit and converse mingle;
For mind's best rays, like sorrows waves,
    Ne'er rush to meet us single:
Bright fancies strike on minds alike,
    That fade not with the fleeting,
For wards that thrill grow deeper still
    When glance with glance is meeting.

It wakes within the melting soul
    Time's lost or buried pleasures,
Old friends, old books, old songs, old joys,
    And all life's garnered treasures:
Bereft of pain, 'twill softly gain
    Old Memory's haunted places,
While o'er us rise, in angel guise,
    Soft smiles on vanished faces.

As one by one our guests depart,
    Left with remembrance only,
We scarcely sigh that time flits by,
    And leaves us sad and lonely;
Hope's morning breaks, and joy awakes,
    Life's gloomy page to brighten,
As on our quiet silent hearth
    The dying embers lighten.

Then on the pillow softly sinks
    The head with visions teeming,
And many an eastern pageant floats
    Before our gorgeous dreaming;
To see life pass in fancy's glass,
    With moonlight radiance beaming,
It seeks the breast divinely blest
    Through misty mocha gleaming.

V

Discursive Thoughts on Chowder

BY JOHN WATERS

JULY 1840

'THERE are more things in heaven and earth, Horatio,
Than are dreamt of in your philosophy.

WHEN THE soul of man, relieved from the last trace of materiality, as that term is understood on this nether side of Uranus, shall revisit the solar system and the earth perhaps, upon some excursion of pleasure from the realms of upper heaven; and all the latent affinities of nature are exposed, unveiled, before the piercing rays of its glorified existence; I often think it will be a vast satisfaction to know why a tree should live and bourgeon in shady luxuriance under one man's planting, that will die if the hand of another place it in the same ground: why flowers flourish under one woman's care, that fade if another, perchance more beautiful, possess them: why dogs growl upon one man, and instinctively attach themselves to another not more kind toward them; and why, with the same ingredients, one man only out of a whole fishing party can build and season, and successfully concoct, a chowder.

The facts themselves are undeniable. No man of a certain age but has observed the truth; and no philosopher, but has wondered at it. Why is it, *humanly speaking,* as the Presbyterians say, why is it that the same alternate layers of pork, of haddock, and cod, and sliced potatoes, and the one onion cut into rings, and the same hard biscuit soaked for five minutes in cold water before it takes its place in the pot; with the same black pepper throughout; and salt if you will, when your pork is not salt enough; with the self-same flour and butter, shall refuse their charms under one man's management, that gratify, with a joy and a flavor, and a fragrance untasted and unknown before, the careless and unhesitating distribution of materials that form these successive strata of good things from the hand of one of these favorites of nature? *Favorites of Nature!* — the word is a good word! No member of the family of the Blenkinsops could ever blow out a candle; none but a Creole could ever make a pepper-pot; and the chowder-builder and the poet must alike be born, each to his 'art unteachable, untaught.'

Dear, dear JIM! — the cove of dark rocks upon that shore in the old Bay State, near which our boat had grated upon the harsh and pebbly sand, is before me at this moment; the hum of cheerful voices thrills upon my ear, and the glow of youth — youth, sparkling youth that borders upon immortality, and is almost as free as it is from ache or care — again warms the old heart that loved thee in its better days, thou *Favorite of Nature!* I never thought that any idea connected with a pot of chowder; or as thou wert wont to explain the etymology of this uncouth word, a *chaudière;* styling it the best of those ragouts à la matelote, which French culinary art has derived from the happy invention of the sailor; I never thought that any recollection of the sort could have been otherwise than gay or joyous; and yet at this moment my hand falters, and the air has not breath enough for me, as I remember how thou wert taken from us in a moment of such youth; thou, our pride; the beautiful, the gifted, and the brave! GOD bless thee! The universe contains no constellation too bright for thine abode; and when I look up at night to Heaven and love a star, I fancy it to be thine own!

We were all despatched by thee, I remember, on different errands; some to shoot sand-snipe, and others to collect driftwood for fuel along the shore, or to stroll about and do nothing, if we preferred it, so that we were kept out of the way of interfering with thy functions; equipped as thou wert in a moment in a linen jacket; a napkin round the waist; a face of calm determination;

the gazette of the day (called the Columbian Centinel,) curiously folded as thy cook's cap, and resting on thy dark rich locks; the smoke of the lighted fire slowly tracing its way upward by the precipitous rocks as by a chimney, and thyself kneeling beside the chaudière, with fish and implements about thee, and the boatman in attendance at thy side.

Nature turns over to the ordinary journeymen of her busy workshop the countenances of most of the human race. Doughfaces are they for the most part, shaped with a trowel; the point of which, being inserted, cuts to the required length the aperture, which *is* called, by courtesy, a mouth. But she watches, in her studio, with a jealous care over the features of *her favorites,* her artists, her poets, the man of taste that is to be, the intuitive being chosen to decorate and to refine society; and her chisel was in her own right hand, and her thoughts were dwelling upon the bow of Cupid unbent and held horizontally, when she marked out the contour of thy mouth, and planted its terminations deeply in the cheek, and saw that her work was beautifully done; and, with a kiss, light as the fall of *the* damask rose-leaf that she left upon thy lips, awoke thee into life, dear chowder-builder!

I mention this feature of Jim's countenance particularly, because my heart insists upon it; and yet his eyes were singularly fine, and changed like a thought from falcon into dove, as he turned from man to rest them upon woman.

Do the words vibrate deeply on the chords of the heart of anyone who hears me, when I repeat from one of the grandest effusions of the human mind, 'THERE SHE STANDS; LOOK AT HER!' Then I shall be understood when I say, that upon the ocean shores of Massachusetts, every noble passion of the soul may find a tongue! The illimitable reach of waters; the azure sky that over-canopies it; the waves inviting man to enterprise or to command; the distant sail half-gilded at the approach of sunset, and the unbroken glories of the rising day; and then the long anthem peal that often, when the shores are calm and tranquil, takes possession of the air, and tells of the distant or the approaching storm. The sea-birds come for refuge near us at the sound; the cattle leave the distant pasture, lowing for shelter at the hand of man; and even to himself the joys of home, his own free home, rise with an unwonted delight as the roof of his dwelling then opens to his returning gaze. These are among the objects and the thoughts that 'feelingly persuade us what we are,' or that occupy the soul with cheerful musings, during the cookery of a chaudière.

JOHN WATERS.

VI

Correspondence Concerning Chowder

BY HARRY FRANCO

AUGUST 1840

To the Editor of The Knickerbocker:

SIR: The enclosed letter was sent to me by the writer, with the request that I would forward it to JOHN WATERS; but as I am ignorant of the address of that gentleman, I enclose it to you, and beg that you will see that he gets it.

Your obedient Servant,

H. FRANCO.

Letter to John Waters.

Nantucket, July 10, 1840.

ESTEEMED FRIEND JOHN WATERS:

I have read thy piece of writing in the KNICKERBOCKER Magazine, which thou callest 'Discursive Thoughts on Chowder,' and I now take my pen in hand to give thee my sentiments in relation thereto. If thy writing had made its appearance in a less popular journal, or one numbering fewer intelligent readers, it is probable that I should not have felt myself moved to communicate with thee and the public on the subject; but as it is, I feel an inward yearning to do so, lest a wrong impression be made upon the minds of a multitude of persons ignorant of the matter on which thou hast undertaken to enlighten them.

I am fearful, friend Waters, that thou art wholly and entirely ignorant of what Chowder really is, and that thou hast never so much as smelled of the dish in thy life; for if thou hadst, thy thoughts would not have been discursive when thou wast writing of it. Can a mother's thoughts wander from her child, when its first cry sounds in her ear? Can a miser think of the next world, when his eyes are fixed upon the glittering dust of this? Can fire forget to seek the sun, or water turn back from its parent ocean? No. And I do confidently affirm, that no man's thoughts will ever wander from a pot of Chowder, when they have once been attracted to it; either by the pleasing reality itself, or only by the unsubstantial shadow of it which his memory may retain. And then to call this simple yet savory dish by a finical French name, *Chaudière*, as if the concoction of Chowder had ever entered into the culinary conceptions of a befrizzled Mounseer! No, friend John, Chowder is a dish of greater dignity than your friend James had an idea of. It is a dish of great antiquity, too. It was known in the days of Barclay, and Fox, and Woolman. And notwithstanding that I have searched diligently through the chronicles of Obed Macy, and other conscientious Friends, yet I have not been able to find that any mention has been made of the discoverer or inventor of this excellent dish; hence I have been led to believe that it was neither invented nor discovered, but that it was an inspired dish: for there were giants in those days: and doubtless some Friend was moved by the givings out of the inward light to confer the great blessing of a pot of Chowder upon our sinful race.

From the manner in which thou enumeratest the ingredients of thy friend James' Chowder, it is very evident to my mind that he too knew nothing at all about the matter. Such a mixture might do well enough for a codfish stew, or what we denominate on this island a 'Frank Gardner mess;' but it is not worthy to be called by the name of Chowder. Thee may call it *Chaudière,* or any other outlandish name, but do not call it Chowder. Didst thou never read the ode of the poet Southey, beginning thus:

> 'Full of my theme, O Muse! begin the song!
>   What though the sunbeams of the west
>   Mature within the turtle's breast
> Blood glutinous, and fat of verdant hue!
> Give them their honors due, ,
>   But, *Chowder,* thou art best!'

And dost thou think that a vile compound of fish and potatoes would inspire such a noble strain? And what presumption in thee to assert that thy friend James could prepare the dish better than anyone beside! Now, friend Waters, I have eleven daughters, and either of them can cook as good a pot of Chowder as a reasonable man could desire to dip his spoon in. Although I must confess that my youngest daughter Hepzabeth hath perhaps the most skilful hand of either, since my daughter Rhoda, who is married to Amaziah Green, a Newport Friend, removed from the Island. Even my eldest son Libni, who is now absent on a whaling voyage in the ship Barclay, I have been told by his former shipmates, was a very good hand at making Chowder; and I have heard that he once made a very good Chowder out of an albatross, that he shot near the Island of Tristan d'Acunha, off the East Cape.

I have shown thy 'Discursive Thoughts' to my daughter

Hepsabeth, and she says that one onion is not sufficient; that the biscuit ought not to be soaked in water; that the potatoes should be omitted altogether; that there should be no butter, and that the pork should not be put in layers, but that it should be cut up very fine, and fried brown.

For my own part, friend Waters, I must confess to thee that my mind misgives me that one who errs so greatly in his opinions about Chowder, cannot be altogether correct in his views of religion. I hope, for thy soul's sake, that thou art not one of the Hicksite persuasion; but I fear, I have a ship now on the stocks at Mattapoiset, which I intend to call after my youngest daughter Hepsabeth Starbuck; and I shall necessarily be absent from the island until she is launched; but when I return, I shall be pleased to see thee at my house in Coffin-street, and thou shalt then decide whether thy friend James could make a better Chowder than my youngest daughter Hepsabeth. And remain, thy friend, with esteem,

HEZEDIAH STARBUCK, THIRD.

VII

The First Oyster-Eater

BY RICHARD HAYWARDE

MAY 1851

THE IMPENETRABLE veil of antiquity hangs over the antediluvian oyster, but the geological finger-post points to the testifying fossil. We might, in pursuing this subject, sail upon the broad pinions of conjecture into the remote, or flutter with lighter wings in the regions of fable, but it is unnecessary: the mysterious pages of Nature are ever opening freshly around us, and in her stony volumes, amid the calcareous strata, we beheld the precious mollusc — the *primeval bivalve,*

—'Rock-ribbed! And ancient as the sun.'

Yet, of its early history we know nothing. Etymology throws but little light upon the matter. In vain have we carried our researches into the vernacular of the maritime Phoenicians, or sought it amid the fragments of Chaldean and Assyrian lore. To no purpose have we analyzed the roots of the comprehensive Hebrew, or lost ourselves in the bathing labyrinths of the oriental Sanscrit. The history of the ancient oyster is written in no language, except in the universal idiom of the secondary strata! Nor is this surprising in a philosophical point of view. Setting aside the pre-Adamites, and taking Adam as the first *name-giver,* when we *reflect* that Adam lived inland, and therefore never saw the succulent periphery in its native mud, we may deduce this reasonable conclusion: viz., that as he never saw it, he probably never NAMED it — never! — not even to his most intimate friends. Such being the case, we must seek for information in a later and more enlightened age. And here let me take occasion to remark, that oysters and intelligence are nearer allied than many persons imagine. The relations between physiology and psychology are beginning to be better understood. A man might be scintillant with facetiousness over a plump '*Shrewsbury*,' who would make a very sorry figure over a bowl of water-gruel. The gentle, indolent BRAHMIN, the illiterate LAPLANDER, the ferocious LYBIAN, the mercurial FRENCHMAN, and the stolid, (I beg your pardon,) the stalwart ENGLISHMAN, are not more various in their mental capacities than in their table aesthetics. And even in this CENTURY, we see that wit and oysters come in together with September, and wit and oysters go out together in May — a circumstance not without its weight, and peculiarly pertinent to the subject matter. With this brief, but not irrelevant digression, I will proceed. We have 'Ostreum' from the LATINS, 'Oester' from the SAXONS, 'Auster' from the TEUTONS, 'Ostra' from the SPANIARDS, and '*Huitre*' from the FRENCH — words evidently of common origin — threads spun from the same distaff! And here our archaeology narrows to a point, and this point is the pearl we are in search of: viz., the genesis of this most excellent fish.

'Words evidently derived from a common origin.' What origin? Let us examine the venerable page of history. When is the first mention made of oysters? Hudibras says:

> —'the Emperor CALIGULA,
> Who triumphed o'er the British sons,
> Took crabs and OYSTERS prisoners, (mark that!)
> And lobsters, 'stead of cuirassiers;
> Engaged his legions in fierce bustles
> With periwinkles, prawns, and mussels,
> And led his troops with furious gallops,
> To charge whole regiments of scallops;
> Not, like their ancient way of war,
> To wait on his triumphal car,
> But when he went to dine or sup,
> More bravely ate his captives up;

Leaving all war, by his example,
Reduced—to vict'ling of a camp well.'

This is the first mention in the classics of oysters; and we now approach the cynosure of our inquiry. From this we infer that oysters came originally from Britain. The word is unquestionably *primitive*. The broad, open, vowelly sound is, beyond a doubt, the *primal*, spontaneous thought that found utterance when the soft, seductive mollusc first exposed its white bosom in its pearly shell to the enraptured gaze of aboriginal man! Is there a question about it? Does not everyone know, when he sees an oyster, that *that is its name*? And hence we reason that it originated in Britain, was Latinized by the Romans, replevined by the Saxons, corrupted by the Teutons, and finally barbecued by the French. Oh, philological ladder by which we mount upward, until we emerge beneath the clear vertical light of Truth!! Methinks I see the First Oyster-Eater! A brawny, naked savage, with his wild hair matted over his wild eyes, a zodiac of fiery stars tattooed across his muscular breast — unclad, un-sandaled, hirsute and hungry — he breaks through the under woods that margin the beach, and stands alone upon the seashore, with nothing in one hand but his unsuccessful boar spear, and nothing in the other but his fist. There he beholds a splendid panorama! The West all aglow; the conscious waves blushing as the warm sun sinks to their embraces; the blue sea on his left; the interminable forest on his right; and the creamy sea-sand curving in delicate tracery between. A *Picture*, and a *Child of Nature*! Delightedly he plunges in the foam, and swims to the bald crown of a rock that uplifts itself above the waves. Seating himself, he gazes upon the calm expanse beyond, and swings his legs against the moss that spins its filmy tendrils in the brine. Suddenly he utters a cry; springs up; the blood streams from his foot. With barbarous fury he tears up masses of sea moss, and with it clustering families of testacea. Dashing them down upon the rock, he perceives liquor exuding from the fragments; he sees the white, pulpy, delicate morsel half-hidden in the cracked shell, and instinctively reaching upward, his hand finds his mouth, and amidst a savage, triumphant deglutition, he murmurs — OYSTER!! Champing in his uncouth fashion bits of shell and seaweed, with uncontrollable pleasure he masters this mystery of a new sensation, and not until the gray veil of night is drawn over the distant waters does he leave his rock, covered with the trophies of his victory.

We date from this epoch the *maritime* history of England. Ere long, the reedy cabins of her aborigines clustered upon the banks of beautiful inlets, and overspread her long lines of level beaches; or penciled with delicate wreaths of smoke the savage aspect of her rocky coasts. The sword was beaten into the oyster-knife, and the spear into oyster-rakes. Commerce spread her white wings along the shores of happy Albion, and man emerged at once into civilization from a nomadic state. From this people arose the mighty nation of Ostrogoths; from the Ostraphagi of ancient Britain came the custom of Ostracism — that is, sending political delinquents to that place where they can get no more oysters.

There is a strange fatality attending all discoverers. Our Briton saw a mighty change come over his country — a change beyond the reach of memory or speculation. Neighboring tribes, formerly hostile, were now linked together in bonds of amity. A sylvan, warlike people had become a peaceful, pisciverous community; and he himself, once the lowest of his race, was now elevated above the *dreams* of his ambition. He stood alone upon the seashore, looking toward the rock, which, years ago, had been his stepping-stone to power, and a desire to revisit it came over him. He stands now upon it. The season, the hour, the westerly sky, remind him of former times. He sits and meditates. Suddenly a flush of pleasure overspreads his countenance; for there, just below the flood, he sees a gigantic bivalve — alone — with mouth agape, as if yawning with very weariness at the solitude in which it found itself. What I am about to describe may be untrue. But I believe it. I have heard of the waggish propensities of oysters. I have known them to clap suddenly upon a rat's tail at night; and, what with the squeaking and the clatter, we verily thought the devil had broke loose in the cellar. Moreover, I am told that, upon another occasion, when a demijohn of brandy had burst, a large *'Blue-pointer'* was found lying in a little pool of a liquor, just drunk enough to be careless of consequences, opening and shutting his shells with a 'devil-may-care' air, as if he didn't value anybody a brass farthing, but was going to be as *noisy* as be possibly could.

But to return. When our Briton saw the oyster in this defenseless attitude, he knelt down, and gradually reaching his arm toward it, he suddenly thrust his fingers in the aperture, and the oyster closed upon them with a spasmodic snap! In vain the Briton tugged and roared; he might as well have tried to uproot the solid rock as to move *that* oyster! In vain he called upon all his heathen gods — Gog and Magog — elder than Woden and Thor; and with huge, uncouth, druidical d—ns consigned all shellfish to Nidhogg, Hela, and the submarines. Bivalve held on with 'a. will.' It was nuts for him certainly. Here was a great lubberly, chuckle-headed fellow, the destroyer of his tribe, with his fingers in chancery, and the *tide rising!* A fellow who had thought, like ancient Pistol, to make the world his oyster, and here was the oyster making a world of him. Strange mutation! The poor Briton raised his eyes: there were the huts of his people; he could even distinguish his own, with its slender spiral of smoke; they were probably preparing a roast for him; how he detested *a roast!* Then a thought of his wife, his little ones awaiting him, tugged at his heart. The waters rose around him. He struggled, screamed in his anguish; but the remorseless winds dispersed the sounds, and ere the evening moon arose and flung her white radiance upon the placid waves, the last billow had rolled over the First Oyster-Eater!

I purpose in my next to show the relations existing between wit and oysters. It is true that Chaucer (a poet of considerable promise in the fourteenth century) has alluded to the oyster in rather a disrespectful manner; and the learned Du Bartas (following the elder Pliny) hath accused this modest bivalve of 'being incontinent,' a charge wholly without foundation, for there is not a more chaste and innocent fish in the world.

But the rest of our poets have redeemed it from these foul aspersions in numberless passages, among which we find Shakespeare's happy allusion to

'Rich *honesty* dwelling in a POOR house.'

And no one now, I presume, will pretend to deny that it hath been always held

'Great in mouths of wisest censure!'

In addition to a chapter on wit and oysters, I also may make a short digression touching cockles.

VIII

How to Cook a Black-Fish

BY JOHN WATERS

DECEMBER 1840

PART FIRST

COURTEOUS AND gentle Reader, before the retina of whose philosophic vision this correctly printed page of our favorite journal now presents itself, didst thou ever partake of a thoroughly well dressed black fish? I anticipate thine unhesitating, but perhaps incautious, answer: 'Certainly, most certainly.' 'Then let me tell thee, that at the moment when thy fork was flourished for the first time over the happy plate, in the center of which lay that delicious portion, the star of thy destiny was in the ascendant, and that the day itself should henceforth be to thee an *alba dies* in the history of sublunary enjoyment!

> 'To *live* with fame
> The gods allow to many; but to *dine*
> *Upon a well cook'd black-fish* is a blessing,
> Jove, among the choicest of his boons, reserves,
> Which but on few his sparing hand bestows!'

My lamented friend, the late Alderman B—, once observed to me, that although the market abounded in them, 'his youth was gone before he knew what that fish was!' 'I was staying,' said he, 'at —, on Long Island, at a farm house, surrounded by a shady orchard, with the barnyard within a few steps, so that you could always hear from the hen herself the right time to get a fresh egg.

199

We had got down from town in the afternoon, had had a charming ride, the weather warm, but not uncomfortable; the night fine; my room was on the lower floor, with the window a little up, and we all breathing blossoms! Should you not have thought I could have slept soundly? Sir, there was a cock in the barn! — a pretty bird, but a wonderful noisy one. If he had cried fire! I suppose I should have slept on; but making such an unaccountable noise, such as I was no wise used to in the night, I was forced to get up; and so we got the people up, and I took an uncommon early breakfast. I did not, upon the whole, regret it, when I was seated upon the stoop with my segar, and the morning breaking beautifully all around, with a slight movement upon the surf as if there had been a wind in the offing, and the smoke rising up by the side of some dark rocks upon the curve of the shore in the distance. The farmer said that the fishermen were preparing their breakfast; and as I had finished my segar, and wanted a walk, I thought I would go down and see what sort of fare they were making it of. It was a pretty long pull, so that they had nearly finished before I arrived. They asked me if I had come to breakfast? They were in a nook of the rocks, with nothing but a few coals of fire, a square bit of board, a small toolbox, a paper of salt, a roll of fresh butter, a biscuit or two, a pepper-castor, and a basket of blackfish; but they were so pleasant that I hated to say no, and so I said yes. The head man — they were all three nice, young, handsome fellows, I wish they had all three been my sons, and I could not help telling them so at the time — the head man chose a fish out of the basket; it had an eye like a seal, and a skin as black as a wolf's throat; rich pouting lips, and almost as thick down at the lower dorsal fin as he was across the shoulders; it was a pleasure to look at him as he lay quite satisfied like in the hands of a man that knew how to take hold of him; he breathed a breath or two, and each time such gills! If ever you have seen a pomegranate in your life opened in the heart, you know the true color of the gills of a first-rate blackfish.

The skipper laid him upon the board as if he had been helping himself to jelly, so balanced and quiet was his one hand, while with the other he took up his knife. There's a natural division in the middle of the upper jaw of a black fish, just broad enough for a sharp knife to enter; he touched him there with the edge, and before you could say Jack Robinson, the fish was cut down the back to the flapper of the tail, the board turned over, and he opened, tacked and toasting, inside outward, before the coals. As soon as he was done, the fisherman took a small piece of the yellow fresh butter and spread it over the fish, threw a cast of black pepper over him, and 'your fish is ready,' said he.

'Some salt,' said I.

Yes, but eat your salt always in crystals, and put it on the last thing, otherwise it is salt-water, and not salt that you take into your mouth; remember that all your life.

'Well, Alderman, did you eat the fish?'

'The fish! I scooped two of them out of their jackets, and I have been growing fat from that day.'

But is this the way to cook a blackfish? Gentle reader, it is not; it is *a* way, but it is not THE way. Then what is the meaning of all this cock and bull story about a barn and an alderman? It is merely to introduce you to the fish, which I propose to teach you how to cook.

PART SECOND

I HAVE endeavored to impart to the aspirant after culinary happiness some idea of the more striking and ostensible characteristics of the individual Black Fish: the soft, deep, mazy eye; the luxurious and pouting lips; the peculiar thickness across the lower dorsal fin; the pomegranate gills, and the blackness of the skin, which should designate the object of his choice.

The scene is in one of our own markets: the contract is closed; the fish is found to weigh four pounds and a half; scaled; opened in front about three inches; drawn; and cleansed by one, and see that it is not more than one, rapid immersion in pure water; and Mr. Fishmonger, not being one of the Alderman's Long Island friends, takes me up incontinently a clumsy sail-needle, and is upon the point of ruining all our hopes, by inserting a tarred string through the lower jaw. Had he accomplished this, vain were all our subsequent exertions! Not all the waters of the multitudinous seas, nor all the spicy perfumes of 'Araby the blest,' could have removed, however they might possibly overwhelm, the effects of his incaution. Latterly indeed some of our market men have provided themselves with white strings purposely for this fish, which is a great improvement upon past usage; but far better is it if your fish can be brought home without any string, in a nice napkin, and laid folded in the covering unbruised, upon your white dresser table, in the light and cheerful kitchen, where I will now suppose it to be.

And now, fair ruler of the destinies of dinner! (for if thou beest a man I have no sympathies toward thee,) smoke-compelling Betty, Mary, or whatever else may be the happy appelative in which not only thou but all of us rejoice, thou hast lying extended before thee one of the most delicately absorbent substances in nature, imbibing flavor from everything which surrounds it, whether of adverse or of propitious tendency; subject, as Warren Hastings said of the tenure of the British possessions in India, alike 'to the touch of chance, or the breath of opinion.'

Thou hast it, my choice Mary! The small, deep stew-pan —with its thin cullender or strainer, on which the fish is to be lowered to the bottom, that it may, when stewed into soft delight, be gently raised again, without injuring its integrity of form — glows with brightness in front of thee! Thy vigorous arm of mottled red, thy round wrist, and small compact fingers grasp the sharp-pointed knife with which thou followest the rude course of the saw-like weapon of the fish dealer, to complete his endeavor, and satisfy thyself that not one scale remains around the head, the fins, the tail.

Now tail, and fins are nicely shortened in their termination, not hacked off. A little salt is thrown over the fish, merely to *harden* and *not salt* it, and it lies two hours for this purpose. It is then scored, that it may not break when it swells, and browned well upon the gridiron: from which it is carefully taken up, and laid to repose upon a bed of nicely peeled and very fresh mushrooms, daintily spread over the strainer.

While the fish was hardening, Mary has had a communication from upstairs. An extra bottle of the Chateau of twenty-five had been unavailingly opened the day before, to tempt a total temperance friend who had arrived from the country. Good part of it remains, and at this moment it is decanted into the stew-pan; the freighted strainer descends into the wine; and the fish, entirely immersed in the amethystine element, regrets no more its loss of life, of liberty, and youth. A white onion or two is sliced into rings, that fall as decorations over him; a few berries of pepper thrown in; six cloves; two blades of mace; an echalot, if you think proper; and cayenne or not, according to your taste. The stew-pan is then covered, and a careful, slow, epicurean simmer completes the work.

At dinner the best friend you have in the world is offered, but declines, *the head;* you refresh your thoughts with all that can be recollected of Gall and Spurzheim, and gelatinize your way neatly but scientifically through bumps, indications, and developments.

But my friend WATERS, where are we to get mushrooms? Beautiful inspiration whom we call Woman, whose smile can obliterate every disappointment in life except a bad dinner:

'Quand on n'a pas ce que l'on aime,
Il faut aimer ce que l'on a.'

You will find in article number four hundred and thirty-nine, Harper's edition of Kitchener's Cook's Oracle, the best recipe for making the double catsup, or, as he calls it, the dog-sup, and this is your substitute. Use substitutes. Take a bottle of Medoc instead of Chateau Margaux, or use beef gravy instead of either, only realize that we have in the Black Fish or Tautog from April to October, an unfailing solace against many of the cares of everyday existence.

The most judicious comment that any foreigner has made upon our national character is, that we neglect and overlook our real advantages, while we pique ourselves upon those which we do not exclusively possess. Let not this be said of us in reference to this precious offering of the ocean to our happy shore.

PART THIRD

SONG

*OF MARY THE COOK-MAID TO THE BLACK FISH, WHILE
SIMMERING IN CHATEAU MARGAUX.*

FULL fathom five thy father floats,
 With all his school around;
O'er the blue wave, the fisher boats
 Reach now an anchorage ground:
  See, see! — 'tis cast!
  The boats are fast —
 The anchors ground; the school is found
  At last! at last!
 The school is found at last!

The morning breaks with clouded light,
 But gay are fishers' looks;
And all with dew their decks are bright,
 And countless are their hooks:
  See, see! — 'tis cast!
  The boats are fast —
 The anchors ground, the school is found
  At last! at last!
 The school is found at last!

No ravenous shark with monstrous throat,
 No porpoise that way wends:
But o'er thy race from fishers' boat
 The baited line descends:
  See, see! — 'tis cast!
  The boats are fast —
 The fish-leads sound, the school is found
  At last! at last!
 The school is found at last!

In health, in sport, in deeps profound,
    Thine artless race delight;
But the rich baits that hang around,
    Tempt fish by fish from sight:
        See, see! — 'tis cast!
        The tide is past —
    Late wears the day, the anchors weigh
        At last! at last!
    The school is caught at last!

But mourn not thou that swim'st in wine,
    For those who breast the wave;
One common fate marks ours and thine,
    The groundling or the brave.
        See, see! 'tis fate!
        Some glittering bait —
    The camp, the state, gold, love, fame, hate,
        Teach all too late,
    They can't resist a bait!
        A bait! a bait!
    We can't resist a bait!

IX

Deipnologica Variosa

BY C.T. CONGDON

JULY 1859

A GREAT many years ago, when, like Mr. Halleck's Fanny — who must be, if surviving, a positive Sarah of longevity, and like many gentlemen who were my contemporaries in my primitive baldness and toothlessness — I was younger than I am now, and perhaps prettier, my eating was made a part of my moral education: by which I am very far from meaning to say, that any Brillat-Savarin moulded my inchoate palate, or guided my infant gusto. The reader, if his memory of juvenile experiences be reasonably good, will remember several dietetic abominations, which are the peculiar pride of New England tables; and which, having come into high fashion in those dreary Pilgrim days, when there was nothing else to eat, have been eaten traditionally and from a sense of duty ever since, and not in the least from relish, or the satisfaction which they afford to the inexperienced.

There was at least a propriety in eating pork in default of beef; and the Pythagorean beans, when green peas were wanting; or potatoes, if one could get no cauliflowers; or salt cod, well flooded with the essential oil of pig, if one could compass no provent more salutary or savory; or in drinking sour cider in the absence of Haut Barsac, or St. Juhen Medoc. Dwelling among savages, this band of exiles, after they had moored their bark on the wild New England shore, and had performed the proper devotional exercises, however high their previous taste, were obliged to eat

as the savages around them did; and thus to expose themselves
to fearful attacks of gripes, and a general disarrangement of
that 'raging canawl,' scientifically known as the alimentary, by
devouring quantities of the *sickishuog*, or clam, which the ALL-WISE
undoubtedly meant for fish-bait, as he meant oats for 'horses
and Scotchmen;' or of green corn, which will do occasionally,
when the Asiatic cholera is not imminent; or of fish, which must
be cured, and is spoiled in the curing. I wish it to be distinctly
understood, that I do not blame the Puritans for eating of these
things, when they had Hobson's choice only; but why it should
be thought necessary to celebrate the LORD's Day by the weekly
devouring of these dainties; why persons of wealth should deem it
a religious duty to charge themselves with fish-balls well wadded
in with chunks of brown bread, in these times of tender chops and
savory steaks; why they stick by beans, which do so fearfully stick
by them, with 'the finest market in the world' — I refer to that
less imaginatively known as 'Funnel,' and occasionally spoken of
as 'Old Funnel,' as if it were a miracle of antiquity—is what I do
not comprehend. But I do not find it so difficult to understand
the fierce wrath of the Puritan soul, and the turbulent stomach,
when rumor came of the riotous doings of Squire Thomas Morton,
formerly of Furnival's Inn, and afterward of Mount Wollaston,
otherwise called *Mare*-Mount, or Merry-Mount, [THOMAS himself
spells it *Mare*-Mount; and I incline to the belief, that he meant
Sea-Mount, or Sea-View, and not Merry-Mount at all.] and then
Mount Dagon. I can imagine the indignation of some saintly but
still human Puritan, who had not had a drop of comfortable strong
waters for a month, when he heard of the roysterings and revels
of the jolly dwellers upon that delectable mountain. The Maypole
did not, of course, have a depressing effect upon his gorge; but
when he was told of 'ten pound worth of wine and spirits in the
morning,' the news was too much for his hissing-hot stomach.
So the jovial Thomas was first 'set in the bilbous, and after sent
prisoner to England,' where he drank *Rosa Solis* with Ben Jonson,
and consoled himself, as so many unhappy gentlemen have

done, by writing a wrathful little book called 'The New Canaan,' which, in its coat of rusty black, I have seen reposing in its old age upon the shelves of an eminent statesman, who treated it with more respect than he bestowed upon many a stately folio — causing it to be continually dusted with great tenderness, and to be sedulously protected from the marauding of moths, and the light fingers of bibliomaniacs. Nor does it seem that our Puritan friends, whenever there happened to be policy in it, disdained to do as Master Morton did; and with profound philosophy, to find the Indian heart through the Indian stomach; the favor of many a truculent warrior being secured by judicious presents of tobacco, of beer, and of mugs from which to drink it. In this way was the Sachem Chickatabot partially disarmed; and when the advantage was followed up by a present of pantaloons made after the English fashion, the stern warrior at once joined the Peace Society, or at least contented himself with scalping his rival redskins, who had shown themselves proof against the blandishments of British breeches. Unfortunately Mr. Thomas Morton mixed gunpowder with his donative rum; an operation which is traditionally declared to have had a marvelously encouraging effect upon the brave tars of the frigate 'Constitution,' but which, however excellent the ingredients, could not have rendered the Massachusetts aborigines particularly pleasant neighbors.

The truth is, your Englishman has a natural, although I admit a not over-delicate appreciation of creature comfort, and goes about the world conquering and to conquer, with a sword in one hand, a spit in the other, and the formula in his pocket for melted butter — that sole sauce which Voltaire placed in startling antithesis to the hundred Anglican religions. There is a coarse passage in 'Venice Preserved' which positively declares, if an Englishman be furnished with beef, a sea-coal fire, and one other comfort, which we cannot name to ears polite, that he will be ready for all manner of treasons and conspiracies. Indeed, it is curious to notice how much eating and drinking there is in the English drama, and how small a figure these accomplishments make in the plays of other languages. In Colman's 'Inkle and Yarico,' when Mr. Trudge is left in the wilderness, with the usual stage propriety, he sings a comic song — not at all comical — in which, after a touching allusion to 'the gay chop-house signs' of London, he warbles after this fashion:

'FOR a neat slice of beef I could roar like a bull;
And my stomach's so empty, my heart is quite full.'

It will be found, indeed, that the highest as well as the lowest English literature has a dietetical squint. I am not about to say that this is, *ex necessitate*, coarse or animal; and, if 'I should say so, everyone who has read the sensuous reverberations of Milton, or his softer but still epicurean sonnets, might encounter and vanquish me in a 'veni-vidi-vlci'-eous way. But everywhere, in the best and in the worst company, one sees how much the kitchen has done for all writers; or failing the cook, how much the tapster has accomplished. 'Tis the same in tragedy or in comedy, and 'tis not wanting even in the records of religion. You may miss it in Aaron Hill's frigid reproductions of French tragedy, but you do not miss it in the rantipole interludes (which are emphatically Hill's own) sung between the acts of 'Zara,' and intended to fit French claret for English stomachs, by giving it a dash of brandy; and in which 'He' tells 'She,' that men

—'dream not that eating will appetite tire.'

In 'High Life below Stairs,' one of the cleverest farces of the last century, the offence of the servants is, that they have, at their master's expense, 'had a smack of every sort of wine, from humble Port to imperial Tokay.' There is a rivulet of wine running upon its sparkling course, from the beginning to the end of Congreve's matchless comedies. Valentine plies Trapland the scrivener, who comes to arrest him, with wine, and 'cannot talk about business upon a thirsty palate,' and plies him to the good purpose of a reprieve from arrest. All the metamphors of the play shoot in that direction. Sir Sampson Legend complains that his spendthrift son 'has organs of digestion and concoction large enough for a cardinal;' and goes on, in his grief and wrath, to inquire: 'Why was I

210

not a bear, that my cubs might have lived upon sucking their paws?'
How charmingly, to refer again to Milton, is Comus described:

> 'Offering to every weary traveler
> His Orient liquor in a crystal glass,
> To quench the drought of Phoebus.'

This is a different affair, of course, from the maudlin fun of Sir
John Vanburgh's 'Provoked Wife,' in which Col. Bully sings some
things which we cannot quote, and this which we can and will,
because it is a fair specimen of English bibulosity fairly run to
senseless seed, and of what our ancestors chanted in their cups,
to be found in old songbooks, now very rare, which once lay in the
window-seat beside 'Hale's Pleas of the Crown,' 'Burns' Justice,' and
'Tusser's Husbandry' — *sic* sang Bully:

> 'We're gayly yet, we're gayly yet,
> And we're not very fow, but we're gayly yet:
> Then sit ye awhile, and tipple a bit,
> For we's not very fow, but we're gayly yet.'

This charming canticle so delights Sir John Brute, that he
incontinently declares, that he 'would .not give a fig for a song
that is not full of sin and impudence;' and concludes by exclaiming,
as well as his thick tongue will let him: 'No morality — and damn
the watch! And let the constable be married!' And so he goes out,
like a true gentleman, reeling drunk, to encounter the citizens
airing themselves of a Sunday night, with this pious declaration:
'He that says Sir John Brute is not as drunk, and as religious as
the drunkenest citizen of them all, is a liar.' In the touching letter
which announces the death of Sir Roger de Coverley to the Club,
we are told that he, first of all, 'lost his roast beef stomach.' And
in contrast to this homely touch, is the vigorous Bacchanalian
pard-like ferocity of honest Nat. Lee's 'Alexander.' How he rolls
out, after his flourish of trumpets, into the merely mortal ears of
Perdiccas, Cassandra, and the rest:

> — 'While the bowl goes round,
> Mars and Bellona join to make us music:
> A thousand bulls be offered to the sun,

211

White as his beams; speak the big voice of war;
Beat all our drums, and sound our silver trumpets;
Provoke the gods to follow our example
In bowls of nectar, and replying thunder.'

This is extravagance; but it is at least superb extravagance. Even in protesting against luxury, it is curious to notice how luxurious the English dramatists grow. In 'the Chances,' by Beaumont and Fletcher, the Duke cries out:

—'is there any
Amongst us of so fat a sense, so pampered,
Would choose luxuriously to lie a-bed,
And purge away his spirits; send his soul out
In sugar-sops and sirups?'

which half-converts one to sensuality, like — —'s last novel against *crim. con.*, or Mrs. Flamingo's 'Poems of Passion,' recently collected. There is a mad merriment in the later comic dramatists, which might almost make an epicurean of St. Simon Stylites; and of these, Farquhar pleases one the best, because he is the most cleanly. We take hugely to honest Sergeant Kite enticing the bumpkins 'round the Wrekin,' with 'a purse of gold,' and 'a tub of humming ale,' 'to pull down the French king,' who of course is contemptible, partly because he is a tyrant, and partly because he eats frogs. The gallant Sergeant, when asked, 'What induced him to turn soldier?' replies: 'Hunger and ambition.' The answer has the merit of truthfulness, and moreover, puts one in mind of Falstaff's exquisite: 'What! A young knave, and beg? Is there not wars? Is there not employment?' I suppose, by the way, that all lovers of Shakespeare have remarked what a fine aroma there always is of the taproom and the kitchen, when Sir John trundles in with his roguish tail of followers. The very smell of larder and cellar exhales from the printed page, and the breath of beer and sack comes up to us from sightless flagons. The metaphors are of meat, and the tropes all seem to jump from the durance of tankards. All Eastcheap sings:

'Nunc congregatum nobis est,
Edendum et bibendum.'

There is Corporal Nym's sword, which is 'a simple one; but what

212

though? It will toast cheese.' Bardolph, to make friends, will 'bestow breakfast.' As for the Knight himself, he is always talking like the cleverest and wittiest of cooks or of drawers. The Prince is 'a sneak cup,' but he has a Roland for that Oliver, and Sir John is 'my sweet beef.' Hal says to his 'fat friend' in another place: 'What a devil hast thou to do with the time of the day, unless hours were cups of sack and minutes capons,' etc. If a very hungry man can thrive without cost, and snub his own impecuniosity by sniffing the steam of a cook-shop, surely some fasting scholar in his heavenly attic might find a feast for an emperor in the fat sentences and oozing wit of Sir John Falstaff, while gentlemen and ladies of the vegetarian persuasion might eat 'much good, dry oats' and 'a bottle of hay — good, sweet hay' — with Bottom.

Since it came into fashion either to take no note of the unquestionable fact that we have, even in these our most mortal and contemptible bodies, stomachs, spleens, and omentums, and pyloric orifices and chymes, stimulating our duodenums and our livers, and peristaltic machinery, and all that sort of thing: or to remember these facts, only to see with how much success we can mortify our inward forces into flat revolt and a perpetual jostle — since, I say, all this came into fashion, nobody is allowed to speak of what he eats, unless he pleases to eat like the beasts that perish; and then he may make an immense noise in private circles, or, upon his personal responsibility, convoke a convention. When a man has lived for two years upon sawdust and molasses, he considers that circumstance of sufficient importance to be mentioned in the newspapers, or even in the monthly magazines; and he will be more than usually modest if he calls no convention to pass five-and-twenty resolutions upon the subject of his successful starvation, and to present him with a silver pudding-stick. Another gentleman, who has scorned stint, and who has consulted no table to discover that wild turkey is digested in two hours and eighteen minutes, while the domestic bird requires two hours and twenty-five minutes; who does not know how his food is introduced into his stomach, and has not the least notion what is done with it after it gets there; who eats

213

partly that he may drink, and who 'drinks liquor' (as they say in New England) of the best accessible vintage: this good liver, I say, albeit upon his genial barbarities he grows stalwart and jolly and contented and benevolent, never thinks of writing to the editors — for which they are much obliged to him — and attends no conventions save those of the political party of which he is probably an ornament and valuable defender. He is discreditably vigorous, has a most infamous chance of achieving longevity, and will probably be ingloriously lamented by his friends, who will send him to his dishonored tomb without deeming it to be at all needful to glorify and magnify themselves upon the occasion of his exit.

For my own part, whenever I am engaged in any research, biographical, historical, geographical, or ethnological, I invariably experience great inward comfort and refreshment from what I may call the edibilities and potabilities of literature. When I was a boy, I read the life of Abyssinian Bruce, and the fact which stuck in my tender memory was that, when other provision was unattainable, he ate raw beefsteaks 'cut from a living cow.' In 'Poor Robin's Intelligencer,' London, 1675, 1 find an enterprising victualer of Moregate advertising the same thing, save that he cooked the beef after he cut it, for which I sincerely trust that he was taken to the Compter, or compelled to flee into Alsatia. My ancestors, or at least one of them, had the honor to be sent to Leicester jail, with George Fox; and I am pleased to learn that George, rather than buy beer of the inhuman jailer, extemporized a decoction of wormwood, which answered well enough for those who found sin and perdition in drinking healths. There was a certain Wiltshire parson, one John Fox, who, being of the Presbyterian faith, was sometimes mistaken for George, and who uttered this most unchristian sentiment, when charged with preaching for hire, 'Fill my belly with good victuals, then call me false prophet, or what you will, or kick me about the house if ye will' — to the intense disgust of the true and original Fox, who records the dreadful admission with becoming indignation. But if George was an anchorite at the table, his present representatives, particularly in the agricultural regions of Pennsylvania, have bravely apostatized. But how refreshing is it to meet a great one in his cups, or a hero at his trencher: Domitian, dining so heartily that he had no stomach for his supper; Vitellius sitting down to a banquet of two thousand fish and seven thousand birds, with his centerpiece of' 'The Shield of Minerva' made of 'the brains of peacocks and the livers of fishes;' Nero, with 'his big belly and slender legs;' fierce, hungry emperors snatching meat from the altar; of Masaniello, whose life has been so musically rendered by Mons. Auber, letting his beloved country go to the bow-wows, while he drank Lachrymae Christi to the extent of 'twelve bottles before breakfast;' of Ferdinand asking his uncle, the Admiral Henriquez, 'to stop and dine, for they had a chicken for dinner;' of Charles at Yuste, with his 'potted capon before he arose, served with sugar, milk, and spices — after which he went to sleep again' — dining at noon, and dining again after vespers, sending leagues upon leagues for sausages of a particular kind, and then reduced *eheu!* to a mess of 'barley water, the yelks of eggs, and senna wine;' of George IV. brewing Regent's Punch; and of the amiable Victoria over the domestic muffin; of King (sartoris gratia) Brummell begging biscuit in his banishment, of soft-hearted pastry cooks; of Napoleon at St. Helena, walking every morning, with his silver cup in his hand, to drink from his favorite spring; and of Gen. Andrew Jackson smoking a corn-cob pipe, and smashing the United States Bank at the same instant. And the Kings of Letters eat and drink in a way which is equally entertaining. Milton was not a gourmand, but many passages in his poems prove that he was an epicure. Bacon lost his life by catching cold in making an antiseptic experiment of stuffing a fowl with snow. Swift got a headache for life by eating stone fruit at Sir William Temple's. James Thomson devoured the sunny side of peaches which he was too indolent to pluck. Steel, as a palliation of his playing truant, sends his wife a present of walnuts. Dr. Johnson threatened to write a cookbook which should drive Mrs. Glasse out of the market, and loved Mrs. Thrale because she gave him 'roast veal stuffed with plums.' And to crown all, when the noble and illustrious Launcelot Langstaff, Esq., collected those immortal works which are called 'Salmagundi,' did he not place upon the title page this extract from the great Psalmanzar, namely:

'In hoc est hoax, cum quiz et jokesez,
Et smokem, toastem, roastem folksez,
    Fee, faw, fum'?

which being interpreted metrically, by Pindar Cockloft, Esq., signfieth:

'With baked and boiled and stewed and toasted,
And friend and broiled and smoked and roasted,
    We treat the town.'

And is there anything in this delicious book more affecting than the death of' 'the Little Man in Black'? 'He pointed to his mouth with an expression of dreadful meaning, and, sad to relate, my grandfather understood that the harmless stranger, deserted by society, was perishing with hunger.' I quote a passage which everybody must remember, because, alas! How many years ago, I was wont to weep over it, particularly about the blessed Christmas time, when I was usually in a condition of turkey and pudding proper for its appreciation. Irving, like all sensible men, does not despise deipnological aid. Witness the glorious supper which preceded the dreadful catastrophe of Mr. Ichabod Crane — which may not have been a banquet for gods, but was certainly something better — a banquet for men! It would take us a pretty time, I fancy, to grow fat upon ambrosia and nectar; and talking of nectar, let us end by remembering pretty Evangeline — gentle, black-eyed Evangeline — fair, in sooth,

'When in the harvest heat she bore to the reapers at noontide
Flagons of home-brewed ale, ah! fair in sooth was the maiden.'

But it is time to rise from our humble repast. '*Nunc est bibendum!*' This glass only to dear memories — to those who will no more gather about the old domestic board with gladsome sunrise shining in every face; to the brave and true and generous who once rang their empty glasses upon the hospitable mahogany, when life was young and hearts were hopeful, and we had not tasted the fennel in the cup! The lights are all extinguished — the dust of time has dried the wine which was spilled from the tossing flagons; there are no flowers now upon those stricken brows! Here in my chamber I call you, dear friends of youth and manhood! I call, but you 'answer not again.' And so, since I must drink only to what is left of the wealth of life, I call with Christopher Sly, 'for a pot of small ale.' Away with 'sack cups' and 'conserves' — 'a pot of small ale!'

X

A Chapter on Eating

MARCH 1848

— 'HUNGERING man,
Fretful if unsupplied.'

MR. LEONIDAS BOYD had partaken of a plentiful breakfast; he had read the morning papers through; he had stood directly in front of the fire, with his hands clasped under his coat-skirts, and was thoroughly warm; he had kicked off his slippers, and drawn on his nicely polished boots; he had muffled up in his sack, neck-cloth and gloves, put on his hat, and was passing down the door-steps, when a voice from behind arrested his progress; for Mrs. Leonidas Boyd exclaimed, 'Don't forget the salt, my dear!' and a moment after, 'nor the salaeratus and starch!'

As men go, Mr. Leonidas Boyd was a good man, a kind husband, and an indulgent father. Not a day passed but his handkerchief was tied into a half-dozen knots to remind him of things he never would remember; not a day in which he did not say, 'Yes, my child,' and 'I will, my dear,' to requests he was sure to forget. The butcher's bill, the coal-man's bill, the flour-man's bill, the house rent, were all quickly settled, and cheerfully he bought cotton cloth, new dresses, bonnets and schoolbooks; but there was ever a mystery to his masculine understanding. He could not comprehend what became of the minor groceries that went into his house; and as he paced with quick steps the road leading to his place of business, his meditations ran thus:

'Don't forget the salt, my dear!' No, I won't forget the salt; but I wonder what has become of the last I bought! 'Starch and salaeratus,' too. I never taste salaeratus in anything; the cook must just throw that away; and starch — let me see; that goes into my shirts; but it can't take a pound for a shirt. There's 'soap,' too, and 'a few more eggs, my dear.' Last week it was 'some indigo, and a new mop; a little sand and some soda;' tomorrow it will be 'Bristol-brick and a pound of ginger.' What women want of so many things I cannot imagine; but my wife shall have what she wants if she is rational about what she calls 'house-keeping.''

Every town has its Mr. Leonidas Boyds; men whose perceptions are obtuse on the subject of small domestic needs; men to whom little wants are no wants at all, and to whose minds what they do not see used is sure to be wasted; men who wonder where the salt goes, men who think women make too much ado about housekeeping; men, in short, who are great connoisseurs of the culinary art in general, but have no conception of its multiplicity of details, and who buy butter, sugar, lard, pepper and spice, and verily think that they are doing their wives a great favor. Eating is on the whole a serious business. When we take into consideration the sustaining of vital energies and the consequent actions, the office of cook becomes one of solemn interest; and the incessant demands made by that orifice with which the 'human face divine' is garnished, seem but reasonable. The republican sometimes wonders if royalty condescends to roast potatoes and bread-and-butter, and thinks that Victoria should, like the fairies, be fed on broiled rose-leaves; or, if mortal, on pound cake and custard; at the farthest, should Her Majesty choose a bit of flesh, let it be a 'squab-angel' or some cherub oysters. Prince Albert might have 'four-and-twenty blackbirds baked in a pie,' and have high precedent therefore; and Montezuma, we read, relished his stew or fricassee of tender little children; a dish difficult to be furnished often in a private family. But common people with common appetites will submit to coarse fare; and ever since our great-grandmother Eve got into the foolish habit of waiting upon Adam and handing him apples, it has fallen to woman's lot to be a cooking animal. Ages ago it was established as a fact that the way to a man's heart was through his stomach. The Irishman sitting by his peat-fire, begrimed with smoke, thinks

'The very best comfort, under the sun,
Is to sit by the fire till the 'taters is done.'

A Dutchman smiles when he sees snits and scralls, and tastes sourkrout. The Southern Negro will dance after eating his poke-greens and bacon. The city loafer is only happy when

'Some faithful she
Is fryin' sassengers for he.'

The city merchant cries:

'A Fine leg of mutton, my dearie,
    I pri'thee have ready at three;
Have it smoking and tender and juicy,
    And what better dish can there be?'

The city 'merchant-lord' must have his many courses; the fisherman his 'lobscouse,' and the backwoodsman his 'chicken-fixins'' and 'shanty-cake.' The careful housewife, 'taught by experience, soon discerns what pleases, what offends;' and with this experience before her eyes, what wonder that her heart is often in a greater tumult than the pots boiling tempestuously over the fire, and that her spirits will rise and fall with the bread in the oven? A kitchen; what is it? In the words of another, 'it is not a warehouse, nor a washhouse; a brew-house, nor a bake-house; an inn-house, nor an outhouse, nor a dwelling house. No; 'tis absolutely and bona-fide neither more nor less than a kitchen; or as the law more classically expresses it, 'a kitchen is camera necessaria pro usus cookare cum sauce-pannis, stew-pannis, scullero, dressero, coal-holo, stovis, smoke-jacko, pro roastandum, boilandum, fryandum, et plumb-pudding mixandum, pro turtle-soupus, calves'-head hashibus, cum calipee et calipashibus.' And to be captain of this establishment, keep each boiler from bursting, and make three regular trips daily, and found, from thence to the family table, requires some skill, fortitude and patience; yes! and 'sugar and spice, that's very nice.'

A man's theory of cooking consists in 'stirring up something' and baking it until it is done; carried into practice, it would be worse even than the French 'olla podrida,' wherein 'a little of *anything* you have got is put into a pot half full of water, boiled an hour, seasoned with salt and pepper, and served up hot;' or on a festival day it might amount to the Spanish recipe for the same dish: 'Take a little of *everything* you have got, boil it hard for an hour, season it to your taste, and garnish it with parsley.' There is little romance about a kitchen fireplace. The beautiful theory of living upon the fruits of the earth is charming to the young maiden on the eve of matrimony and housekeeping. She will regale herself and her husband on apples, peaches and pears for breakfast. She will never become a drudge in her own house — not she! No doubt but a turnip field and a good well of water would sustain life; but we opine that our lord of creation would find his way to a cook-shop and our lady fair seek for consolation where the Duchess of Orleans said she could always find it in her times of affliction; in eating ham and sausages. Yet, after all, there is a satisfaction in having 'got up one's victuals' nicely, apart from the mere eating of them. A trifle, a stick of green wood, a falling of a little soot from the chimney, a grain of salt or pepper too much or too little, and alas for the dinner! Or if the housekeeper has done it by means of her independent proxy, viz.; 'help,' then the trifle of a soft or hard word, and the whole family circle must be happy or unhappy. Happy it is, and she rejoices over her dinner, and feels thankful when it is over. Had Madam Nature (a pretty good world-keeper, we think,) hung dinners on apple trees and made vines to bear good cooked breakfasts, caused the earth to send up bubbling springs of good hot soup, and made turkeys to run about roasted and chickens to issue fricasseed from the white houses of their infancy, we doubt whether man or womankind would have been as well satisfied. Did not Pat Tigg enjoy himself hugely when he thought,

''Tomorrow I'll kill my fat pig,
   For I'm sure he'll make illigant mutton
So then he goes into the hovel,
   And hangs the pig up by the heel,
Cuts his throat so nate with the shovel,
   And cries, 'This is the way to dress veal!'

And did not the cobbler's wife bustle about and feel consequentially happy when her lame-legged spouse hung out his little shingle?

   'Here Kake and Pise and Bier I sell,
   And oysters stoo'd and in the shel.
   And frighed uns tew for them that chews,
   And with despatch mends Butes and Shews!'

Then hear how like a connoisseur the black man tells us the best way to cook the pearly grains of rice: 'Wash him well, much wash in cold water; rice flour make him stick; wash all quite away. Water boil very fast; throw rice in, boil quarter-hour, or more, rub one rice between thumb and finger; if all rub away, him quite done. Put rice in cullender, hot water go away; pour cup of cold water on him; put him back in saucepan; keep him covered by fire; then he all ready. Eat him up—he very good!' Yes, Mr. Pompey, Cato, or Plenty, whatever your name be, 'he very good,' and you love to cook him.

For every dish there is a time and season; Solomon the king said so before we did, and the Spanish proverb regarding oranges, 'gold in the morning, silver at noon, and lead at night,' will hold true of other things. Charles Lamb discourses like a lover over his roast pig, with its delicate crackling and tender flesh, with which he delighted himself at the midday meal; but hear the Dutchman's experience of the same dish for supper:

   'Sometimes when 1 eat von pig supper, I treams
   Dat mine shtomach ish filt full of shtones,
   Und out in mine shleep, like ter Tivel, I schreams,
   Und kicks off de ped-clothes, and groans!

223

'Den dere ash I lays, mit de ped-clothes all off,
  I gits myself all over froze,
In de morning I wakes mit te het-ache and koff.
  Und I'm shick from mine het to mine toes!'

Who wants buckwheat cakes on a hot summer morning, chicken pie when they are ill, or gruel when they are well? The man who desires green peas in December and relishes cucumbers in January is one who would turn the world upside down, and ought himself to be put under a forcing-glass until better tastes and aims are developed. We like a dinner in style, with its bit of biscuit and napkin, its silver fork and finger-glass, its soup, its fish, its roast and boiled, its game, its salad, its pies and jellies, its fruit, its wines; but deliver us from it on Thanksgiving day! Give us then the roast turkey and cranberry sauce, the boiled chicken and apple sauce, the well-boiled ham with its little pepper and clove bouquets, the chicken pie and pickles, and a fine array of well-cooked vegetables, and let us eat plentifully of each and all, and save only room and appetite for the snow-like pastry, so sure to follow. How readily then will one cry, 'Temperance is true luxury!'

If every dish has its times and seasons, no less truly hath every person their likings and their antipathies. What man likes a 'picked up dinner,' or will not consider it as tasting of the cupboard? How mincingly will a child pick at its plate of boiled dinner — 'pot luck,' the grandmothers call it. How many like the old maid's hash-up,' where that same boiled dinner appears the second time, salt beef, pork, potatoes, turnips and cabbage all finely minced, and warmed with the melted butter, a little salt, pepper and vinegar? Who has not seen the eyes of the boarding school boy almost suffused with tears as he gazed upon the codfish dinner, alias 'Nantucket owls?' What American loves sour-krout, and what Dutchman does not? Or what Jew will eat pork?

Americans have few national dishes, saving and excepting those made of the Indian corn. What better dish than a good Johnny cake?

'Sissing. steaming;
Up the water liquid boils,
Kettle in, o'er hanging coals.
Now the cook, so kindly careful hasty takes the spoon,
With a tow-cloth, up the kettle see her take.
Pour the water, none demurring.
On meal yellow, keep it stirring,
Till 'tis fit for making cake.
On round tin
Outspread thin,
Down she puts it before the fire,
The flame outbreaking rises higher.
The inward spirit of the mass is moving,
And all its mighty energies is proving
It swells, it swells, oh smack your lips,
The crust begins to brown.
Take care; oh! me, it moves, it slips
There, there; 'tis falling down!
Oh! how tempting; oh! oh! how it
Seems to woo the butter standing near!
Think'st thou, thankless reader, think'st thou
Johnny cakes no more to tell thee?
Know then, feel then, somehow, no how
Higher, deeper thoughts should swell thee.
One big universal large
Johnny cake the world contains,
Huger than one rehearsal
Could be told in many strains,
Oh! the noble, all including transcendental make
Of inward, outward, upward, great world,
Johnny Cake!
Sure there'll be a new creation.
Sure there won't be no starvation.
Spirit aiding; heart up-moving;
Life reviving; health improving.
New Ideal;
Super-real
Indian Johnny Cake!'

Would that all the Paddies and Paddies' wives but believed this! The French are the great cooks of the world, and Paris the great cook-shop. Mons. Moustache in his hotel boils his biggin of coffee over the spirit-lamp, buys his egg, and sheet of paper for firewood to cook it, and breakfasts with grace and goût, morning after morning. Taste if you dare the fricandeau he serves you for dinner. It may be cat, dog, or a piece of his grandfather, who knows? But the gravy who but a Frenchman could compound such a gravy? And 'gravy is to meat what a veil is to a homely woman,' or shade trees to an old house! We are content in France to live as Frenchmen do; but give us here in our glorious republic dishes that can do without so much gravy, and that we may eat without fear and trembling in our hearts. Hotel keepers in Yankee-doodle-dum, oh! give us Yankee-doodle fare! and thrust no more in our faces your long bills of fare (that we cannot read,) of dishes that we cannot relish! Let the Englishman ask as long as he pleases,

'Who hath not seen homemade bread
A heavy compound of putty and lead!'

We don't have that kind, since the 'price of putty is riz;' but we have the fine white loaf with its golden crust; yes, and we have even feasted on its sweetness before a morsel touched our lips. We have seen, too, delicate slices of broiled ham, the potatoes like snowballs. We have eaten Yankee baked beans and fried hasty pudding, the nicely broiled shad; and the more elaborate meal of chicken pie, roast sirloin or spare rib; but each and all have we known and greeted like old acquaintances, and they spoke to us in their and our vernacular, and asked us, as little Red Riding Hood did the make-believe grandmother, 'What have you got such a great mouth for?' and we, wolf-like, have answered, 'To eat you all up with,' and felt that we would reverse the stoical maxim and cry, 'We live to eat, not eat to live.'

But lest any Mrs. Leonidas Boyd should think that, after all, we have not told where the salt goes, let us give the great Sidney Smith's recipe for dressing salad. He knew, if anybody did, the best way of getting up pungent, smart dishes:

'Two largo potatoes, passed through kitchen seive,
Smoothness and softness to the salad give;
Of *mordant* mustard add a single spoon.
Distrust the condiment that bites too soon;
But deem it not, oh! man of herbs, a fault,
To add a double quantity of salt:
Four times the spoon with oil of Lucca crown,
And twice with vinegar procured from town;
True flavor needs it, and your poet begs
The pounded yellow of two well-boiled eggs,
Let onions atoms lurk within the bowl,
And scarce suspected, animate the whole
And lastly, in the flavored compound toss
A magic spoonful of anchovy sauce.
Oh! great and glorious; oh! herbaceous treat;
'Twould tempt the dying anchorite to eat
Back to the world he'd turn his weary soul,
And plunge his fingers in the salad bowl!'

Potatoes, mustard, salt, Lucca oil, vinegar, eggs, onions and anchovy sauce, articles to the number of eight, just to make *a dip* wherein to put the 'herbaceous' feast; upon which man could never thrive, hardly live, and never relish without his bit of bread! Oh! murmuring man, slack provider for a family, contemner of small wants, slanderer of woman's economy! Mr. Leonidas Boyd, would you have thought it?

Angola, Iowa, Jan. 15th, 1838.

XI

My First Dinner Out

BY R. M'PHERSON, ESQ.

JULY 1833

"So may ye gain to your full great renowne
Of all good ladies through the world so wide;
And happy in her heart find highest rowme
Of whom ye seek to be most magnifyde."

— *Faery Queene.*

ON LOOKING over some old papers, a few days since, my attention was arrested by a nicely folded note, gilt-edged, and bearing upon its broken seal the remnant of a most sentimental motto. On opening the paper its contents recalled to mind a scene that neither time nor circumstance can entirely eradicate from my memory. The note was a mere card of invitation to dinner: it had lain, undisturbed, among a host of other interesting documents for years, but no sooner did my eyes glance over it than the recollection of circumstances connected therewith, came upon me with all the freshness of reality, and an involuntary cacchination burst from my lips at the remembrance. At the time this note was received, I was a student, residing, for the time being, in Branton. There was one great man in this village, at that time — one man, I mean, especially great — a candidate for a seat in the State Legislature! He was, moreover, a colonel of militia, — owned large tracts of land somewhere between the Mississippi and the Rocky Mountains; and possessed, withal, a considerable estate — the homestead of his family, where he then resided. This gentleman was a sort of "lord of the manor" with the villagers; he had a warm heart; was a man of a kind, liberal disposition; and if he had a fault it was one possessed by greater men than Colonel Bronson. He was ambitious, — so was Julius Caesar. He wished to represent the "free and independent electors" of Branton, in their state assembly, and he would stop at nothing fair and honorable to accomplish his object. Party spirit ran high at this time, and the "free and independent electors" of Branton were divided in their opinions. The opponent of the Colonel in this political strife was a blacksmith, a most worthy man; true and firm as the steel he hammered, and about as easy to bend. This man was a federalist of the old school — so was *not* Colonel Bronson. The smith was on the point of success, in consequence of a flaming speech that "went home to men's business and bosoms," and was sent there by a certain lawyer, who had an eye to the smith's daughter, and over her shoulder to a fair proportion of the smith's goods and chattels. I know not how it was, whether influenced by that *"cacoethes scribendi,"* which, since my first graceless efforts at school, has haunted me like a ghost, or whether it was to shine in the admiration of a certain "blue-eyed Mary," who called the Colonel "father," or to tickle the embryo-senator himself, but from some cause or other I was influenced to write a reply to the lawyer's speech. It appeared the next week, and the subtle reasoning, bold argument, and doubtful truths of the aforesaid attorney were (to use his own elegant expletive) "used up." This was my first public literary attempt; if a furious political tirade, filled with patriotic sentiments, and breathing red-hot democracy in every line, deserves such a *soubriquet*. The Colonel was mightily pleased; he considered his election a thing decided, and forthwith betook himself to the study of Burke; assumed a dignified senatorial air, set his house in order, and began to make sundry necessary arrangements for a six-month sojourn in the capitol. He was not disappointed. The election shortly after took place; — the exquisite morceau of which I was guilty, was printed on handbills, and dignified with a conspicuous situation on the town pump — opposite the handle, and was read aloud by the village tailor, mounted on a stump. The little "man of nine" seasoned my patriotism with sundry oratorical flourishes that were irresistible; and the Colonel was after the canvass, declared "duly elected." This was a great triumph for democracy! Colonel Bronson was a grateful man; he gave a dinner to the "free and independent" democrats of Branton; and for my services on the occasion — which somehow or other became known — I received an especial card of invitation. Now, although I had been "through college," I was at that time — strange as it may appear — troubled with bashfulness, and the idea of facing a public assemblage of all the notables of the county, (and there were a good many,) was, to my delicate imaginings, as agreeable as the idea of facing a full-mouthed battery. I considered the matter long and seriously. I thought of the elegant attitudes which my *mauvaise honte* would probably place me into, — attitudes to be criticized, — it was probable, — by sundry female virtuosos to be then and there present; Mary among the rest. I thought of being called upon for a toast, and imagined my own graceful figure (four feet and a fraction) behind a pitcher, I thought of *a stool!* And yet I dared not decline. Mortal offence would be taken in a quarter where I had particular reasons for wishing to appear amiable. Mary might think — Go I must. I "screwed my courage to the sticking place," and at half-past two precisely, with a trembling hand, I gave the finishing *pinch* to a pair of invisible whiskers, that I was then endeavoring to coax into a promising existence, and wondering, the while, whether Adonis was troubled with bashfulness — I adjusted my hat fiercely on my brow, and set out for the mansion of the great man.

Not having, in the course of my experience, ever faced an enemy's front, nor in my soarings after immortality, addressed a crowded house from the stage of a theatre, I cannot draw a comparison between the daring bravery of the one, and the moral courage of the other; nor can I, from the experience of others, find anything like a similitude to my feelings, as I entered the withdrawing room of Branton House. There stood my host in the midst of an assemblage that, to my eyes, had all the horrors of Pandemonium. He stretched forth his hand as I entered, with a self-possession that astonished me. "Ah, Mr. McPherson — allow me, sir, to —, Miss Tabitha Bronson, Mr. McPherson, —My daughter Mary, sir, — Mr. Fitz Fugle, my friend Doctor Ipecac, — Squire Botherum, Mr. McPherson — Mr. McPherson, Squire Botherum — sit down, sir; sit down and be acquainted with the rest of our friends here."

I sat down. Not knowing exactly what to do with my *hat*, I fixed it firmly between my knees, where, for some moments I gazed upon it, as it shook between its trembling supporters. This was agreeable, and I felt as if, at that moment, 1 would have sold myself, hat and all — cheap! I made an effort to speak, and addressed myself to Mary, who, it happened, sat at the farthest extremity of the room, by the side of the gentleman to whom I had been introduced as Squire Botherum — a tall, gaunt, upright backwoodsman, — a relative of the Colonel's, and about as rough a specimen of humanity as I ever looked upon. "You have a pleasant view from this window, Miss Bronson." She did not hear me. I might have expected that, for the backwoodsman was just then emitting an observation in his double; bass, that would have silenced a moderate thunderclap. I tried again. "This window, Miss Bronson, commands a pleasant prospect." The squire held his breath this time, but still she did not hear me. I trembled more than ever. At this moment the servant offered to take my hat — I gave him my *handkerchief;* — Mary laughed; it must have been at my awkwardness; nothing, I thought, but that, could at such a moment have awakened her risibilities. I was astonished at the rudeness of some people. Suddenly, mastering my timidity, I made another desperate effort. "I observed, Miss Bronson, that you had a fine *view* from this window" — she heard me. "No, sir," said she, "'tis not a *yew* — 'tis a poplar!" I felt uneasy; I moved quickly in my seat; and, as if to fill up the measure of my confusion, a villainous snuff box rolled from my pocket, and scattered, as it fell, a thousand pinches of Bolongaro, full in the face of Miss Tabby, who, if she "abhors anything," as she afterwards observed, "abhors snuff." The lady (oh, breathe it not in Askalon,) sneezed; the gentleman next to her sneezed; the Colonel sneezed; the infection spread through the rooms, and one general sternutation shook the air. I seized the unlucky snuff box, and in a fit of mortification, hurled it through the air; some particles of the tillittating compound must have remained in the box, for, as it passed from my hand, I saw the doctor spring from his chair with a whirl — such an one as Forrest might make in Metamora — and uttering a pithy anathema, apply his handkerchief to his blood-shot eyeballs. ****** I cannot proceed. Apologies were applied to the company; cold water to the eyes of the doctor; and the *coterie* moved to the dining room. Here I was especially honored; a seat was placed for me at the right hand of the senator-elect — a most conspicuous situation at the top of the table. I would to heaven it had been less conspicuous, even had it been *under* the table. There were several ladies near me, to whom — having by this time, in a measure recovered myself — I *did* intend to be particularly amiable. Everything went on smoothly, and I felt quite at home. Indeed, so far did my self-possession carry me, that I was astonished at catching myself in the very act of sporting, with the air of an improvisatore, sundry bon-mots and exceeding smart witticisms, which, for the last two days, I had been excogitating from the dry remnant of my college reminiscences; and it was certainly with a degree of amiable complacency that I listened to sundry complimentary remarks from the lower end of the table, on the uncommon talent evinced by the *unknown* author of a certain political essay. I began to flatter myself that an impression had been made, not only on the minds of the male politicians, but also on the hearts of the *ladies* (dear souls,) by the said political essay. Miss Tabby sat opposite to Squire Botherum, and being herself a little bit of "a blue," she was endeavoring to set off the sparkles of her wit, by making a foil of the man of law.

"Are the waters of the Black River, in your backwoods, Mr. Botherum, literally *black?*" inquired the damsel. "Black as a thunder cloud, madam." "Is it possible! What a contrast to the waters of the Black River, are the translucid waters of Helicon!" "Hel— what, madam?" "Ah, I perceive, Squire, you have not wandered, in imagination, along the banks of Castaly: delicious streams, made immortal by the pen of Esculapius, the Stagyrite! Where bowers, shaded by the myrtle and the vine, invite to heavenly repose; and where cluster the golden grapes, whose exquisite juices fill the soul with ethereal imaginings; where" — "I'll trouble you for a potato, madam?" Miss Tabby turned in disgust from the monster, and settled upon Mr. Fitz Fugle, who, secure in all the gracious puppyism of a New York dandy, was ensconced in an armchair beside her. A gentleman of consideration was Mr. Fitz Fugle, the graceful twist of whose mustachios struck an agony of awe to the hearts of the unsophisticated damsels of Bronson. He wore the latest New York fashions, his hair "à la Brute," and his moustache "à la Cussaque." Mr. Fitz Fugle was, in short, an exquisitely finished gentleman. What brought Mr. Fitz Fugle to a place, which, to his gentility appeared, (as he was pleased to say,) an "untamed wilderness," I knew not, unless it was to procure for his hair some unadulterated *bear's grease* — an article then in great demand with "perfect gentlemen."

"I have heard," said the dandy, addressing Mary, "I have heard that you have some aspiring *geniuses* in this part of the country, Miss?" "Indeed! We are plain people here, sir, and I believe our *genius* consists principally in" — "Raising large turnips!" interrupted Botherum. Mary smiled at her uncle, and the conversation was continued in a rather low tone. When Mr. Fitz Fugle spoke of *geniuses* I pricked up my ears, and began to feel some respect for him; but the discourse afterwards was carried on in such an undertone, that I could only now and then catch a word. They were evidently speaking of some promising youth in the neighborhood. The words, small stature — promising look — ambitious — gold cup — beat his opponent, only, I could distinctly hear. I never flattered myself without cause, but I was *tolerably* certain that *I* was the subject of their commendations; "small stature," — four feet to a fraction, — "promising look," "ambitious," — me exactly, — "gold cup," "beat his opponent — aha, there could be no doubt of it! Colonel Bronson, as I said before, was a grateful man; and he, in gratitude for "*the* political essay," was, undoubtedly, about to present me with a "gold cup" for thus assisting him to "beat his opponent" at the hustings; and it was *this* then—oh, it must be *this*—they were talking of, and in a whisper, too, that I should not hear them. I was delighted! The world would hear of it!

Only think, a "gold cup!" — my name in German text on one side, — Genius placing a wreath around my brows on the other — neat device — sentence of gratitude—Anno Domini—Glorious! I would not have exchanged situations with the author of Waverley! I listened to hear more. I seemed to stretch the drums of my ears almost to bursting. I leaned forward, but all was still. They had undoubtedly observed my attention, and would not speak for fear of embarrassing me. I pretended to be wholly absorbed with the wing of a fowl, but all my ears were open. Suddenly Botherum broke out — "Yes, that *was* a fine colt!"

A COLT! The ladies were about to retire; the Colonel arose requesting them to remain. Would to heaven they had retired, or that their eyes and ears had become inanimate, and every sense of observation palsied — that they might not have been witnesses of my shame. The Colonel made a speech; his health was drunk; he made another, and then, — oh, horrible, — gave a toast! Why, in the name of decency, these villainous compounds of trash are countenanced and encouraged, I invoke the spirit of Chesterfield to answer! But I was prepared — thank the gods! I had "written out" a toast expressly for the occasion. I had *learnt* it, and I knew I could give it with effect. Alas, how far from just is a man's conception of his powers; how little does *he* know who has not ventured. But I was brimful of resolution. Few hearts quail *after* dinner; why should mine then!

My turn came. The Colonel had, in his toast or speech, I forget which, complimented the author of *the* political essay. So much the better—*my* toast would be the more appropriate. I seized the decanter; I poured forth the liquid which was to be the usher of my confusion; I arose; all eyes were upon me. I was cool as one of Contoit's ices. I raised the glass: "Ladies and gentlemen permit me to return thanks for the honor done me on this very flattering occasion, and offer" — Here, — oh, horror! — in advancing my left foot, in order to assume a more Demosthenian attitude, I stepped — oh, most unlucky chance — upon the hindmost extremity of a *cat!* A short, vituperative yowl, to which the roar of a lion seemed a whisper, issued from the lungs of this villainous rat catcher! I could have crept into a wine glass! I wished myself with Vanderdecken or Dr. Faustus — anywhere but there. The ladies elevated their handkerchiefs, and turned their heads — the gentlemen, ditto. There was a bursting desire to laugh — confound them — but I recovered myself. "Ladies and gentlemen," (I spoke as loud as a town crier,) "permit me to offer our honorable host — the worthy head of the *cat* — confusion — beg pardon. Ladies and gentlemen, our honorable host — the worthy head of the free and independent — Demo-*cats* of Branton!" This was too much. There was a roar from one end of the table to the other. Mary Bronson laughed! The glass was to my lips: — in utter agony I dashed it to the earth, and rushed — I know not where.

On returning from the wedding of Mary Bronson and Frederick Alonzo Fitz Fugle, two months after the event related above, I had the felicity of planting a ball exactly between the ears of a certain feline quadruped, whose "still small voice," as she leaped a fence was not to be mistaken.

XII

Knowledge for the People

GASTRONOMY

FEBRUARY 1840

GASTRONOMY, properly speaking, is the science of the table, but among seamen it is known as panthology, their food being always served up in pans.

We have no institution in which this art is taught, but in England they have an Eaton College.

The feeding establishments connected with our literary institutions are termed 'commons,' in consequence of the inferior quality of food served up.

Starvation or absence from food is a very popular mode among physicians of ridding themselves of troublesome patients.

Gruel is a common expedient in such cases. The term is a corruption of 'growl,' from the effect which it produces upon both tongue and stomach. It is made by thickening a teaspoon full of flour or meal with a gallon of water.

A few years since the physicians, fearing that the demand for food would be greater than the supply, invented a new disease, called the dyspepsia, which is a patent method of starving men to death by a slow but sure process. The dyspepsia is first cousin to the 'hypo,' and connected to the 'hysterics' by marriage.

Women were probably intended to do all the carving, since we are informed that Eve was given to Adam for a help-meat.

With regard to the usances of the table, we would remark, for the benefit of the uninitiated, that it is considered to be a breach of etiquette to use the napkin (a tablecloth) in lieu of a handkerchief, especially if one has a cold in the head; that toothpicks should not be applied to the car should the fingers be washed in the wine glass; and that silver forks are not intended to eat soup with.

Gastronomy and astronomy are different, although both are illustrated by a series of plates; yet persons who have been indulging in the pleasures of the table are very apt to see stars, and examine intently revolutions both of celestial and terrene bodies.

XIII

Outlines of Phaceology

BY J.E.G

FEBRUARY 1840

'Let me have a luncheon of bread, and about four pounds of raisins, for really and truly, I cannot live without eating. The stomach supports the head, and not the head the stomach.'

— Sancho Panza.

PHACEOLOGY IS the science which treats of the appetites, and certain marks upon the human countenance corresponding with them. This science cannot fail to commend itself to every inquisitive mind. An acquaintance with it will reveal the habits of men by a glance at the countenance, so that the main points in the character of an individual may be known almost instantly. Upon the importance of such an acquaintance to the merchant, the mechanic, the professional man, the lover, the *lovee,* the bachelor, the maid, in fine to all classes of persons, it is unnecessary to expatiate. It is true that Phrenology, in this respect, is in a measure useful; but when we consider that the head is almost invariably covered with hair, natural or artificial, we shall decide, once and for all, that Phaceology is *the* science on which we are to rely for an immediate knowledge of the human character.

There are implanted in the breast of every individual of the human family, appetites; and these appetites acquire strength in proportion to their gratification. Between them and the physiognomy there is a connection so mysterious, that the indulgence of the former, to an improper extent, will produce evidence thereof in legible marks upon the latter. These marks are ORGANS. There may be some captious individuals disposed to doubt this, or even deny it *in toto;* to such I will say, that I cannot waste my time and talents in endeavoring to prove what is self-evident.

Phaceology is divided into:

I.   MASTICATIVE PHACEOLOGY, which relates to the appetite for food.

II.   BIBATIVE PHACEOLOGY, which relates to the appetite for drink.

Masticative Phaceology has two organs: those of GUSTIFULLNESS, and GORMANDIZABILITY.

I. GUSTIFULLNESS. This organ is a lateral distension of the mouth, accompanied by a sly, inquisitive, cast of countenance. It is peculiar to individuals who are in the habit of tasting whatever of an eatable nature is within their reach, and continue tasting to the great gratification of their palate, and to the great annoyance of the owner of the thing tasted. Such individuals are egregious nuisances in society, and may be readily known by a little attention to the organ. Good housewives and retail grocers will find an acquaintance with the organ particularly useful; the former in ascertaining the character of 'help' that may offer for employment, and the latter in acquainting themselves with the habits of their visitors!

II. GORMANDIZABILITY. There is a great inclination in some men literally to cram themselves with food. They have a peculiar relish for the good things of the table, and indulge their appetites to such excess, that soon the countenance loses its naturally healthy look and proportions, and becomes inflated and inflamed. The organ of gormandazibility may be traced in each direction, from the summits of the cheeks, to points between the eyebrows, and in the chin. It is of a Spanish-brown hue, and is scabbed. A knowledge of this organ will be of vast importance to gentlemen who are in the habit of having dinner parties and suppers; especially if they are economists, from choice or necessity.

The organs of Bibative Phaceology are:

I. SANGAREETIVENESS. II. EGGPOPSTABILITY. III. VINEFRETABILITY. IV. BUSTIVELOCITATIVENESS. V. PUNCHVOLUBLENESS. VI. TODDYTIVENESS. VII. BRANDIFORMITY. VIII. CARBUNCLIVITY. IX. POTHEASIVENESS.

I. SANGAREETIVENESS. There is a luscious drink, the chief ingredients of which are port-wine and loaf-sugar, known by the musical cognomen of sangaree. This drink is sipped with much gusto by people just indulging in the use of alcoholic stimulants. Its flavor is such, that the drinkers of it, frequently before they are aware, become victims to insensibility. The organ of Sangareetiveness is a slight flush of the countenance. It will not be recognized by anyone who is not familiar with the science of Phaceology.

II. EGGPOPSTABILITY. There is another drink, of which rum and eggs are fundamental ingredients, bearing the abrupt name of egg pop, or eggnog. It is much desired by those who are in the early stages of intemperance. The organ is a slight redness of the eye, added to the organ of Sangareetiveness. Men in whom this organ is found, are inclined to instability of mind, and sometimes of body, and may with propriety be called men of Eggpopstability.

III. VINEFRETABILITY. Persons who indulge habitually in the use of wine, and frequently to excess, are subject to fits of irritability; and ultimately the countenance assumes a severity which, with the two preceding organs, forms the organ of Vinefretability.

IV. BUSTIVELOCITATIVENESS. Those who are addicted to the use of sangaree, egg-pop, wine, and drinks of similar character, are more or less in the habit of indulging in wild scenes of inebriety, commonly called 'sprees,' or 'bu'sts;' probably a contraction of *bursts,* signifying a breaking away from sobriety. These persons are called '*bus'ters,*' and are gregarious. When several of them are congregated together, they indulge themselves to such an extent, and their spirits become so elevated, that they find pleasure only in extreme obstreperousness, jactitations of the body, braggardism, and mischievous caperings. 'They have *gymnasia bibonum,* (as old Burton hath it,) schools and rendezvous; these Centaures and Lapithae toss pots and bowls, as so many balls. .... So they triumph in villainy, and justifie their wickedness, with Rabelais, the French

Lucian; drunkenness is better for the body than physick, because there be more old drunkards than old physicians.' Such persons may be known by their blowzy countenances, and inflamed eyes, which together form the organ of Bustivelocitativeness.

V. PUNCHVOLUBLENESS. There is a disposition in excessive drinkers of punch to punch their neighbors, as well as great volubility. They are known by a slightly contracted brow, fiery eye, and half-opened mouth, which compose the organ of Punchvolubleness.

VI. TODDYTIVENESS. There is a warm drink called Toddy, of which old bachelors and old maids are extremely fond. The former, especially, imbibe it until their ratiocinative disposition has oozed out, and they are left in a state of blissful obmutescence. The appetite for this drink may be discovered by the organ of Toddytiveness, which is situated upon the nose, and is vulgarly known by the name of Toddy-blossom.

VII. BRANDIFORMITY. It is not difficult to find this organ in the brandy drinker. The deep vermilion hue of his countenance, and the strong development of the organ of Vinefretability, are always sufficient indications of it.

VIII. CARBUNCLIVITY. This is truly a wonderful organ. It is almost always to be found upon the nose of the old brandy and gin toper, and is composed of shining pustules, of various sizes and hues. When the possessor of this organ has been long addicted to inebriety, it extends itself to the cheekbones and forehead. It has been said that it is used in dark nights, as a lantern to light its owner from the barroom to his cheerless home. Whether we credit this or not, we may safely believe that it is the only lantern with which he should be trusted. For a farther, description of the organ, I refer to Sir John Falstaff.

IX. POTHEASIVENESS. Those persons who make pot-houses their constant resort, and drink the chief part of their subsistence, are always possessed of this organ. It is too well known to require any description here. Look at the confirmed drunkard, and in his countenance you will see the organ of Potheasiveness.

I have thus given some of the outlines of this wonderful science; a science before which all other sciences will hide their diminished heads; a science which, for simplicity and definiteness, certainly cannot be equaled; a science which for sublimity is unrivalled, and for usefulness cannot be matched; a science which requires no bombastic parade, no fulsome panegyric, to obtain for it immediate and lasting celebrity. Time shall be no longer, when it shall cease to exist!

XIV

The Good Wine

BY WILLIAM B. TAPPAN

FEBRUARY 1838

'O thou only God of wine,
Comfort this poor heart of mine,
With that nectar of thy blood.'

ALEXANDER ROSSE, 1650

CYPRIAN wine is not for me,
Nor the juice of Italy;
Nor Atlantic's luscious pride,
Prom Madeira's sunny side;
Nor from Caprea's royal hoard,
Nor from Lisbon's modern board,
Nor from elder Egypt's crypt,
Which Mark Antony hath stripp'd;
Nor from Rhrine or laughing France,
Where Garronne's blue ripples dance,
Nor from banks of classic river,
Winding Po or Guadalquiver.

THE GOOD WINE

All the grapes in vintage crushed,
Could not satisfy my thirst;
Purple flood in chrysolite,
Where it moves itself aright.
Freely pour'd in princely hall,
Sparkling at high festival.
Well refined or on the lees,
Could not my ambition please;
Draught that passing pleasure brings,
Leaving ever-during stings.

When my lips the beaker kiss,
I have other wine than this.
Taken from the fruitful hill.
Which doth live in poesy still;
Where for vine, a cross of wood.
Guarded by the Roman, stood;
Whose rich spoil was gathered when
Triumphed hell and triumphed men:
Crushed and mangled was whose grape,
While the heavens look'd agape,
And in sackcloth hid — whose wine
Streaming dimm'd the mid-day's shine,
Fermented in nature's sigh.
Ripened in the earthquake's cry.

How it stirs my languid blood!
How it cheers my soul, like food!
Drink ye kings! and cares forget,
Drink ye sad! and triumph yet.
Drink ye aged! strength renew,
Drink ye children! 'tis for you.
Drink ye pilgrims! While 'tis nigh —
Drink, nor in the desert die.
Drink ye fainting! thirst ye never,
Drink ye dead! and live forever.

Boston, August 21, 1850.

246

XV

Anecdote of a Bottle of Wine

BY JOHN WATERS

OCTOBER 1843

TRINOULO. Oh Stephano! Hast any more of this?
STEPHANO. The whole butt, man!
CALIBAN. Hast thou not dropp'd from Heaven?
STEPHANO. Out of the moon I do assure thee: I was
    The man in the moon, when time was.
CALIBAN. I have seen thee in her, and I do adore thee;
    My mistress shew'd me thee, thy dog, and bush.

I CONSIDER the wines of France to bear the same rank in comparison with those of other countries that the highest order of lyrical effusion sustains in the world of poetry. Ordinary Rhenish wines are its satires and pasquinades; Port is didactic verse; while among the first growths of the Rheingau, of Madeira, and of Spain, are to be sought the Shakespeares, the Homers, the Miltons, Virgils and Dantes of the wine-crypt.

It is in conformity with this poetical disposition of things, that, when I expect a visit from my friends, I descend into my wine-vault or mount the stairs of my attic. There, with keys in hand, I unloose the spirits of the mighty past, and restore in their happiest temperament and condition, and to their bright and animated destiny, the effulgent glories of the grape.

It was not always thus, dear John! 'I do assure thee,' as my motto says, 'when time was,' a few cobweb'd bottles of old Madeira

247

upon the upper shelf of a chamber closet not too near the surface of the earth, and a case or two, and basket or two, in a distant receptacle, were, in the golden days of thy better manhood, but faint precursors of thy rich and cherished hoards; thy vaulted cellar and thy loaded wine-chamber — fraught as these now are with the result of distant voyages, of curious tastings, of patient research, and of elaborate choice illustrated with a benignant and happy fortune. And yet those were glad days, bright days, precious days; were they not? What a flavor, what a zest the wines wore when thou and I were young! And the cookery! Dear Sirs, how well dressed things were in those days!

We were living in a French boarding house celebrated for its *cuisine.* Our wine of course depended upon our proper self, but I have never met with a better *table d'hôte* than we were wont to be seated at, particularly upon any intimation to our worthy host that we expected friends, and wished to entertain them with our best. There was nothing of the 'busy hum of preparation,' nor any anxiety about the successful practice of the cook, nor disappointment in the marketing, nor rising in the dawn of morning after a feverish night to acquire, at any cost, the first specimen of the season; nothing of that state of perturbed feeling which a tourist among us well calls 'stirring Heaven and Earth to give a dinner;' but the hour came, the guests were punctual, and we sat down with young hearts, young spirits, and above all, young palates to the board.

Among those few cobweb'd bottles that I have adverted to, upon that upper shelf, in that chamber closet, of that upper story, there might in those days have been discerned one that stood, like a star, APART; the treasured, cherished, garnered bottle that should upon some *alba dies* occasion grace our bachelor's repast. It was twin bottle to one that had been opened for us in that City of Refuge of good wines, Charleston South Carolina, in those days not less certainly than now, the abode of the hospitable, the accomplished and the brave. Our host there had produced its fellow as a specimen that he was desirous his friends should appreciate. 'Oh Stephano, hast any more of this?'

When I arrived in New York after ten days and ten nights of

continuous posting, (the distance is now accomplished I am told cleverly in three,) the flavor of that wine still regaled my palate; there was a spiritual vineyard flourishing within my heart; the fragrant blossom, the young grape, the purple cluster, the yielding pressure, and the nectarous juice; the autumnal grape leaf with its magic dyes, and all the long history of joy which it is given to one or two rare specimens of the wines of this life to impart to the spirit of man; to impress upon his nerves; and to be recalled in sensations that make glad the fountains of his heart, and dispense his affections among his fellow men; all these were present to my senses, and delighted me with a varied, an intellectual, and constantly reviving joy. I had never known so perfect a beverage; and I wrote at once to my friend, offering him in exchange any description of wine that he could name to me, bottle for bottle.

He returned for answer an expression of regret that one only bottle remained of the batch; and entreating my acceptance of what I prized so highly, sent it on without delay. This was that lonely bottle that stood, in vague and uncertain light like a Hero of Ossian, upon that upper shelf, in that chamber closet, of that upper story. Often did I gaze upon it, often apostrophize it, praise it with a recollected gladness, remember its acquirement, delight in its possession, and wonder when the time might come, and when the friends, that should deserve the peerless, the incomparable offering.

Upon a certain memorable day, and punctual to the moment, came a chosen party of my most honored and distinguished friends. The dinner was beyond praise, and all the appointments good. No crowd, no tumult, no excuse, no delay in serving, no vacant seat, no chair with small open hexagons of split rattan to disfigure the person of the guest for three successive days when the dress is thin, or to torture him when the weather is cold with pains which he is ashamed to complain of or even to mention — a practice, Mr. Editor and all who hear me, still obtaining in some houses in New York, and at times, especially in winter, more abhorrent to the thoughts than is the martyrdom of St. Lawrence, since heat upon a gridiron is in many of its appliances preferable to cold upon sharp rattan. No; each guest had his cushioned chair, 'with ample room and verge enough;' and coarse after course, and wine after wine, appeared, and was enjoyed, discussed, and quietly disappeared, alike without want or waste.

Well, the time of the repast came for my selected wines: they were all prepared, and all in the finest order and condition. The series was a perfect one; a veritable ladder of transport; up which the spirits of my guests ascended gracefully, step after step, as each higher and higher flavor presented itself to their gratified and entranced palate. At the last, sole remaining bottle of the list, came my Charleston acquisition. It is certainly in bad taste to expatiate upon one's wine from the chair, but as this was the only bottle of its kind in the World, it seemed necessary to introduce it with a word that should at least perform that ceremony.

I told the story of its acquisition, and expressed the pleasure it gave me to present on this occasion the one remaining bottle of the world. We had been conversing a moment or two before, I remember, on the comparative advantages in drinking wine, between the sip and the throw, and had come to the conclusion, (which I think every man of sense must ultimately arrive at,) that the latter is the true way to enjoy the full *aroma* of the beverage, and at once to gain that gratifying descent, and that ascent to the wits; in short that satisfying blessedness of taste, which the mere sipper of potations of whatever kind must vainly aspire to know; say what you may to the contrary, Mr. T. G.!

"The bottle was uncorked, decanted, and the wine came forth, in the profound silence and expectation of the guests, bright as the beam of your mistress' eye! The attention of all present was so absorbed by their interest in this only bottle, that until every man's glass was filled, hardly a sound was perceptible except the gurgling of the long-necked decanter as it distributed its glorious contents and passed with wings from hand to hand around the board and returned drained to the head of the table. Toasts were at that time in vogue; and as soon as I had said, *'Our hospitable friend in South Carolina, may his own last bottle reward him for the pleasure of this gift,'* each man did ample justice to the wine.

How shall I recount the catastrophe that ensued! We are all sinful men born to trouble as the sparks fly upward, and it seemed as if the wine had also dealt ample and instant justice upon us! Every soul present was struck through the heart and liver to the spine! All rose instantly from the table, speechless, aghast, and terrified with the effect! There was a napkin or handkerchief over the mouth of each, and if we could have articulated a word, we might have exclaimed with the sons of the prophets at the feast in Gilgal, 'Oh my Lord, there is death in the pot!'

But it was impossible to relieve ourselves by words; it was literally in tears and groans that the guests made for the door, vanished from the room, escaped from the house, and left me, appalled, transfixed, incapable of utterance, standing at the head of my deserted table, and feeling that 'No man said, 'God bless him!''

For a fortnight, three weeks, a month, no one of my guests had his mouth *right!* I was afraid to walk in the streets lest I should meet one of them; there was a paralytic stricture in the countenance of each member of that sad party; in some it wore an expostulatory, an admonitory, in some a remonstrant, and in all the look of *a much injured person*. I must except one gentleman whom, however, I did not get a glimpse of until six weeks had elapsed. He was a well-bred Frenchman, with all the suavity and grace of manner that belongs to his class and nation. I shall ever feel grateful to him for the first kind word I had received since the discomfiture; though I have sometimes had doubts, judging from the reinstated appearance of his lips, whether he had taken more than half a glass: 'My dear Sir,' said he, 'when I had the pleasure to dine with you at your very agreeable party, there was one wine that had flavor very exemplary, ma foi!' I acknowledge it, I said. 'I think you did say it was American wine?' I did, I replied. 'What is the name if you please, as I pay much attention to the *sujet* of wines?' I named it. 'Will you be so very kind as write it in my tablet?' I prepared to comply; and telling him that I was not quite certain of the correct orthography of the word, wrote in large characters, the word, 'Scuppernong.'

JOHN WATERS.

XVI

Grave Thoughts on Punch

BY JOHN WATERS

NOVEMBER 1843

IT WAS a nice remark of the distinguished French General Moreau during his residence in this country, that the next thing in the world to a shock of cavalry is the English word, WHAT! There exists in it an irresistible abruptness, that frequently puts to flight at once the whole array of thoughts of the foreigner whose nerves are assailed by it. 'I can stand,' said he, 'anything better than your word. WHAT! It is impossible to reason against it; I seem to have nothing to do, when I hear it, but to submit!'

It certainly is one of those short words of power, one of those words of pistol-shot energy that characterize our grand tongue and give it originality and force. It is a word to conjure with; and has many a time raised Truth out of the depths of the heart of the double-dealer: it is a word of defense — and not infrequently has it overturned or repulsed in one utterance the half-formed scheme of some wheedling knave endeavoring to make a confederate, or nefariously to win the heart of a pretty girl. May you and I, dear Editor, never hear from lips we love, in the overwhelming accents of astonishment and of disappointed hope, the English word, WHAT!

The word at the head of my Essay, and which by the way I mean to make the subject of it, is another of these short English words of great strength and pith. This carries however no disfavor with it; no discourtesy; nor does it raise up one association that is otherwise than bland and attractive to the mind: and yet how forcible is it, alike in sound and in effect! Let us listen to it — PUNCH! — To the ear of my Imagination it is altogether irresistible! How impossible to parry it! What a possession it takes of the faculties, and how entirely it seems to get the better of one! Then how intrinsically, how essentially English it is in all the strength and vigor of the tongue! — PUNCH! Turn the word into the French, and behold how pitiable is the effect — *ponche!*

Now it is a curious fact in the Natural History of Liquids, that a similar and not less remarkable result occurs in the noble beverage which this short word is intended to designate! Try over the whole continent of Europe and wheresoever else the English language is not the vernacular, try I say to get PUNCH, and it invariably comes out *ponche* or something still more despicable! I have essayed it repeatedly and have always found the result the same; and yet I am neither a young, nor an inexperienced, nor, if you will allow me the word, an *inextensive* traveler!

On the other hand, the moment you recross the channel and 'set foot upon the sacred soil of Britain,' or come home quietly to our own unassuming United States and lay your hand upon the right ingredients, out of the sound of any foreign language, the mixture succeeds as a matter of course, and at once becomes virtually and essentially. PUNCH — PUNCH proper; PUNCH itself; in short, PUNCH!

> 'Tout Éloge d'un grand homme
> Est renfermé dans son nom!'

The native merits and distinctive propriety of the word being thus established; before I enter into any consideration of the drink itself, I cannot refrain from chiming in with the general feeling of the day on this side of the Atlantic so far as to observe, how incontestably this proves the mutual interest and common origin of 'the two great nations;' and should the dark day ever arrive, when letters shall be obliterated; printing forgotten; and language lost; it is still consolatory to reflect, that a mutual and inborn affinity between the two last representatives of 'the MOTHER and DAUGHTER' might be satisfactorily shown and most agreeably demonstrated by means of *two lemons; four tumblers of Croton or filtered spring water; one of double refined loaf sugar well cracked; and one of old Rum!*

Gentle Reader! Hast thou carefully dwelt over this list of ingredients? Are earth, air, fire, and water, more dissimilar in their elementary properties than are Lemon, Sugar, Water, and Rum? And has it ever before occurred to thee, to what supernal brightness of original and fortuitous Genius thou must have been indebted for this astonishing combination? Art thou alive to the grandeur of the original conception? Alas! The name of the architect of the Temple of Ephesus might as well at this epoch be sought for as that of the author of this stupendous compound, but the irrefragable word which is universally attempted to be attached to it indicates beyond the shadow of a doubt the land that claims the honor of his birth!

I am writing to thee from the attic of the house in which I have my abode. Canst thou tell me the name of the first artificer who planned the building of a second story? Who first contemplated or imagined STAIRS? Or changed the tent and the cabin into the fabric of diversified flights? The scheme of this was taken from the invention of the Beaver — But where throughout the animal creation was the instinctive indicator to the man who first conceived the thought of PUNCH?

NEWTON by the fall of an apple is said to have determined the Theory of Gravitation: how vast and limitless in its application has been the discovery! Yet is the whole but the elucidation of one principle or element of knowledge — while four different and antagonistic elements associate and are made to combine homogeneously in the glorious beverage of PUNCH!

DAVY, in his wonderful invention of the Safety Lamp, went with it completed in his hand from the laboratory to the mine, and found his reasoning true! Throughout the terraqueous globe his achievement is cited as the conquest of abstract Science over Physics. But vain is all abstract reasoning here; all distant experiment; all knowledge of the gases; all study of the powers of repulsion; — here four palpable and repulsive reasons are placed in presence of the chemist and philosopher, and the irresistible argument of all is — PUNCH.

These are hints for reflection to thee, Gentle Reader, in the quiet and solitary concocting and brewing of thy Pitcher, during the two hours that thou shalt diligently pour it from one glass receptacle into the other. When all is finished, and thy star hath proved benignant to thee; and thy beverage shall have become like the harmony that steals away thy heart; gushing from four musical instruments where the sound of neither predominates; — then drink to the memory of the great original Genius who planned and inspired thy joy; and forget not to favor, with a passing thought, the verdant Spirit who would gladly be Thy Companion; and who here subscribes himself, Thy Friend,

JOHN WATERS.

XVII

On Champagne Wine

BY J.M. SANDERSON

SEPTEMBER 1856

AN ARDENT admirer, from my earliest hoblledihoyhood, of that sparkling cup which cheers, and, I regret to add, sometimes inebriates, it was with more than ordinary gratification, and pleasure I received and accepted an invitation from the principal of a well-known firm in the Champagne wine trade, to visit the city of Rheims, and post myself up in the secrets of this my favorite tipple. Accordingly, one fine day early in the month of June, in the year of grace 1855, 1 bestowed myself and my wardrobe on the cars of the 'Chemin de fer de Strasbourg,' and in due course reached my destination, was welcomed by my friend, and comfortably installed in my lodgings. After devoting the usual time to a proper and respectful examination of the town, its cathedral, its promenades, its monuments, and its inhabitants, I turned my attention to the principal object of my trip, and after a careful investigation, obtained the information herein set forth, which 1 trust may be as interesting to you in the hearing, as it was agreeable to me in the collecting.

Champagne wine, although indubitably a factitious article, holds in the estimation of wine-drinkers, physicians, and connoisseurs, a high place in the catalogue of beverages, its sparkling qualities and agreeable sweetness attracting the first, its diuretic and tonic properties rendering it valuable to the second, and its delicate flavor, delightful aroma, and refreshing

257

bouquet endearing it to the third. But from the fact of its being a manufactured wine, there has been an attempt to throw around it a mantle of mystery which I have never, in my mind, been able to penetrate satisfactorily, either by reading the numerous books written on the subject, or by conversing with intelligent persons from the immediate locality. This mystery has been carefully fostered by persons interested in the manufacture or sale of the article, who, fearing the truth might possibly lessen the demand, when asked as to the modus operandi, have generally either flatly denied the addition of sugar and brandy, or if admitting it, asserted that it was only done occasionally, when, in consequence of a cold or wet season, the produce of any particular vintage did not possess sufficient saccharine matter or body, but on no account would they acknowledge this addition to be a matter of rule, and in fact necessity. This version has been handed down from one author to the other until finally it has grown into a belief, and as every other detail of the mode of manufacturing this wine has been clearly described by almost every writer on the subject, the only originality I can claim for my paper is the dissipation, in some degree, of this mystery, and the verification of another point, which, until this moment, has been denied, in some cases most emphatically, namely: that the produce of different localities are intermixed. To enable me, however, to do this understandingly, it will be necessary to travel lightly over the same ground as my predecessors, trusting, also, that among my hearers there may be some not as 'learned in the lore' of wine-making as others.

The vineyards of Champagne cover an expanse of territory of about thirty miles in length and two miles in breadth, thickly interspersed with gentle elevations and shallow streams, the river Marne, which passes through its entire length, being the exception. The vine generally employed is called the 'Pineau,' of which there are two varieties, the black and the white, the former, however, being the favorite. The grapes known as the ' Burgundy Grape' are of a rich, deep purple color, and in size resemble our chicken grapes. The soil in which they are planted is formed of a calcareous loam strongly impregnated with lime, and thickly incrusted with small stones. The location most sought after is the side of a hill, having a southern or southwestern exposure, of which the midway portion is preferred, the top and bottom being most liable to frosts and dampness. The vines are planted quite close together, and are but sparingly manured. After every vintage they are cut down close to the ground, leaving but three or four inches so as to preserve the eyes; the stump is then buried, and on the following year makes its appearance three or four inches higher up the hill; and on the new wood, which springs up, is produced the grape; some roots are known to be forty feet in length, and a few have reached the respectable age of two hundred years. The plant must be four years old before it will yield fruit; at six years it has attained its maturity; and at one hundred years will still produce good merchantable grapes. Every third year new vines are planted at the bottom of the hill, to replace those promoted by time and growth. A French vineyard possesses but slender claims to the picturesque. At the period of my visit the vines were about eighteen inches high, and consequently nothing met the eye but the thin sticks planted near each root, to which they are attached by bands of straw as soon as they are sufficiently high to cause the heads to droop. These sticks, having acquired, by long exposure to wind and weather, a hue somewhat between whitey-brown and sky-blue, give to the hillside a dingy, furzy appearance, not at all calculated to call forth on the part of the observer either an eloquent or a poetic description. Late in the season, however, when the grapes have ripened, and the tops of the vines have covered their cerulean-hued supporters, the vast expanse of green foliage is at least refreshing to the eye, if nothing else. If the season has been favorable, each vine will produce from two to five small bunches, but when the reverse is the case, as was the vintage of 1855, a single bunch is with difficulty discovered. Many, on the contrary, yield no fruit; still the labor and attention can by no means be spared or relaxed, an unproductive vine requiring as much of both as its more richly-freighted neighbor, in hopes that on the following year it may make amends. The latter part of September and the beginning of October is generally the period chosen for gathering the grapes, an operation requiring the assistance not only of all the inhabitants of the district, but affording also ample means of employment for an immense number of stragglers who rush, in from every quarter. This event is by no means the pleasant, romantic, and picturesque affair we have been taught to think it, being, on the contrary, regular hard days' work and plenty of it. It must be done in a hurry, too, as a heavy rain or frost would be a great damage to the ripe grapes; therefore when the gathering commences, no delay is permitted in bringing it to a final close, and from all I can learn, and I state it for the benefit of my bachelor friends, the season of the vintage is not conducive to lovemaking, other authors to the contrary notwithstanding, the young females engaged therein being, generally so fatigued after the labors of the day, and, I blush to add, so dirty, that the soft side of a plank is much preferred to the blandishments of Cupid, or worshipping at the shrine of his naughty mamma. After being picked, the bunches are carefully culled over by the old women of the establishment, and the choice ones being placed in casks containing one hundred litres — a litre being a fraction more than a quart — are sold to the buyers from the different houses, although in many instances a large proprietor will have his own pressoir or wine-press, through which, for a consideration; his poorer neighbors are permitted to pass the produce of their little patch. This system, however, is fast falling into disuse, as the better and heavier houses in the trade invariably object to purchasing in that shape, preferring much to buy the fruit in bunches, and make the pressings themselves. The press most generally used is the old-fashioned perpendicular affair, but of late years, among other improvements, the lateral press has been introduced, and when once used is invariably preferred.

When the grapes have been delivered to the purchaser, great care being taken to avoid any unnecessary motion, they are heaped up on the platform of the press, through the bottom of which openings are left for the rapid escape of the juice to the vats below, and that portion of it which is first produced without artificial pressure, and denominated 'the first droppings of the grape' is placed aside and reserved for the highest grades of wine, the quantity of which, of course, is very limited. The lever is then applied with moderate force so as not to discolor the wine by bruising and mashing the skins. This pressing furnishes wine of the first quality, known here as the Cabinet and Imperial brands; another turn of the screw produces material for the second quality wines, sold here at from twelve to fourteen dollars, and rejoices under an infinity of names and brands, whilst still another yields the lower quality, and finally, some white grapes being added, the screws are put on to their utmost tension, producing a strong, piquante, red wine, which is reserved for the use of the workmen of the establishment. The various pressings are then put into casks, properly marked, and stowed away until the first fermentation (which takes place almost immediately) is over, after which it is sacked and fined twice, and oftener if required, and, if the summer has been wet and cold, or the season backward, so that the wines are deficient of the required amount of the saccharine matter, a knowledge of which is arrived at not only by tasting, but also by the rise of an instrument known as the 'Sacchometer,' the deficiency is made up by the addition of pure sugar candy. This, however, does not often happen, and is only resorted to when the juice gives unmistakable evidence of its necessity; and it is at this point, when Nature apparently languishes in a measure in her operations, that Art is called in to her assistance, both by the addition of foreign substances, and the intermixing of the produce of different localities. Redding, in his 'History of Modern Wines,' says: 'Mixtures are not often made of the effervescing wines. They generally remain the pure production of the spots the names of which they bear.' So far from this being true, exactly the reverse is the case, for no Champagne wine would be considered even second quality that did not possess delicacy of flavor, a well-defined bouquet, and a certain degree of body. To obtain these requisites it has been found absolutely necessary to commingle the produce of various vineyards, each of them possessing in an eminent degree one of these characteristics, and by this means infuse qualities into the wine artificially which cannot be acquired naturally. To achieve this satisfactorily, the taster of the establishment, who must, of course, possess a fine taste and approved palate, prepares a mixture by taking a certain portion of the juice from the Verzinay district as a basis, to which lie adds a portion from the Aij or Bonzy vineyards, and another from those of Mareuil, Avizes, or possibly Epernay, carefully noting the proportion from each. This mixture is then tested and discussed, and if, in his judgment, it lacks delicacy, bouquet, or body, the quality lacking is furnished by the addition of so much of the product of that district possessing the required characteristic necessary to remedy the defect. It will thus be seen that a most important element in a good house is the possession of an accurate and experienced taster, for on his judgment and taste depends the character of an establishment and its brand of wine. The details of the mixture once arranged, a large vat or tun, holding from seventy-five to one hundred casks, is then filled, the same combinations being closely observed in the enlarged proportions, and the contents are thoroughly blended and amalgamated, so that every bottle of that *cuvie* or lot may be exactly alike. Formerly, and in some large establishments the practice holds good to this day, it was the custom, after ascertaining the proportions of the mixture, to effect the combination in casks containing one hundred and sixty litres, rendering it impossible to get more than two hundred bottles of uniform quality. To remedy this evil the huge tuns used in the Rheingan for equalizing the German wines were introduced, (by the old house of Mumm, Geisler & Co.,) which not only removed the defect, but also, by rendering the other operations more perfect, materially improved the character of the wine. After a proper interval, the wine is drawn from this vat into hogsheads, and thence immediately put into bottles, which are placed away in deep cold cellars, constructed with great care and at heavy expense, expressly to receive them. Early in the spring they undergo the secondary fermentation, which produces the mousse, or sparkling qualities of the wine, and it is at this period that the carbonic acid gas, sometimes proving too powerful, causes the immense destruction of bottles and loss of wine, so large an item in the sum of expenses. Of late years the average has been from twelve to fifteen per cent; in 1842 it reached the incredible amount of fifty per cent. Having been carefully corked, twined and wired, the bottles are stowed away on their sides, in lots of from one to twenty thousand, for the period of eighteen months, during which time a thick, muddy deposit is precipitated to the lower side of the bottle; they are then placed in horizontal racks, perforated with holes so shaped that, place them in whatever inclination you may desire, they are always secure and firm; and every day a workman, especially charged with that duty, shakes them gently, and at the same moment raises them slightly, until by slow degrees they obtain a perpendicular position, and the sediment finds its way to the neck of the bottle, accumulating on the end of the cork, leaving the wine as clear and as bright as crystal. In this position they can, and sometimes do, remain for years; in fact, they are never removed from it, although such removal would entail no injury to the contents, until it is wanted for export or sale, as the wine will keep without deterioration, if unmixed with sugar, for at least twenty years, but after the sugar has been added it will depreciate sensibly in five or six years. The next operation is that of the *dégorgement*, or cleansing out of the sediment, which is the most difficult and delicate, as it is the most curious, requiring great skill and precision in the handling, for by this time the wine has become so highly effervescent, that in the hands of the unskillful and uninitiated it would either be made cloudy or every drop would suddenly quit the bottle. The practiced *dégorgeur*, however, takes it carefully from its perpendicular position, and inclining it slightly, with its mouth towards the ground, divests it of the wire and twine, and, with an instrument resembling a brad-awl, quickly displaces the cork, which flies from its resting-place with a sharp report, carrying with it all the deposit, and a small portion of the wine; seldom as much, however, as is necessary to give place for the liquor which is immediately afterwards added. Up to this moment, the wine generally, with the exception of such assistance as has already been mentioned, remains free from any artificial mixture, but on leaving the table of the *dégorgeur*, it passes at once into the hands of the mixer, who adds to each bottle, according to the country it is to be sent to, from eight to twenty-two percent of a liquor composed of crystallized sugar candy of the finest quality, dissolved in wine of a character especially intended for this use, and a certain percentage of very fine old Champagne brandy, for which a fabulous price is paid. For America the allowance of brandy is never over one per cent, whilst for England three and sometimes four is added. For the Parisian consumption one percent is also the quota, but for Russia and Germany a very spirituous wine is employed instead. As the addition of the liquor is greater than the escape of wine and deposit, the necessary quantity is generally poured out into bottles which are slightly fortified, and sold to the Parisian restaurateurs, who readily retail it, under the name of 'Tisanne,' at four francs the bottle.

In defense of this addition of sugar and spirits, it is alleged that it is employed not only to give sweetness and body to the wine, but also that it is absolutely necessary for the purpose of destroying certain deleterious qualities appertaining to it in its natural state, which, unchanged, would render it both disagreeable and unhealthy; in other words, that a certain quantity of sugar is required to correct the malic acid which forms a constituent element of the wine, which, if drank pure, would inevitably cause in the stomach of the imbiber thereof, a sensation painfully reminding him of the ' belly-ache ' of his boyhood. From the mixer the bottle passes to the corker, who, with the aid of a powerful lever, reduces the cork, which is previously soaked in wine, to about half its original size, and forces it into its place; it is then secured by twine and wire, which gives it the knobby-looking head it possesses when released from its prison by the consumer'; and finally, after being tin-foiled or leaded, as the case may be, and labeled, it is packed away in cases or baskets to await orders for shipment. The average day's work of a large establishment is one thousand bottles. The report of the Minister of the Interior states that the annual export of genuine Champagne wine is about thirteen millions of bottles, which are distributed as follows: To Germany, which includes Austria, Prussia, and all the States belonging to the Germanic Confederation, between four and five millions. To America the exportation amounts to very nearly three millions, and to Russia about two millions. In France and Belgium the consumption averages about two millions, while in England the demand is very limited, seldom exceeding half-a-million, leaving about a million and a half for the rest of mankind. The class of wines sent to Russia and Germany, as a general rule, are of the first quality, possessing delicacy of flavor, light body, and highly effervescing, with from eighteen to twenty-two percent of sugar. In America, which offers no fixed standard of taste, every grade and quality, from the Heidsick, with its eighteen per cent of sweetened liquor, to the 'Grand Vin' of Moot, with its two percent of brandy a l'Anglaise, are exported, and find admirers and advocates. The general standard of the first-class houses, however, is from fourteen to sixteen percent, (and an experiment is now being made by the well-known firm of G. H. Mumm & Co., to introduce into this market an article with but a moiety of the usual addition of sugar, approaching, as near as possible, to the French standard, which ranges from eight to twelve percent.) To England, however, is sent the driest, strongest, and poorest quality of wine, for although an English wine merchant will assure you that he receives none but wine of the first quality, it is a notorious fact, in the Champagne district, that an order for anything above the third quality rarely finds its way from London, and as no labels are permitted on wine intended for that market, the manufacturer has no means of designating the true quality to the consumer, who is thus left to the mercy of the dealers, who are, beyond contradiction, as a class, the greatest rogues in Christendom.

Of late years it has been the fashion, on the part of would-be wine oracles and pseudo-connoisseurs to talk learnedly and inveigh bitterly against what they are pleased to term 'the extraordinary depreciation in the quality of Champagne wine,' some of them even going so far as to assert they don't believe 'there is a single bottle of genuine wine ever reaches our shores,' quoting, in substantiation of their dictum, their recollections of the 'celebrated I. C. Champagne,' the 'famed Cornet brand,' and a host of fancy names 'long since dead and passed away,' any of which could be had for fourteen dollars or less. In the 'dollar sense' of the case, these gentlemen are very nearly right, but they forget that during that same period of time, flour, 'the staff of life,' to quote that elegant remark of the classic Baggs, 'isn't what it use to was,' and it is vividly within the recollection of many suffering housekeepers, that a shilling loaf of bread, twenty years ago, was esteemed food enough for a growing family, while now it barely suffices to stay the stomach of a sturdy stripling. But that feeling fact certainly does not prove that the Genesee of today is inferior to the common brands of other and cheaper times, nor is it a convincing argument that the bakers of yore had more conscience than the modern dough-faces, or still less that Young America is a better feeder than his father; it simply demonstrates that the demand is greater than the supply, and, as an inevitable consequence, prices go up or quality goes down, just as naturally as water finds its level, or that two and two make four. Now, apply the same rule to Champagne wine, and you have the same result, for how is it possible that, with, a limited and frequently a diminished supply of the raw material, and a constantly increasing demand for the manufactured article, prices and quality should remain stationary. It certainly cannot be supposed that gentlemen engaged in the wine trade are going to invest from one to five hundred thousand dollars of capital, merely for the fun of hearing the corks pop, and as it is impossible for them to export *profitably* the same article which cost them in 1846 (the most famous vintage on record) at the rate of *four sous the bottle*, for which they now pay *forty sous*, and sell it at the same price, it will readily be understood why first-quality wine has appreciated in price, and why fourteen dollars now will not buy the same wine as it did years ago. If gentlemen must have the best article, they have got to pay for it, and, comparing it with every other article of trade or consumption, subject to the same vicissitudes, at eighteen or twenty dollars the dozen, it does not yield as liberal a profit as when sold at the minimum price so pathetically lamented for by the old fogies in question. Ten years ago the connoisseur placed before his cherished gastronomical chums, claret of the premiere cue at fifteen dollars the dozen, brandy of a fabulous age and undoubted purity, at five dollars the gallon, and segars of the choicest brands and most delicious fragrance, at fifty dollars the thousand. Why, then, should he object to pay twenty-five dollars a case for the best Champagne, which the great De Thou so appropriately termed 'Vinum Dei.' But, at the same time, I would not be understood to say that a very fair wine, good enough for any man's drinking, cannot be had at the stereotyped price of fourteen dollars. On the contrary, there are several brands sent to this market, and held at that price, which have puzzled many excellent judges, even when placed in competition with higher grades; but I do maintain that, under that price, the thing is impossible, and as Champagne is somewhat

'LIKE JEREMIAH's figs,
The good are very good, the bad too bad to give the pigs,'

the consumer had better err on the right side by buying the very best, as he may rest well assured that neither his friends nor his stomach ever find fault with a wine for being too good. Much more could be said and written on this genial topic, but although the subject is not exhausted, the audience probably are, so we will rest here for the present.

XVIII

Drinking Song

BY HENRY DE WITT

FEBRUARY 1833

If Jove, when he made this beautiful world,
  Had only consulted me,
An ocean of wine should flow in the place
  Of the brackish and bitter sea,
Red wine should pour from the fruitful clouds
  In place of the tasteless rain,
And the fountains should bubble in ruby rills
  To brim the sparkling main.

No fruit should grow but the round, full grape,
  No bowers but the shady vine,
And of all earth's flowers, the queenly rose
  Should alone in her beauty shine;
I'd have a few lakes for the choicest juice,
  Where it might grow mellow and old,
And my lips should serve as a sluice to drain
  Those seas of liquid gold.

XIX

A Hotel Dinner

FROM NOTES IN PENCIL,
ON THE BACK OF A BILL OF FARE

SEPTEMBER 1838

HOW STARTLING is the sound of the dinner gong! The tympanum suddenly recoils beneath the swell of the brazen instrument, and echoes the alarum to its fellow member of the lower house, of which Appetite is the speaker. In a large hotel, the effect is magical. What a rush from all quarters of the house to the dining room! Chambers, offices, and closets, are hastily deserted by their occupants that the elements of an unspeakable hurly-burly may mingle at the *table-d'hôte*. Loungers in the street catch the sound with wonderful acuteness, and hasten homeward to the hotel. The boarder under the barber's hands frets at the practitioner's slowness, gets out, while uttering a violent oath, starts up, looking daggers, and wiping the soap hastily from his half-shaved chin, seizes his hat, and rushes to the place of feed.

In one dense crowd, they pour in at the door, pushing and squeezing, jostling and swearing, as if life itself depended upon the celerity of their entrance. Dignity is nothing; decency is nothing. A choice seat at the table is everything.

The twenty or thirty individuals who are already seated at the head of the board, and in the immediate vicinity of the choicest eatables, are 'old heads;' they have 'cut their eye teeth;' they are 'up to snuff;' or, to cut the classics, and descend to homely English, they know how to live in an American hotel; an accomplishment by no means to be lightly regarded. Every day, about half an hour before the dinner hour, they station themselves near the door of the dining room and with a patience worthy of Job, await its opening. Barely does John, the waiter, have time to sound the gong, the notes of which I have said are so magical, before they dart by him, and the last vibration of the brazen monitor finds the men of brass seated at the table. Some unsophisticated persons may think this a contemptible subserviency to the appetite; if so, they do the worthies much injustice. Their motives are of a high order; an honor to themselves, and a great light to the world. Example is everything. Punctuality is a jewel. WASHINGTON said so, and he was a man of veracity. The hour to dine, as specified in the rules and regulations, posted up in the 'office,' was three. Not one minute before nor after three, but three precisely. Some inconsiderate man may think that a minute or two out of the way could make no material difference. Don't trust such an one with the conveyance of your wife and five small children to a steamboat pier! Ten chances to one he misses the boat. 'Time is money,' and two minutes lost daily, is seven hundred and forty minutes per annum. At this rate, supposing a man to live seventy years — a fair computation when we consider the caoutchouc case of Joice Heth — thirty-five days, eleven hours, and four sixtieths, are wasted in a lifetime, by being two minutes behind hand at dinner! Shades of Washington, Franklin, and Dr. Alcott! — what a dissipation of money! It was of this that the men at the door ruminated. They wished, like Washington, to set a good example, in being punctual. If, in virtuously striving to excel in such a cause, they tread on each other's corns, and tumble over each other's heels, making themselves appear excessively ridiculous, it is our business not to laugh at, but to condole with them, as martyrs who suffer for our sake. Many a gouty toe has been ground into torture, in its owner's generous emulation to be the first and most punctual at the dinner table. What disinterested martyrdom.

The crowd have squeezed themselves into the room. Such a scrambling and jostling for seats! Spare the crockery. The din — from din comes dinner—redoubles. Such an outcry! Babel is music to it. 'Waiter!' 'Waiter!' 'John!' 'Waiter!' 'Thomas! Thomas!'

'Waiter!' 'John!' 'Thomas!' 'Soup!' 'Soup!' 'Soup!' were iterated in all octaves, from contralto to soprano. I was a 'looker-on in Vienna,' when the scenes which follow occurred, and I 'speak the things which I do know.'

'Give us a. stout, hearty plate of soup, William!' said a short, crimson-faced man, with an abdominal periphery like a semi-globe. As he gave this order for a second plate of soup, he shoved into the waiter's hand, open to receive the plate of a gentleman who had as yet secured nothing, his own dish, and bade him make haste. Ignorant of 'dinner etiquette,' as Fanny Kemble styles it, a dozen of those around us had at once commenced on the solids; which of course made the rest work like beavers to finish their soup; and some of those at the end of the table, who, having but just received the initial liquid, were still sipping after their luckier friends at the favored head of the table had concluded, were admonished of the necessity of making haste, by the removal of their plates by the impatient waiters. Waiters are systematic. People should be more simultaneous in eating soup. A polite man swallows his, scalding hot, that he may keep pace with his more fortunate neighbor.

'Here! Here! — You rascal, bring back my soup!' bawled out a man with a thin, vinegar aspect. His plate had suffered abduction. The waiter feigned not to hear. The wrinkles on the pungent face visibly sharpened. That look would have soured an entire dairy. In a voice thin and sharp as his features, he exclaimed: 'Here! Here! You unmannerly Irish scapegoat! (Ah! You hear at last, do you?) Bring back my soup, instantly!'

'It's ag'in' the rules, Sir-r; I can't do it, Sir-r! But here's a beautiful arrangement!' replied the Irishman, passing a bill of fare.

'D—n you and your rules, and your bill of fare, in a mess! I want my soup, you Irish blackguard!'

'Can't do it, Sir-r; the rules must be observed. Can't give ye any more soup, Sir-r; the *mates* is on, Sir-r; them must be ate nixt; them's the rule, Sir-r;' and the waiter ran to answer a call farther up the table.

The discomfited man swore as terribly as if he had formed one of the celebrated army in Flanders. 'Pretty hotel, this! Excellent regulations! Polite servants! *Must* eat meat, must 1? I'll see 'em hanged first! Here, you chowder-head, bring back my—'

'Green peas, gen'lemen — green peas!' squeaked a bean-pole waiter, with a nose like a sausage, and little twinkling eyes. A dozen hands grabbed convulsively at the dish. Green peas were a great rarity; a fact sufficiently evinced by the complacent air of the servant, as he announced them. A dish of gravy and a bottle of catsup were upset in the scuffle, much to the annoyance of the sour man, in whose lap a greater part of the first sought a dépôt. 'You have got your soup, I find, Sir!' said a wag, opposite, at which everybody laughed, and one individual, at an untimely moment, when his mouth was full of Scotch ale, whereby a great gurgling and spluttering ensued, ending by a general spirt upon the 'fixins' of all who were near him; a most impartial division, for all received a portion. As soon as he could make himself heard above the discord, the person to whom the wag's remark had been addressed, answered, with much asperity, 'That's *Irish* wit, I s'pose; I hate Irish!'

'Peas, waiter!' 'Waiter, peas!' 'Peas! Peas! Peas!' exclaimed a hundred voices in a breath. Reasonable souls! They looked to be all helped at once!

'Pass those peas?' said a score of impatient voices to the gentleman with the crimson face, who in the scuffle had succeeded in securing the dish to himself.

'Ha, ha!' he spluttered, complacently, with his mouth half full of salmon, 'I hav'n't eat any of these 'ere for a long while!'

'They *look* very fine!' said the next but one adjoining, in a manner that implied a strong desire to ascertain whether they did not *taste* respectably.

'Very, *very*!' replied the fat man, as he scooped nine-tenths of all there were in the dish onto his own plate. Sundry eyes glanced pitchforks at him. They were evidently astonished. They should not have been. The gentleman came from a western pork-growing district. He fatted his own swine. 'I'm special fond of peas!' said he, half in enthusiasm at his own appetite, and half as a sort of an apology.

'Split me, if I shouldn't think so!' exclaimed the wag.

'Well, it's nothing strange!' snapped out Vinegar, taking the part of the obese, and chuckling at the discomfiture of the others.

'Some people will eat, until, being unable to help themselves, we shall be compelled to lift them out of their seat!' exclaimed one of the disappointed, giving the fat man a look that was not to be misconstrued.

I looked about me for some peas, but saw none. As I was scrutinizing, my eyes encountered the rueful and bewildered face of a modest young man, with an empty plate. In all probability, he had never dined before in a hotel; at least, the diffident manner with which he received the inattention paid to his modest requests, seemed to say as much. A constant fear, too, lest he should not behave quite like the rest, appeared to haunt him; and the longer he was neglected, the more he appeared embarrassed. Poor fellow! He had not yet received a mouthful to eat. What a bore is modesty! Brass is, emphatically, an accomplishment. The young man looked very ridiculously for the lack of it; and I pitied him.

''Waiter!' said I, winking peculiarly to an Adonis with squint eyes, and a mouth like a codfish. He sprang to my side. The wink had touched his feelings. I knew it would. A waiter's heart is open to a wink, when words are useless.

'Get me some peas, and fresh salmon, on a clean plate.'

The fellow's eyes concentrated into their deepest squint, as he looked inquiringly, first into my face, and then at the space between my thumb and forefinger. Apparently not seeing there what he had expected, his sprightly, helpful manner died away very suddenly, and his answer, as he stared mechanically up the table, was unqualifiedly brief.

'Guess there ar'n't any here; don't see any.'

I pointed to my thumb and forefinger. A quarter-dollar filled the space so lately vacant.

'Do you see any now?'

The mouth opened wide, and assumed an amiable grin, and the

eyes an extra squint, and for half a minute glanced scrutinizingly around the table.

'I think I does!' said he. His sight was completely restored.

'I thought you would,' said I, dropping the coin into his horny palm. What wonders the 'root of all evil' can accomplish! It makes the best vegetable pills in the world, and 'may be used with equally astonishing success in all climates.'

'Here, you squint-eyed rascal!' roared out Vinegar, who for the last ten minutes had been unceasingly cursing every servant within hearing, 'I saw you take that bribe! Bring me my soup, or I'll expose you. Pretty joke! Have to pay landlord exorbitant charge for dinner, and then pay, beside, a lubberly set of lanthorn-jawed waiters for helping you to it! I won't submit to such treatment, and those who will, are ninnies! *I* won't stand it. I'll make them change their tone. I'll publish the landlord. I'll blow his hotel to the devil. I'll — I'll — I'll have my soup! Here, you laughing hyena, with your teeth out of doors, bring me my soup!'

The disinterested servant brought me the peas and salmon, with great alacrity, and looked as if he would like to have the silver dose repeated, but I had no farther use for him, and stared coldly upon his enthusiasm. He was a philosopher, and a deeply read student of human nature. He understood that cold look, as readily as he had done the wink, and, to adopt a western phrase, quickly 'absquatulated.' Helping myself to a portion of the viands which I had been so fortunate as to obtain, I passed the remainder to my modest neighbor. He appeared very grateful, but was too much embarrassed to thank me. Having helped himself to salmon, he was proceeding (leisurely, lest he should seem indecorous,) to take some peas, when the dish was unceremoniously seized, and carried to the obese, who had bribed the waiter with a shilling to execute the maneuver. Whereupon my modest friend looked very blank, and Vinegar took occasion to dilate sarcastically upon the expense of feeding pigs in the west; in which the fat man, unsophisticated, and seeing no allusion, coincided with fervor. He had swine to sell, and crying up the expense of fattening them, would tend to increase their value in the market. And here ensued a confab between the wag and the obese, in which the latter was made the unwitting butt of a thousand and one small shafts, touching his professional and personal affinities.

'Clear the tables!' sang out the authoritative voice of one decked in a short white apron, who brandished, in a masterly manner, a huge carving knife and fork. This was no less a personage than the headwaiter, or 'butler,' as he directed his fellow servants to style him. He knew the responsibility of his situation, and filled it with great dignity. His own talents had raised him, step by step, from the comparatively low office of a knife-scourer and cook's errand boy, to the high stand which, knife in hand, he now occupied. His history is an excellent illustration of the old maxim, that 'talent, like water, will find its level.' I could dwell upon the hopes and aspirations of the lowly knife-scourer; his surcharged bosom overflowing in the lonely watches of the night, as he plied his rag and 'rotten stone;' his longings for the birth of porter; 'the attainment of his Wish; his enthusiasm upon his first début with Day-and-Martin; his still craving ambition; in short, his whole rise and progress, and final attainment to that pinnacle of usefulness, the situation of head waiter.

My modest neighbor, supposing that the last-named order was intended as an insinuation that the guests had ate enough, arose and walked off. Upon reaching the door, and turning round, he seemed to perceive his mistake, and that the order was but for the clearance of the meats, to make room for the pastry; but, ashamed to expose his ignorance of 'etiquette,' by returning to the table, he left the room, hoping, I doubt not, from the bottom of his soul, that those he had left behind him would ascribe his withdrawal to surfeit rather than ignorance. He probably adjourned to a neighboring eating-house, to appease his tantalized appetite.

'What pudding is this, waiter?' said a gentleman opposite.

'It's a *pud*-ding, Sir-r,' was the satisfactory reply.

'We know it's a pudding, but what *kind* of a pudding is it? Find out *what* pudding it is.'

'That's aisily done!' said he, as with the utmost *sang froid* he perforated the crust of the doubtful dish with his dirty thumb.

'Sure, gintlemen, it's a rice!'

'You ignorant ape! — don't you know better than that? You ought to be lynched!'

'He would be, if he was in our parts!' said the fat gentleman, swallowing a glass of champagne, which he had taken, uninvited, from my bottle.

'Look here, cabbage head!' said Vinegar, tweaking the offender's ear; 'bring me my soup!'

I left the table. It was my last hotel dinner.

XX

Wine-Song: From Lanjou

BY HASCLER VADENROPT

JANUARY 1858

Now, while the wine in the gleaming glass glances,
See through its mimic waves floating fine fancies:
　　Down in the seething flood
　　Of the grape's purple blood
　　Is the Mirth-god's abode:
　　　　Deep in the chalice
　　　　Joy has his palace.

Now moving fitfully, whirling in dances,
Oh! How my senses the sweet sight entrances!
　　See, glides a merry band,
　　Strays from a fairyland;
　　Love, with a ray-like wand,
　　　　Leading the chorus,
　　　　Flitting before us.

Ripples, like drapery, now seem concealing
Shapes traitorous bubbles would fain be revealing:
　　Spirits most delicate,
　　Keeping their tiny state,
　　Wavering, seem to wait;
　　　　Tremulous groups,
　　　　Like uncertain hopes.

279

WINE-SONG

Here is a Lethe for cares that oppress us;
Here is a gladness waiting to bless us:
    E'er any envious slip,
    Lift to the ready lip:
        Let Jove his nectar sip,
        Red wine be ours,
        Cups crowned with flowers.

XXI

The Chicken Club: or, Stories After Dinner

STORIES AFTER DINNER

JULY 1852

ONE WORD will explain why the club was called the 'Chicken-Club.' The planters visited their crops twice a week on certain days, and not residing on their estates in the summer, they ordered a chicken to be killed and ready for them after looking over the crop; and as many of them planted near enough to meet at dinner, and often to look at each other's crops the same day, someone gave the familiar invitation: 'Well, gentlemen, you'll take your chicken with me today;' and this was done alternately through the season. The doctor of the several plantations thought it a very proper and agreeable time to make his report, and never failed to make one of the party. They were all (then as now) men of education, and many 'of travel;' and while agriculture was the leading subject, the conversation often became general, and all matters in dispute were decided by the host of the day, who was president for the occasion. And this was the simple constitution of 'the Chicken-Club.'

Thus it was with their fathers and uncles, (blessed be their memories!) but with the present generation and proprietors, anyone would smile, and a hungry man rejoice, to 'take chicken' with them. It is true, the chicken is there, perhaps half-a-dozen of them; but in the drains of our rice fields, from June to frost, are found in great abundance the 'soft-shell,' which, under the skillful compounding and practiced tasting of the doctor, makes a plate of soup that throws the chicken and all his feathered kindred into the shade of shades; that no man, Major-General or not, could be *hasty* in enjoying, but rather would rally, and charge again; that satisfies, but fills not, leaving your digestion quickened only for dishes yet uncovered, and gives them a subdued flavor and a relish, like lemon to a pudding. Nowadays, also, a lamb is killed, and a quarter is retained for the club, while the other is sent home for the family, the *fore* being distributed to the sick and the old. Green peas, and corn, and vegetables of every description, abound in well-cultivated gardens in the ever-dry squares, and rock-fish and trout at the mouths of the river-trunks are caught without trouble by the winders; hams of their own curing, and juicy as a peach; and in the early harvest the bird of all birds, the rice-bird. This, I think all will admit, is an improvement upon the time-honored chicken. The wine which the old gentlemen boasted in their cellars, is now toasted at the table, though in the moderation of extreme propriety, it being their habitual observance, and prudent withal, having to return to their wives in the evening. A good cigar, and a story from the doctor, who is always ready, adjourns the club for the day.

Number One.

'Our conversation, gentlemen, a few moments since, on *destiny*, brought to mind an incident of my life in which my fate, as predicted by an old fortune-teller, was near being fulfilled, which I will tell you, and also the singular manner of my escape:

'In my infancy, I was called the 'little cub,' not from any rudeness of temper, or clumsy extremities, (for I enjoyed the common reputation of being 'a very fine child,') but from this circumstance: My father had a fancy for pets of all kinds, and among them was a well-grown bear, as tame and gentle as a kitten; and during the height of the hurricane of 1804, while the family were retreating from the dwelling to the kitchen for greater safety, it being lower to the ground and a stronger frame, my nurse was blown over with me in her arms, and in the fury

282

of the storm, and in the blackness of darkness, she lost her hold of me, and I could not be found. The family had reached the kitchen, and was soon followed by my nurse, screaming higher than the wind; but her terror and that of my parents was gone in a moment, for the bear stepped in, walking uprightly, and holding me safely and softly in his embrace. Hence, for many years after, I was known in the family and the village as the 'little cub.' Now this, with all the perishable record of nursery tales, had passed out of my memory, when I was most disagreeably reminded of it; and I introduce it because it furnishes the key to my story. While a student at Philadelphia, I accompanied two young ladies from Georgia then finishing their education at a boarding school, to a 'fortune teller' in Callowhill Street, who had great notoriety for her wonderful disclosures of the past, and fulfillment of her predictions for the future. I need not say that I went merely for the pleasure of waiting upon the girls, and to gratify them, for they had been looking to the appointment impatiently, and were full of rose-colored anticipations in the coming examination of their fair but treacherous palms. We were admitted separately into her presence; and when it came to my turn, I stood before the prophetess with the same indifference I would before an owl, which she very much resembled. She noticed this, and was angry, for she expected great awe and deference. She took my right hand and traced its lines minutely, then consulted her chart, and with much form and solemnity pronounced 'my fortune.' I paid the accustomed fee, and laughed in her face. She sprang from her seat and caught my left hand; hers was cold and trembling with rage. She made a hasty survey, and then darting at me a look of black revenge, she muttered between her snake-like teeth: 'Your life was saved by a bear, and it will be taken by a bear! Now go!' said she, and she waved her bony arm toward the door. But I was motionless, pale, and confounded. She saw my discomfiture, and in turn she giggled in my face, and left me to my reflections. I recovered in a few minutes from the amazement in which she left me, and joined the young ladies in the reception room. I found Mary very happy, and Jane very sad and in tears. Mary controlled her joy in sympathy for her companion, and we left the house in silence, nor was it broken until we reached the seminary. We rested on the steps, and told our fortunes to each other. Poor Jane tried to laugh at my pleasant prospects, and I took my leave.

'I graduated the following spring, and returned to Georgia. The young ladies also completed their course, and returned to their homes. It is useless to say I was not annoyed at the old woman's allusion to my infant adventure, for it happened a thousand miles off, and twenty years before, and I had almost forgotten it myself. More important matters, however, engaged my attention, and, regarding it only as something very singular, I dismissed it from my mind. Ten years after, I was present at an inauguration ball at Milledgeville, and among the gay, fashionable assemblage of ladies, I was delighted to see my Philadelphia friend, Mary; she was leaning upon the arm of a distinguished member of Congress, whom I knew very well, and with that ease and confidence which at once assured me he was her husband. I took the earliest opportunity to approach her and renew our acquaintance. She seemed sincerely glad to meet me, and, as was natural with friends separated for so long a period, our inquiries were directed to our histories in the intervening time. She told me she had crossed the water, had seen strange people, and heard strange languages, for her father had taken his family with him while minister at a foreign court; that she had lost a near relative, (her mother;) had married young, and the man of her choice, and a statesman whom the people were pleased to call distinguished; 'all of which, you will remember, was predicted for me on our visit to Callowhill Street, to the very letter;' and she added, hurriedly, 'You have heard of poor Jane? She went step by step, as was foretold for her on that same evening. She had many suitors, married injudiciously, was neglected and almost deserted; lived unhappily, and died young. Is it not strange?' she asked; then looking earnestly at me, she said: 'Do you ever think of that dreadful bear?'

'I left Milledgeville a few days afterward, and, having no traveling companion, I thought a great deal of what I had heard from Mary, and determined, if extreme prudence and caution would avail anything, I would at least falsify the old hag's prediction in regard to myself. And I confess, gentlemen, in your repeated bear hunts nothing could have tempted me to join you. But with all my management to avoid my threatened destroyer, I was fairly caught at last. One morning, when returning from one of the upper plantations, and passing the western angle of Colonel Dick's rive -bank, I heard a piercing scream of distress; and it was repeated again and again. The Negro who was paddling the canoe exclaimed: 'Master, what's that?' And again the cry rung in our ears. I directed him to paddle up quickly to the spot; and taking up my rifle, (which I always carry in alligator season,) I jumped ashore and ran down the bank a hundred yards or more, until opposite the spot from which the screams proceeded. I was excited by curiosity to discover the sufferer and the hope to relieve him; and I leaped into the swamp and forced my way in some distance, when I came to an open space, and in the middle of it were two dogs and a wildcat in desperate conflict. I recognized at once the scream of the cat, which is more like the human than any other animal. I enjoyed the fight exceedingly, which ended in favor of the dogs. The cat was prostrate between them, and they sat very near each other, panting, and watching any signs of returning life, to seize him again, seeming to know his deceitful and nine-life character; but he was dead. In the next moment the *dogs* were struck dead by an alligator with one sweep of his tail. I had not seen him before, as he lay concealed in the thicket close to the combatants. He whirled around, and facing his victims, he seemed to enjoy the prospect of the meal before him; but he was not to realize it, for I was but ten yards distant, and, leveling my rifle, I sent a bullet through his heart. There was a log near by me, and I sat down to review the scene of death that had transpired in so short a time around me; and this version of the children's story of the 'bread and butter' came unbidden to my mind: 'Where's the cat? The dogs killed him. Where's the dogs? The alligator killed them. Where's the alligator? The Doctor killed him. Where's the Doctor? Ah! That's sufficient,' I thought, 'for the present;' and was rising from the log to return, when I heard a rustling noise behind me, and to my horror I saw a monstrous she-bear with two cubs approaching me, and directly between me and the boat She stopped, and, growling, seemed to say: 'Now your time's come. Your life was saved by a bear, and it will be taken by a bear.'

'You will understand my feelings, gentlemen. My rifle was empty, there was no time to reload, and I was otherwise unarmed and alone, for the Negro, as soon as I left the boat, had turned his face to the sun and gone to sleep. I hallooed for him, but in vain. My 'fortune,' like my Callowhill companions', was evidently about to be fulfilled. I felt too young to die. I had every reason to wish to live, and shuddered at the inglorious and miserable manner of my death.

'You all know the nature of these animals: they will run from a man, (or rather walk away from him,) unless wounded, or in defense of their young; and in my case, the bear no doubt looked at the field of the slain, and charged me with the whole 'bill of mortality,' and with the intention of adding her cubs. I would have been too happy to have undeceived her. But on she came, backing her short ears and showing her terrible teeth, rearing up, first to the right and then to the left, but never taking her fiery eyes off of mine until almost in reach of me, when she threw open her arms. I had my rifle ready with both hands round the small of the breech, (the barrel end being the heaviest,) and as she made the next step I let her have it with all my strength directly on her steeple. She recoiled a little, but before I had time to repeat the blow I was pinioned in the dreaded hug. She seemed to know me, and adjusted her hold so as more effectually to secure my hands, fearing, perhaps, I might come the science over her by dividing an artery. I felt the powerful but gradual squeeze, and knew too well that my lungs, once emptied of breath, would never be filled again. I looked for the last time, as I thought, upon the blue sky, and the green woods above and around me; thought of the pleasant world I was about to leave, and the uncertain one beyond, (with no very comforting assurances, I'm sorry to say,) and had fairly given up, when, crack! went a rifle within five paces of us. I felt the bear quiver throughout her whole frame; her blazing eyes flickered for a second, then were fixed, and a film passed over them; her limbs relaxed; she settled on her haunches, and rolled over on her back.

'I was saved by an accurate shot from Colonel Dick, who, with a trusty servant, had gone out that morning in chase of the bear, which had been seen by his negroes in the field. His dogs were put upon the track, but left it for the trail of the cat, whose screams had attracted him as well as myself.

'All was said and done between us as your own minds will suggest as natural and proper upon such an occasion; and I returned with the Colonel and took my chicken with him.'

XXII

Wheat Fields
in Dying Autumn

BY THOMAS E. VAN BENDER

FEBRUARY 1854

Not altogether with a face of gloom
   Does the old Year, when waning, day by day,
      Limp toward his wintry tomb;
But rosy-tinted mists around him play,
      And soft autumnal bloom.

E'en when each brightly-painted leaf decays,
   And Indian Summer drops her vapory robe;
      When garnered is the maize;
When now no longer like a blood-red globe
      The sun in mellowest haze

Shows half his disc behind the mountains blue;
   When dancing lines of motes no more are seen
      With sunset shimmering through;
Then, smiling o'er the land, rise spots of green,
      Oasis-like, to view.

Yes, these are smiles on dying Autumn's face,
   When he forgets his heaps of withered leaves,
      And turning seer, doth trace,
Beyond the coming winter, golden sheaves,
      Bright ripening apace.

WHEAT FIELDS IN DYING AUTUMN

What spots of vivid emerald cheer the eye!
  One lies embosomed in a boundless wold;
    One arches up the sky
Like the grave of a vast giant; hilltops cold,
    With blackening forests high,

Environ one, and shield it from the blast;
  Another, as the sun sinks lower down,
    And longer shades are cast,
Tints itself, artist-like, from base to crown,
    Aye lovelier to the last.

Poised over it, one faintly reddening sphere
  Of cloud is by the skyline cut in twain.
    Thus paints the fading Year,
Glossing with delicate half-tints the fresh grain
    In coloring mellow-clear.

Thus in Life's closing Fall, when coffin-ropes
  Uncoil to let me down to wintery tomb,
    May freshening wheat-green slopes,
Self-shading, sun-gilt, charm away the gloom,
    And kindle deathless hopes.